BEHIND
THE BRICK

SHAUN WEBB

BILL,
BLESSINGS + ENJOY!!

i

Manufactured in the USA

Quality Control and Editing by: Lisa Czyz

ISBN-13: 978-1482739183
ISBN-10: 1482739186

Published by Shaun Webb through In Motion
Publishing

Note: We ask that you, the reader, excuse
any minor editorial errors if you find them. We do
our very best. Thank you and enjoy!

BEHIND THE BRICK

SHAUN WEBB

IN MOTION PUBLISHING

MICHIGAN

ALL WORKS BY SHAUN WEBB:

A MOTION FOR
INNOCENCE...AND
JUSTICE FOR ALL?

BLACK JACKS

BLACK JACKS
(VOLUME TWO):
A KILLER FOR
THE QUEEN

BEHIND THE BRICK

REVIEWS

REVIEWS FOR "A MOTION FOR INNOCENCE...AND JUSTICE FOR ALL?"

I met you last summer mid-state while visiting my daughter and you signed your book for me. Thank you. I really enjoyed it. Thank you for writing about this almost taboo subject. Law and order almost never has any order.

Yvonne

We met you in ***** *** last weekend and bought all 3 of your books. I just finished "A Motion for Innocence." I absolutely loved it! I thought it was very well written and happy that you told this story. Our justice system is in dire need of a total overhaul as I have worked in it many years particularly with juvenile sex offenders. I have watched many of the boys I've worked with struggle to find jobs and make a life for themselves after being convicted. It saddens my heart for those who are truly falsely accused and even those who are guilty but genuinely sorry for their actions someone else. Well, I'm off to start reading your other two books. Will let you know what I think of them. Keep writing. You're great at it and thanks again for telling the "other side of the story".

Sincerely, Angila Adams

I purchased "A Motion for Innocence" at one of your shows last month and read it over the following week on a trip out east. I just wanted to congratulate you on taking me though the legal system and how it works or doesn't. I remember reading a story about a judge here in Oakland County a few years ago that was disbarred for shopping, etc. when she should have been in court. I am sure it is the one Sean had to face. Maybe I am remembering a similar case but I also thought the girl eventually confessed to her lies. It is indeed unbelievable how "anyone" could be falsely accused and dragged through the court system so unmercifully. I have been mentoring at the local High School for the last few years and come across kids that have no idea on what could potentially happen to them if they are falsely accused by a girlfriend, etc. Thanks for giving me this example to talk to young people. Have you ever considered the idea of giving a lecture on this story to such young adults?- **Ed Berry**

There used to be a saying that went the American Justice systems, for all its flaws, is the best in the world. This story is a brutally stark reminder that this is not the case. Through years of apathy, graft, and poor oversight, the American Justice System has become a shadow of itself, with many crying out against it, but the status quo staying just that. This story represents a single example of the overall national problem. Actually, it touches on two HUGE problems...the flawed Judicial system as well as a hugely flawed Sex Offender Registry...and follows the author's nightmarish introduction to what has always been beneath the surface, always out of focus. It is well written and very human. I deduct a star only for not picking either (or both) problem and more properly supplying facts and figures to illustrate just how bad the problem(s) have become. An engaging read, highly recommended.

-kem070396

I guess I have always been naïve in thinking that you are innocent until proven guilty in this country.....get a good lawyer and everything will be okay as the truth will prevail. This book really opened my eyes to what is really happening in our criminal justice system and how false accusations can ruin someone's life (not to mention their bank account). Hearing how the effects of the accusation tear into the family and friends of the accused was heart wrenching. This is an easy read as it flows nicely and keeps you intrigued until the very end...highly recommended!

-Curt, AZ Reader

Naiveté should not be a crime, and faith in the American justice system should not destroy one's life, but that is exactly what happens in Shaun Webb's tale of a simple man up against an overzealous, corrupt judicial system. "A Motion for Innocence" is written in a voice filled with incredulity as a young girl, a girl whose vindictive parents had found the perfect way to "punish" Sean for reporting their thievery from the Church in which they worked, unjustly accuses Sean West of unspeakable acts. From the first accusation to Sean's eventual release, we are brought into a world that an ever-larger percentage of individuals in the United States will experience. Webb takes us on a journey through the degradation of the human soul, when innocence is ignored, and results and votes are the ultimate goal. "A Motion for Innocence" is a definite must-read by anyone who believes that bad things happen only to bad people, and the fates preserve the dignity of the righteous. I would especially recommend this novel to young adults as the statistics alone have great educational value for anyone on the verge of a life of crime. One final thought, don't ever think you are infallible--we are after all, human.

-Patti76

I bought this book a few months ago with a few other titles that discuss the biggest and most expensive problem in our judicial system - false accusations. A false accusation can be the product of a coached child in a custody dispute, a vindictive student at a high school, or a prosecutor using public money to protect a fictitious minor (i.e. entrapment persona). I read a few pages and skimmed through the chapters just like I do every book when I first receive it, and I was able to absorb enough to honestly say that it is a great work-product for a first time author. It will likely be my first "complete" read when I get time, but for now, I'm too busy creating templates for complaint filings against public employees who use their offices to promote no-evidence no-witness accusers and the media outlets they use - so this book will definitely give me better insight into those subversive crimes. I'm not sure why the other reviewer has such a hard time accepting that a 13 year old girl can (and will) be a snot nosed brat, but 13 year olds are capable of much worse behavior she obviously doesn't know much about adolescent behavior.

–Duane Anthony Webb

REVIEWS FOR
THE BLACK JACKS SERIES,
VOLUMES I & II

Another awesome book by Shaun Webb! He is quickly becoming my favorite author! The character development in Black Jacks is fantastic. Shaun is able to develop the characters so well that the reader quickly becomes emotionally drawn in by each one of them. The suspenseful story that culminates in a surprise ending is just the "icing on the cake!" Looking forward to the next book by Shaun Webb.

-Ann Bonde

This is an absolute must read! Very suspenseful and a surprise ending! Love all the twists and turns the plot takes! My only suggestion is to read "Black Jacks Volume 1" first. It explains the main characters and the scenarios that started it all. In Volume 2, you see the characters grow and what leads them to make the decisions (good & bad) that have such impact with their lives and others. You will love both of these books-looking forward to the third installment!

-Mary T.

Being able to see main character Amy evolve is the best part of this series for me. A thrilling sequel to Black Jacks vol. 1. A new town and a new career don't keep the past from following Amy. I loved the suspense and thrill that are a part of this book. I also enjoy seeing a new author develop in his craft. A very creative and scary storyteller that I can't wait to read what's next.

-Bestread

Black Jacks is so good! I could not put it down. The character development, the plot, the entire story is exciting, and brings out every human emotion possible.

-Donna

Black Jacks is an intense thriller that keeps you in suspense until the very last chapters. The characters are well developed and the plot is new and different. A great read! J. Skaife

Shaun Webb did it again. From start to finish Black Jacks compelled me to keep turning pages eager to know what would happen next. His writing style drew me in and painted wonderful descriptions of the scenes in my mind, then introduced dialog so in tune, and intense that I felt I was there and knew the characters. Mr. Webb is a storyteller extraordinaire who weaves quite a tale. I'm looking forward to his next book.

-Don

FOR: ALL OF THE
"OBSOLETE CITIZENS"...
THANK YOU!

"In the hands of the state, compulsory public education becomes a tool for political control and manipulation -- a prime instrument for the thought police of the society. And precisely because every child passes through the same indoctrination process -- learning the same "official history," the same "civic virtues," the same "lessons of obedience" and "loyalty to the state" -- it becomes extremely difficult for the independent soul to free himself from the straightjacket of the ideology and values the political authorities wish to imprint upon the population under its jurisdiction. For the communists, it was the class struggle and obedience to the Party and Comrade Stalin; for the fascists, it was worship of the nation -- state and obedience to the Duce; for the Nazis, it was race purity and obedience to the Fuhrer. The content has varied, but the form has remained the same.

Through the institution of compulsory state education, the child is to be molded like wax into the shape desired by the state and its educational elite. We should not believe that because ours is a freer, more democratic society, the same imprinting procedure has not occurred even here, in America. Every generation of school-age children has imprinted upon it a politically correct ideology concerning America's past and the sanctity of the role of the state in society. Practically every child in the public school system learns that the "robber barons" of the 19th century exploited the common working man; that unregulated capitalism needed to be harnessed by enlightened government regulation beginning in the Progressive era at the turn of the century; that wild Wall Street speculation was a primary cause of the Great Depression; that only Franklin Roosevelt's New Deal saved America from catastrophe; and that American intervention in foreign wars has been necessary and inevitable, with the United States government required to be a global leader and an occasional world policeman."

Richard M. Ebeling

MICHIGAN'S
UPPER PENINSULA

INTRODUCTION

From St. Ignace along Michigan's southern Upper
Peninsula coast to Ontonagon and from Houghton, Michigan
along the Northern coastline stretching back to Drummond
Island, there was a silence that made one wonder exactly what
was going on in the Upper Peninsula of Michigan. There were
few signs of life except for the stray dog or cat and an
occasional deer or coyote sighting. Few signs, that is, except
for the many construction teams spread out along the exterior
U.P. near the Great Lakes Superior, Huron and Michigan. As
for common people, there was none. The towns all across
Michigan's beautiful Upper Peninsula were deserted. A
nuclear war? A famine? Perhaps a debilitating killer virus?
Nobody was quite sure, yet many agreed that it was complete
and utter disrespect of the beauty that permeated the area.

The Canadian helicopter pilot and his two passengers
flew across Manistique, headed toward Ishpeming and
beyond. There were no signs of human occupation. A year
earlier, the residents had been bought out by the Government

1

and moved to other areas of the U.S.A. Despite some detractors, the government was successful, as they paid generously for the property and relocating of the citizens. The people were essentially given offers they couldn't refuse, as not accepting would mean being moved forcefully and *without* compensation.

As the helicopter bore to the right toward Ishpeming, the reality of what was happening began to dawn on each of the four people aboard. Though no one spoke of it in the chopper itself, it was a remarkable sight. What they witnessed from the windows of the copter left all the men inside with their mouths wide open and their disbelief hovering at a new level of horror. They couldn't yet see the entire extent of the walled and barb wired structure, but they were dumbstruck by what was happening to this once wonderful tourist attraction and vacation destination in Michigan.

The construction wasn't complete: The brick wall rose fifteen feet in the air, and thus far, had stretched from St. Ignace west along the southern border of the U.P. and all the way to the small town of Marinette, which sat along the Wisconsin-Michigan border. To the east and north, the wall stretched from St. Ignace up to Ste. Sault Marie, and then extended along the northern border all the way to near the tip of the Keweenaw Peninsula. A fifteen-foot brick wall, along with about thirty-five additional feet of barbed wire stretched three quarters of the way around the Upper Peninsula.

The pilot of the copter and his three passengers had seen enough and bore left toward Thunder Bay; the town the Canadian reporters had flown out of three hours earlier. They all knew that the U.P. was off limits from 2045-2050 and they knew that entering the air space was a violation according to the United States government. Not deterred, the three reporters talked the pilot into the trek with the lure of ten grand, tax-free. Greed won over and off they went. This pilot was confident that he could maneuver the flight plan to avoid detection. He also had the best in radar technology and was small enough to avoid discovery; or so he thought.

*

All the men heard it at the same time: The roar of a sonic boom seemed to come from behind them. They looked up and down, side to side and saw nothing. The men, nearing Lake Superior, hoped that it was simply a sound from a passing airliner, but knew it was unlikely in restricted air space. The pilot agreed with the men's assessment to give them some comfort, but knew in his heart what was happening. He suspected that the army jets had found him and would be forcing them to land. The worst part was that upon

3

landing, they'd surely be charged with criminal trespass and any other myriad of crimes that would come with it. The penalty would probably be years in prison along with enormous fines. The soured pilot kept a smile on his face when to his left, just as he'd predicted, an Army F-15 Strike Eagle pulled to the side of the chopper. He looked to his right, and saw another fighter had flanked him. One of the reporters spoke.

"I thought we were non-detectable. This is bad. I can't go to prison."

The three helicopter riders and the pilot could see the masked faces of the jet fighters and waited for a signal "thumbs down" to start their descent.

The signal never came. The copter pilot, a bit confused, radioed the fighter pilots. He looked left and right, but neither pilot moved a muscle. They instead increased their speed and blew out of sight ahead of the chopper.

"What's going on?" One reporter asked.

"Yeah, what the hell was that?" the other reporter asked.

The pilot, just as surprised and confused as his riders, said nothing. He flew forward, picking up as much speed as possible. He was about fifteen miles from Lake Superior, which would take him out of Michigan. Since there was still land underneath, he knew he had to hold his breath for a few more tense minutes. The horizon in front of him promised water soon. In thinking back a minute earlier, he reasoned to himself that the jets pilots were warning him to get the hell out of the airspace. He tried to smile and cooperate.

One of the reporters was writing, while the other stared straight out of the windshield of the chopper. He saw something in the distance and mentioned it to the pilot.

"Hey. Do you see that way out there? What is that?"

The pilot's eyes shifted to where the reporter pointed and then darted back to his radar. He knew exactly what it was; a guided missile coming straight for the copter. He looked at the reporter as a single tear dripped from his eye.

"What? What's the matter dude? Are we in trouble?"

The pilot nodded yes and cut the engine. The helicopter started a spinning free-fall from the sky. He figured that the reporters would be shocked enough by the maneuver that they wouldn't have to think about the impending impact. Fifteen seconds later, the fiery carcass of the helicopter crashed just outside of Marquette. The debris didn't spread far. It was a job well done, as far as the F-15 fighters were concerned. They gave each other thumbs up and headed back to their base in Ste. Sault Marie.

*

President John Wisecroft shouted on the cell phone while his closest aide sat by idly. "Let this be a lesson that when we say that airspace is restricted, we mean it."

The president was speaking to the Foreign Minister of Canada and pulled no punches. "I informed the international community not to interfere with that airspace while we were working. It was designated a no-fly zone. Those reporters knew what they were doing. Now they've suffered the consequences of their actions."

The Foreign Minister of Canada spoke. "We condemn this action, Mr. President, and we will seek sanctions against the United States for this act of terrorism."

Wisecroft countered. "The United Nations has no power in this situation. Your trespassing was a threat to our national security and our only choice was to respond with force. Now tell the rest of your media to stay out!"

Wisecroft bypassed hanging up the phone; he stood up and chucked it across the room. It smashed into many mille-pieces upon phone-to-wall impact. He took a long look at his V.P., the retired business mogul Henry Jasper, and smiled. Jasper frowned in return, as he hated Wisecroft's reaction. Wisecroft spoke once more. "Do they have any idea who they're messing with here?"

*

6

Construction continued on the bricked facility until its completion in 2050. It encircled the entire Upper Peninsula of Michigan, leaving all of the Great Lakes open for the use of the people of the United States and its Government. The amount of steel re-rod, brick and wire used was astronomical, costing the United States taxpayers over one billion dollars.

The wall stretched along Route 2 covering the southern border of the U.P. It took a sharp left in Gladstone and ran down route 35 to Marietta. From there it moved back up to Route 2 and continued its western trek to Ironwood. The wall then took a jaunt up the western coast of the peninsula until reaching Copper Harbor at the tip of the Leelanau peninsula. It dropped back down into L'Anse before traveling east through Marquette, Munising, Paradise and Sault Ste. Marie. It turned south to Drummond Island and back to its starting point in St. Ignace.

The public didn't know it yet, but the reason for the wall would be made clear after the announcement of what the facility was to be used for; permanent housing for all of the sex offenders living in the United States of America. President Wisecroft anticipated that the populace would gladly finance the facility in exchange for the safety and security of their families.

7

The area was a government secret and the general population stayed away, lest they end up like the helicopter that violated the airspace. The citizens had originally dismissed it as a facility for military exercises and research, or secret installment zones to ensure public safety.

The facility, simply called "The Brick" would have plenty of room for the two million sex offenders living in the country. People accused and convicted of such offenses would start a journey to the facility that would include jails, trains and F.E.M.A. camps. A guilty verdict in a sex crime trial would result in the expulsion of the accused. Because sex crimes had such a harmful effect on its victims, Wisecroft felt this action would save valuable taxpayer's dollars from being wasted on housing the convicted in the nations already bulging prisons, thus eliminating the chance of them being freed back into society.

With so much fear of being near these "types" within the community, Wisecroft was certain that The Brick would be hailed as his greatest contribution to society. Instead of a sense of radically ridding society of the "vermin," which was his plan, he could be seen as "protecting" them from harm. His propaganda plan would see to that. With the number of vigilante attacks against offenders growing daily, he could convince society that this action would be *helping* the offenders by keeping them locked away from the violence growing in the streets. He chose to ignore the fact that these were people with families and children. He also ignored the potential for further violence when society created a class of people without hope for the future.

Outwardly, Wisecroft painted himself as a caring politician working for the good of all, but inwardly he had his personal motivation: revenge and total rule.

NAZI

AMERICA

MEET JONATHON WISECROFT

One of the most handsome presidents since JFK, John Wisecroft was elected in 2044 on a catchphrase of "Cleaning it Up." He knew the American people wanted change and they wanted it quickly. He rapidly rose through the political ranks as his thirst for power and rule continued to grow.

He began his career as a senator for his home state of Texas and impressed on the political floor with his "Conservative Change" party. He pushed hard for the outright banishment of illegal aliens in Texas and won. The Mexican-American population dropped some 70% with his initiative.

"We need to take back our country!" Was his biggest battle cry as a senator.

It started in Texas and moved its way to Washington D.C. as Wisecroft routed his opponents on the way into the Presidency on his first run. Americans liked him and he liked *most* Americans. It was a win-win for the aggressive (yet Conservative Change) man.

*

The 6'5" 220 lb. Wisecroft was solid. He played quarterback at Baylor University and was an All-American for three straight years. Drafted by the NFL's Cleveland Browns, he instead opted for a career in politics.

His wife and high school sweetheart Katie flanked him. It came as no surprise to anyone that they were the most popular couple in school: He the quarterback and she the head cheerleader. They were a good-looking pair of which more than a few "I wish we were like them" quotes were born.

There was another side to the publically docile and friendly Mr. Wisecroft: He was as ruthless as he was serene. It showed with the people that stood closest to him. Whoever or whatever needed running over to reach any pinnacle of command was of no consequence. His charisma on camera, rugged good looks, and no nonsense approach gave him a strong political following among those disenfranchised with the previous "regimes". He was, however, cold-blooded, with more than a few men and women *dying* due to his obsessive yearning for control. He had garnered a formidable army of loyalists who would do anything to see this man through,

14

including, but not limited to, disposing of his competition through deceit, jailing, disappearances and even murder. He was adept at using people as pawns, so he avoided annoying controversies. Other activists and political leaders stopped speaking out against him for fear that they'd be the next victim. The media's attempts to investigate his regime were squelched when his long time crony and multi-billionaire, A. Davis Goddard, and a few other wealthy bankers bought out and monopolized the newspaper and broadcasting markets in the country. Coupled with a political machine adept at social media skills and personal data collection, Wisecroft's ability to shape the minds, beliefs and ideals of the American people became frighteningly powerful.

His speeches and rants touched the hearts of his most ardent followers. Wisecroft was a showman and an excellent speaker. The support of Goddard, and his control of the media on a political stage, was a brilliant move. Referring to himself as a conservative with the conservative change party, he blamed and blamed and blamed while slamming his fists, jumping and squawking like a rooster protecting the henhouse. He used entire stages, not merely a podium placed in front of him. He was outrageous and gifted, smart and sinister.

No matter what the situation or state of the U.S.A., he effectively shifted responsibility onto other parties and citizens. He also promised solutions to the problems caused

by the "Obsolete." The Illegal immigration problem? He
didn't share the details but promised a quick remedy for the
situation (deportation or elimination), as he had done in Texas.
He realized early in his political career that the general
population was not only interested in results, but in being
entertained with some kind of drama, *least of which* being the
political process. He felt it was inefficient to waste a lot of
time and money playing up to the citizens that weren't smart
enough to understand his self-stated superior reasoning. He
saw himself as the epitome of problem solving through the
drama he himself created.

Illegal aliens, however, were not the main problem
Wisecroft planned to "solve". He felt that the offenders were
the culprits responsible for the crumbling of the country.
Having had a daughter raped and murdered by a registered sex
offender before his very eyes was the biggest reason for his
platform. His motivation, like that of John Walsh and Mark
Lunsford, was vengeance.

Back in 2018, at the tender age of twenty-two, he and
Katie had been blessed with a beautiful baby girl, their first of
what would be three children. Eight years later, two men
dressed in dark clothing and wielding weapons invaded his
home. Bound and gagged on the living room floor, he was
forced to watch as his wife and daughter were raped and
beaten by one of the perpetrators. Afterwards, they beat and

shot Wisecroft, leaving him for dead. Katie survived the brutal attack due to her strong physical stature but their lovely daughter passed away a week later. This event changed the core of his being. He vowed retribution against not only the vermin that did this to him and his family, but to all offenders. They would feel his wrath. That fateful day motivated Wisecroft's political career.

After serving as a Senator in Texas, he ran for Governor in his home state, winning election in 2028 using the same excitable speeches and tough as nails attitude he would employ when running for the Presidency of The United States. His first course of action as governor was to establish a much more vociferous sex offender plan. He would lead the nation with his five-point sex offender law made for tightening restrictions and accountability: A requirement for public safety. Knowing the governor's tragic experience and loss, the people of Texas voted it in sympathetically and unanimously.

The 2028 John Wisecroft Sex Offender Law

1. All Registered Sex Offenders are to have a computer chip implanted under their skin to allow GPS tracking at all times.

2. All offenders are to have a barcode tattoo applied to the top of their right hand. When scanned, these codes would allow any government agency access to all personal information regarding the individual. It would also serve as a notification to the public that this individual is an offender.

3. All offenders are banned from any public or private places where kids gather: including, but not limited to: schools, parks, movie theatres, festivals, fairs and libraries.

4. All offenders, no matter what the charge, are to be listed on the Texas Sex Offender Registry for life.

5. All businesses, including, but not limited to; stores, offices, government buildings, etc. are to install devices at each entrance that would sound an alarm if an offender entered. The devices are to be directly linked to the computer chips installed under the offender's skin.

This was the will of the people, according to Governor Wisecroft. He put the law before them and they voted it in with a sense of relief, thinking that their worlds would be a safer place. He would ensure that this code was strictly enforced. His plan wasn't complete. There would be more in the near future.

*

Besides moving towards a solution to the offender problem, Wisecroft's Five Point Plan had another advantage: It helped grease the hands of a few of his Texas longtime supporters.

Ivan Cross, who ran and owned a tether business in Dallas, realized this would undoubtedly make him a multi-millionaire as Texas had the record for the most sex offenders in the United States: over 100,000. He was also helping his Sr. Advisor, Henry Marsh, who established a business and received the government contract for the tattooing and chipping of sex offenders. He opened up over fifty facilities throughout Texas. Once again, a millionaire was born. Both Cross and Marsh would play a big part in Wisecroft's future plans in politics.

*

When the time came to run for president, Wisecroft's speeches always went something like this:

"My fellow American people, we live in the most powerful and beautiful country in the world - but we have

19

some problems that we need to work on and so far I don't see anyone getting them solved. Whether it is Democrat, Republican, Tea Partier, Liberal, conservative or some Independent, I haven't seen anyone roll up their sleeves and get down to business. All I hear are excuses. Well, it's time for a bigger change. It's time for the American people to take back their country."

At that point in the speech, Wisecroft removed the microphone from its cradle and worked the stage like a rock star. He was fanatical and comedic, riling up the crowd.

"I have been the Governor of Texas for a total of four years and in that short time, I've eradicated the illegal alien population in that state. My record speaks for itself. How would you like it if I eradicated all the illegals in the entire country? They're part of the problem in the U.S.A.

The big difficulties I see now are the offenders. We're wasting time worrying about these predator's rights and paying your precious taxpayer's dollars to keep them in jails. What if we stopped allowing them to hurt our children and molest our families? They're not only stealing our innocence, but they are stealing our sense of security. My offender reform plan in Texas has worked. Our streets are safer, our children are safer and any predator that comes there knows

20

they will face major consequences! I want to give back that beautiful sense of security and American value for you and your families."

Wisecroft had his sleeves rolled up, his face was covered with sweat and he manipulated the front of the stage, taking in the applause like that of a hero.

"Hate is a strong word but it does have its place in our language. If anything, it's a word that hasn't been used enough. Do you hate the neighbor that cooks you up a warm apple pie on a steamy Texas evening? Of course not? Do you hate Uncle Jimmy who comes over on his own time to help you out with whatever trouble you may be having? No. However, an offender? A person who abuses our children and then says he or she didn't? You had better damn well hate them or you aren't a decent human being. Join me in bringing family values and security back to the United States of America!"

On and on Wisecroft spoke, swirling up a storm of abhorrence and blame while raining down peace and safety as the logical answer. Revulsion didn't seem so harsh if it was directed at the appropriate people. This strategy would win the hearts of the public, and ignite the flames of revolt in the souls of the fearful.

*"I myself had a family member, my little girl,
murdered by a dirty, scumbag sex offender. I was forced to
watch as my baby and wife fell victim to a deranged lunatic.
Some say offenders can't be reformed; I agree with them.
Offenders are the scourge of our society. Without them, we
would be a much more fluid and calm country. I have a plan
people. The plan is big, the plan is radical, but most of all, I
have a plan that will work. I say "will" because there is no
maybe, might or could about it. The word is "will". I give
you my promise that sex offenders of our country will be dealt
with harshly and with no excuses. No more of the five years
and out routine. My plan will rid this country of the offenders
that hurt our economy, our kids and our consciences. Ladies
and gentlemen, you have my word. This country needs change
and I'm the only man for the job. Thank you all for coming
out today and as I always say; we're in it for the long haul.
Change will be ours. You hold the power in your hands."*

Thus, a seed was planted. The people continued to buy
it and Wisecroft crisscrossed the country making his point. He
continued to dance, swagger and strut on the stage. He
continued to spread his word with aplomb and arrogance;
facets that the American people loved. They loved it so much
they elected him president in 2044.

22

LUTHER'S ELOQUENT WORDS, "THE
INTELLECT IS THE DEVIL'S WHORE," CONFIRM
MY BELIEF THAT THE HUMAN SPIRIT OF THE
GREATEST MAGNITUDE IS TOO SMALL TO
ALTER THE LAWS OF LIFE. AND THE HIGHEST
LAW OF LIFE IS *STRUGGLE*.... NOTHING
COMES FROM "YES, BUT [*ZWAR–ABER*]."

-Walter Buch written to a friend in 1929. Cited from
Richard Steigmann-Gall's The Holy Reich

THE VIGILANTE'S WAR

The meetings held an eerie resemblance to Nazi rallies of the 1930's: A rising of the hand to signal total trust and allegiance to the N.V.A.C., or the National Vigilante Action Committee. Like a "holy" war, their mission was one of protecting the children, and these ends justified whatever means were necessary. Jailing offenders was the primary motivation.

"Save a deer, kill a pedophile." "Why test on animals when you have prisons full of sex offenders?" and pictures depicting hangings and executions were some of the slogans often found on truck and car windows throughout the United States.

The "Vigilantes", as they had been labeled by the media and the advocacy groups, had increased in power and volume with Wisecroft's support. A seemingly blind eye by law enforcement allowed some of their tactics, including, but not limited to threats, intimidation and, sometimes, murder to continue with little resistance.

25

*

The N.V.A.C.: Headquartered in Florida and led by Davis Lowell, a strapping, muscular and heavily tattooed man of twenty-five years. They were the largest threat to the registered sex offender in the entire U.S. The group was accepted and mostly admired across the country for their unyielding protection of children; protection by any means necessary. The general public never saw the dark side of which the N.V.A.C. was involved. They simply heard "protect the children" and went with it. The darker methods included cyber-stalking, harassment, personal confrontations, threats, and in extreme cases, what they considered "justifiable" murder. Although the practice wasn't openly encouraged, there seemed to be an unwritten rule within the group that the only good offender was a dead one. Public sentiment, it seemed to their members, supported their radical actions. The loudest voices, spiked with emotion and fear, overshadowed those who disagreed but were afraid to speak out. The N.V.A.C. social websites included both the vile haters and the logical thinkers. The mix was combustible, as the logical thinkers wanted the offenders to face stiff penalties, but stopped short of condoning harassment and murder.

26

The media feared that by opposing the violence of the vigilantes they somehow condoned the predator. They also became fearful for themselves, as the vigilantes would exact retribution on anyone standing in their way and were now working outside of the law with minimal consequence. As the public panic involving offenders continued to grow, so did the N.V.A.C.'s power.

*

The N.V.A.C. slogan

GOAL: That the Sexual Predator becomes Exposed, Exiled, and ultimately, Extinct

MISSION: The National Vigilante Action Committee mission is to raise awareness about the dangers of sexual predators living free among families in the community. We don't believe that release from confinement should end the surveillance and punishment of sex offenders. Their victims and victim's families have to live with what they did forever, and the predator should too. The United States Constitution ensures all Americans the right to life, liberty and pursuit of happiness. No person can feel free or happy if his or her family and children face endangerment. It is our American responsibility to alert any community when a sex offender is living among them. WE DO NOT CONDONE VIOLENCE! Our logo stands for ZERO TOLERANCE! The N.V.A.C. remains within the confines of the law *at all times*. The police are called to assist in every outing we do. All the information we distribute is public information and we make it readily available to everyone. If there is an issue in a neighborhood with a convicted sexual predator, we assist in whatever means necessary. We do not fear these people. Let all predators know that they are on notice! WE ARE NOT GOING AWAY!

OVERVIEW*:* The N.V.A.C. was founded in October 2009 in the wake of the Somer Thompson tragedy. The loss of a beautiful little girl sparked the inner fire of an entire community and it has been burning brightly ever since. May she rest in peace.

DESCRIPTION: A community united against sexual predators.

*

To the right of Davis Lowell was his number one minion of vigilantism, Sal "The Gal" Parker, a roughneck vigilante also from Florida, the home location of the group. Parker was a computer whiz and incessant pursuer of offenders. She spent at least eight hours per day online harassing the offender, their advocates and their varied groups around the country. She was intense in her work and unyielding in her pursuit. Parker was effective as a "troll", or online infiltrator, because she had no fear when it came to the harassment of offenders. She was also a raving alcoholic, as a full flask of bourbon followed her wherever she ventured. She loosened up after a few drinks, making it easier for her to harass the offenders without fear of potential consequences. Her blood pressure never wavered no matter how much she fought with the advocates.

Sal had an evil look in her eye and a nasty attitude to boot. Standing 5'8" and weighing 160, she was no slouch of a woman. She had large, saggy breasts, a thick, meaty midsection and short stumpy legs. Her hair was cut short, usually just below her ear lobes, while her face was like the toughened leather of a long-time smoker who spent many days in the hot sun. She wore a shirt with the N.V.A.C. logo on the upper right chest along with baggy camouflage pants that gave her the look of a soldier ready for war. She also packed heat in the form of a licensed, registered Glock on her hip.

*

Davis Lowell was less flamboyant than Parker was but shared the same dislike of sex offenders. Having two family members victimized by a rapist along with the Somer Thompson tragedy caused Lowell to pursue his promise of vengeance against all offenders, young, old and in-between. Lowell was a threatening figure. He was responsible for the beatings of at least twenty offenders, most using his bare hands. He also had a propensity for sharing pictures of his bloody knuckles on the internet, and then bragging about his latest beating of an offender.

Rarely prosecuted and never convicted, Davis always had an excuse for his behavior. Whether it was self-defense or a perceived threat against a child, the juries and judges believed him. It didn't matter if it were true or not, as the protection of one child shone in any court's eyes.

He was dangerous to the anti-sex offender law advocates but a Godsend to the public, law enforcement and media. He was free to continue his reign. The police loved him and usually looked the other way when trouble ensued. When the advocacy spoke out against him and his tactics, he always ran to the media for protection. Being called out caused the N.V.A.C. head to become extremely agitated and defensive. Alerting the media to tell them what a great fighter for children he was, along with the urge to look like the "hero", was the salve that soothed his ego.

Lowell and Parker traveled all over the country for demonstrations and the dispensing of flyers that warned neighborhoods of the influx of offenders in their respective areas. They carried signs in front of parks, schools or offenders' homes, and attended local N.V.A.C. meetings. The group Lowell formed had reached an army of fans numbering 500,000 strong. The general public and local municipalities gladly accepted their presence and information. No one questioned the accuracy or sources of their data.

Organized by Parker, their demonstrations took on many different forms. She held a strong and healthy affinity for rabble-rousing and vigorous anti-sex offender hate speeches. Although Lowell usually spoke, Parker, the writer of his speeches, would stand next to him with angst pouring out of every emotional pore of her body. Her eyes blazed, her hands shook (with either D.T.'s, anger or both) and she couldn't stand still for more than five minutes, always fidgeting and wanting to see action in the streets of America. Her favorite anti sex offender phrases included "stick a needle in their arm", "gas 'em", and "they can't keep their zippers up." "Numbnuts" was also a Parker favorite.

The public began assisting them in their crusade: "Outed" offenders were often beaten, bullied, spat upon and

31

kicked. Police were also finding offender's complaints rising dramatically. Investigations rarely took place, but when they did a high number were dismissed. It was just the offenders angered over their "non-violent" treatment. Davis wasn't doing his work with reckless abandon: He thought it through and used the tools given to him to employ his strategies.

*

A problem that *had been created* also had to *be solved*. Just as Nazi Germany's intimidation and eventual encampment and murdering campaign developed, times were changing in a country that may have thought itself too haughty to believe it had the ability for such debauchery.

The public, now informed by a government-controlled media, bought Wisecroft's strategy and carefully turned their eyes in his direction. Some were uncomfortable with the subtle changes, most didn't notice, but few were brave enough to stand for revolution in the building atmosphere of change. As with all the other factions, save for the advocacy, they didn't want to be considered "pro-pedophile," so keeping quiet was the best defense.

*

When the word leaked out of a bricked facility under construction in the Upper Peninsula of Michigan, Lowell and Parker immediately surmised that it was to house the nation's sex offender population, illegal immigrants, or both. They also wondered if the prisons would be emptied into the bricked facility to alleviate over-crowding and escape risks. They never thought about it in terms of military use. The pair sent letters and emails to President Wisecroft pledging their support. They hoped to receive an invitation to attend the ribbon-cutting ceremony in Mackinaw City, Michigan upon completion of the project. Wisecroft's advisory board's response was non-committal, (the president was not yet prepared to make a public announcement), but told the two to keep up their good work in protecting the public from the impurities of the offenders. Lowell and his minions were free to plunder. They took great pride in their quest.

*

Rachel Lyons formed the anti-vigilante advocacy or A.V.A. out of New York State. Rachel, married to a registered sex offender, was adamant about forgiveness, understanding and fixing broken laws that were a hindrance to offenders throughout the entire country. The laws she fought included the registry, the ban on social media and other

33

common rights a non-offender enjoyed. Now that John Wisecroft was president, she knew that the battle would be an all but impossible one. Despite it, she soldiered forward.

Rachel was a tenacious woman of thirty years. Fair skin, strawberry blonde hair and a kind smile all combined with a wonderful personality, which made her a pleasure to be associated with on any level. On the other hand, Rachel also suffered with Obsessive Compulsive Disorder, which caused her to act irrationally (at times) in her perception of the responsibilities she gave herself. The disorder would test her marriage on many occasions, as it fed the obsession she had with sex offender law reform. One had to be careful when conversing with her, as agreeing with murder, torture and other ghastly crimes against offenders brought out her wrath. News reporters who interviewed Rachel and agreed with the vigilantes earned a stern lecture and quick dismissal. It eventually reached a point where it was tougher and tougher to find media who were willing to write columns condemning the vigilante way of law. The press had ignored the problems of the registry so meticulously that unknowing eyes denied it and a public that was unaware of its flaws flat-out supported it.

*

Rachel's husband, Matt Lyons, was a calm man. He allowed Rachel the freedom to pursue her advocacy, even though it brought him major discomfort at times. The pervading thought in his mind was that the police would arrest him or that the N.V.A.C. would interfere with his life and harass him, all due to his wife's undying dedication to reform.

Matt was on the registry for something that happened when he was twelve and his sister was six. Sexually abused by his mother at a young age, a simple game of doctor between Matt and his kid sister turned into a spot on the sex offender list at the age of thirteen. Matt's mother hadn't taught him the difference between right and wrong, as the abuse was all he remembered. She had continually told him it was okay, so Matt assumed it was.

The man of twenty-eight years had already spent fifteen years as an outcast. Most days for Matt felt like sandpaper against raw skin. He was tense, brusque and depressed. The years of soaped up windows with the words "pervert," "Child molester," and other devious quotes were wearing him down. He had repaired his vehicle at least ten times in the previous two years from people coming into his yard during the night with sand for the gas tank, blades with which to slash tires and urine for the antifreeze reservoir. Despite the damage, none of the people who inflicted it approached him, taking responsibility. He and Rachel had to watch their animals closely in fear of poisoning by the very people who preached a non-violent resolution for the pedophile and sex offender problem that plagued the country.

The fights he had with Rachel were legendary, as she wouldn't stand down to her goal of having her husband removed from the registry. Smashed dishes, screaming within inches of each other's faces and stomping out the door angry were the norm for the otherwise quiet couple. They did love each other greatly and always made up, but they had an explosive relationship. It was probably what kept them together.

Despite Matt's fears, Rachel needed to fight for her advocacy. It wasn't that she wanted offenders to walk away from assaults with no punishment; it was that she thought after jail, probation or parole, a person should be considered "clean" or otherwise having paid their debt for the crime. No matter how hard she worked, there were always critics, vigilantes and other non-advocacy sorts that came out of the woodwork to run her down verbally. Despite their best efforts, the determined woman soldiered onward. She refused to stop. Her obsessiveness was her friend.

*

While the vigilantes and sex offender haters were rolling out their threats and occasionally harmful techniques, there existed plenty of N.V.A.C. members who wanted to sit down with the advocates and iron the problems out face-to-face. It was difficult for a non-offender to understand someone who had been accused and convicted of mistreating children, whether the accusation was true or not. Despite that, some tried to be fair and look at the situation from both angles. After all, not *all* offenders were actually offenders, especially the Romeo-Juliet cases. The same strategy applied with Rachel and her advocacy: Some tried to understand from the N.V.A.C. point of view. It still wasn't enough to calm the radicals on each side. The fight had become so personal that the messages to one another described venomous threats and poisonous accusations.

Sal "The Gal" Parker, who refused to negotiate, led those types of attitudes. Advocates and N.V.A.C. members alike collected and often showed the nastier posts to the police in hopes of getting the other faction in trouble. The posts, writings and threats ended up thrown into a file kept by the typically sighing police officers.

"Why don't you guys knock it off? Stop harassing each other. It's like a childish game. Maybe we'll throw all your asses in jail. Of course, the offenders will go first. "

37

On it went. Despite the best efforts of the sensible people, it always turned into a battle of hate and bigotry. Parker continued burning her swath over wherever she traveled while Lowell watched from a distance, smiling menacingly. Rachel fought for her advocacy and changing the laws, while one Steven Smith added his opinions to the Advocacy efforts.

TOWN HALLS ACROSS AMERICA

The people of the United States, from Seattle to Phoenix and from Boston to Miami, plus numerous places in-between gathered to talk about the ideas put forth by President Wisecroft. The registered sex offender took center stage at most, if not every meeting that took place. High property taxes? The offender's fault. Low property value? The offender's fault. Whether they spoke of high unemployment, political strife or the actual crimes being committed across the U.S.A., the offender always took the heat. It also turned into an Advocate-N.V.A.C. fight, with the public adding their two cents to the argument. Wisecroft's plan was taking hold.

Steven Smith went to the town hall held in his hometown of Cincinnati to try to put some reason into the minds of people already set in their ways. Rachel did the same in New York, and many other offenders, along with their advocates across the United States followed suit. This was to be the final chance for the advocates to get their points across. Members of the N.V.A.C felt exactly the same way.

*

Steven Andrew Smith, a handsome and dark-haired thirty-five year-old, found himself convicted of a felony sex offense for kissing and *only* kissing an underage girl. He was under the impression that she was at least twenty years-old but it turned out not to be true *(she was fifteen)*. A felony seemed like an awful harsh conviction in the face of only kissing someone, but the president, lawmakers and other government officials had made it so tough on offenders and potential offenders that it was surprising making love to your own spouse didn't get you thrown behind bars. Steven was not going to take the charge lying down and certainly wasn't going to defend a registry that, in his opinion, was nothing more than a fabricated tool built out of and for fear, along with profitability. Blogging incessantly and with deep conviction, Steven put forth stats every day, wherever he could, explaining the "what's" and "what not's" of a system he believed had gone horribly awry. A computer expert, Steven also had a specialty for infiltrating computers belonging to others and sending in the worst viruses imaginable. He had his own collection of twenty-five laptops and ten desktop computers to avoid detection. He also had the ability to hide the main information his computer held when he did his dirty work. He was the troll of all trolls. He could out-troll any of the N.V.A.C. hackers who threatened him. Most of the N.V.A.C.'s people were smart enough to avoid detection; but if one ever slipped up; WHAM! Steven crushed their entire hard drive with venomous infections. The difference with Steve is that he thoroughly enjoyed his role, mainly because the bitterness inside him was eating him alive.

Having been shot down in flames at every turn, the town hall in Cincinnati offered no hope. He also had to try to devise some kind of a plan to stay under the radar. He knew what was coming: Martial Law, F.E.M.A. camps and a complete government takeover. He was powerless to do any real damage alone and there weren't enough able-bodied, willing offenders or advocates to help him fight the battle. His strength and resolve faced tests each day with new and more brutal messages sent via computer. Death threats, lawsuits and even the promise of burning him at the stake were scary, but Steven took it in stride.

"It's easy to mess with someone from behind a keyboard. Face-to-face, it's an entirely different story."

He and his apartment roommate, Casper, often had knockdown drag-out fights not over the registry, but over Steven's unwillingness to let things go. What Casper failed to understand, according to Steven, was the complexity of the situation. It was more than the registry. It was more than an offender infestation. It was a test to see who were the strongest of the people. Not all offenders could survive the onslaught of a government, in his eyes, that had gone over-the-top with its laws and *didn't know how* to turn it around. The world of the 2040's was different and Steven was a part of it.

He and the rest of the advocacy would soon be tested in the most extreme of ways as the Brick Project in Michigan, along with the gathering of the offenders loomed. It wasn't yet known that Hell was about to break loose throughout the country.

*

In Florida, it was Lowell and Parker that ran the show in their town hall, lathering the people up into a rabid frenzy. When their meeting ended, seven offenders living in the near-by area ended up tracked down, outed and harassed. Egg tossing, mustard squirting and window soaping were the norm as the offenders were powerless to stop it. There were few

41

questions as the police chalked it up as mayhem with no clues or ideas of who had done the deeds. The offenders had no choice but to sit idly by and watch it happen. Resistance could be deadly, as they were overwhelmingly outnumbered.

The attitudes across the states were changing, as had the attitudes of millions of German's during Hitler's reign of terror. As Hitler had angered the people by blaming other factions for the trouble, he fixed or promised to fix said problems. Wisecroft was employing much of the same strategy. He carefully blamed a group of people (offenders), knew he could get the problem under control by building and utilizing the bricked facility (for offenders), and thereby gaining the valuable trust of the society. It was within the blame game portion of his strategy that Wisecroft knew the pendulum of his power would swing back his way when it came time to "fix" the issues affecting Americans east-to-west and north-to-south.

*

In Cincinnati, Steven, careful not to give away his own offender status, pleaded with the people to look into their hearts and forgive the people who had done such awful things in their lives. His plan was to compare molesters with all other common criminals.

"Listen people. We've had ax-murderers, arsonists, people who've killed their wives and children, people who've stole from you and you and you."

He pointed to people in the crowd as he spoke. "We can forgive the murderer, the arsonist, the thief; why can't we forgive the offender? Some were falsely accused and even the ones who did it aren't likely to re-offend."

Steven's logic angered the throng.

"It's our kids they're hurting."

"Burn the sex offenders at the stake."

"Kill them all."

"Maybe you're an offender. Why would you defend such scumbags?"

Steven stood silently shaking his head.

One man stood up and made as much sense out of the situation as he possibly could.

"Murderers murder because they have to ninety percent of the time. Arsonists like fire. Home breakers are desperate. Sex offenders? They're just scumbag people who like to tear up our children's insides, minds and families. I say get rid of them and watch our problems improve dramatically."

The crowd cheered wildly for what they thought was logical. It was a much tougher sell than Steven had anticipated. He knew it'd be hard, but not impossible. He was severely disappointed. He stood with his lower jaw dragging on the ground. What he was hearing was very difficult for him and all other registered offenders. He left the hall early before anyone could figure out his secret.

*

Rachel worked the crowd in New York to the same result. For some reason, people weren't willing to agree with her arguments. The people themselves held the most power and they were the ones you had to convince. Rachel put up charts showing the recidivism rate of a sex offender was less than seven percent. She showed slides with pictures of beautiful children and then told the crowd afterward that the kids they had just seen were children of offenders. Her presentation was studious and precise, the result far less than that. The crowd routed her.

"The offender should have thought about the kids before they acted out."

"Those kids need to be taken away from those offenders. We'll take care of them."

"What kind of woman are you? You're defending the worst of the worst. Get off the stage."

Rachel mulled and argued. Her presentation lasted three hours. The people rejected it in less than five minutes.

Desperate to see a solution that could save her husband, she practically begged on bended knee for the people to see that the offender wasn't the cause of all the chaos going on in the country. She talked of high unemployment for the people but no employment for the offender. The people stuck to their belief that the offenders were taking the jobs. Whether it was true or not was of little consequence. What was real was the disdain for the offenders. Not even Rachel's splendid example could change minds.

Rachel folded up her easel, placed her placards in the boxes and packed up her cards and flyers. She was defeated on this night but would try another bit of strategy soon. Rachel wasn't a quitter.

THE CAMPAIGN FOR FREEDOM

The minute she got home from the town hall, Rachel contacted Steven online with a proposal to form a social page called "The Campaign for Freedom" which was to be a group and site dedicated to the exposing of vigilantes and especially the N.V.A.C. They agreed and worked the site hard from both ends. Steven saved and posted screenshots of the N.V.A.C. social page, which showed hangman's nooses, pointed guns, hunting permits to actually "bag" offenders and other very troubling material. Despite Lowell Davis' promises that he

45

didn't advocate violence, he never pulled any of the nasty comments or posts from fellow citizens who hated the offenders. In fact, while Steve and Rachel diligently tried to drum up support, they attracted just over one hundred followers in a three-month span. During the same span, Lowell's N.V.A.C. site drew ten thousand followers. Lowell still felt the heat and went on local TV to tell the news about the Campaign for Freedom site.

"We don't advocate violence. We want our schools, restaurants and parks sex offender free, that's all. For the pro-offenders to attack is unjustified and downright dirty. We mean to protect children, not be run into the ground by people who hate us for what we do. As for the people that put nooses, guns and other stuff up on the N.V.A.C. page, I can't control everything."

The media bought and paid for Lowell's rant and the country followed suit. Even with Rachel and Steven's best efforts, their last ditch appeared to be going down in flames. A good point for them was that they did get the attention of Lowell and that meant he was watching. The bad was that *his* watching caused the Campaign for Freedom following to drop to forty-five people. The followers were deathly afraid of a shotgun blast to the head. Despite the drop and despite the apparent lack of support, Rachel and Steve continued their fight against the N.V.A.C. They stood staunch in their beliefs.

THE NEW RULE

The time for action was getting closer. For the moment, President Wisecroft had announced a vast revamping of sex offender laws throughout the United States. Out were the old Adam Walsh Act, Meghan's Law and Jessica's Law. They had served their purpose for the previous sixty-five years. Now it was time for the uniform Wisecroft Act. This act would take hold in every state and for every offender, no matter the charge. It would also serve to keep offenders in check until the bricked facility was closer to opening. After that, it was to be a full-scale collection of offenders for a trip to Northern Michigan: A permanent trip.

Under Wisecroft's plan, it became *nearly* impossible for any offender to live anywhere within the U.S. boundaries. Unless an offender chose to live in the middle of Kansas, Montana or wherever there were no children present within a ten-mile perimeter, they would be subject to arrest. Offenders had a computer chip injected under their skin. Not unlike a dog-tracking chip, it monitored every movement they made

47

and served as a warning signal if they passed through a door with a scanner installed. In addition, any offender setting foot within a ten-mile radius of a child's dwelling meant trouble for the offender: Including arrest and/or incarceration.

There were other factors within Wisecroft's Law but the basic premise was to set up the offender for failure. They had no legal access to computers, cell phones or any other device that had mass communication capability. If caught with any of the mentioned electronics, it would mean an arrest and/or incarceration. The House and Senate unanimously passed the bill and John Wisecroft signed it to the delight of the N.V.A.C. members and all others who didn't want the sex offenders near their children. Murderers, arsonists, home breakers and other criminals were not included within the new law. It was exclusively for sex offenders.

Upon hearing of the bill's signing, the advocates felt deflated. No longer could offenders have access to computers to continue their efforts of educating the public. No longer could they live within a ten-mile radius of any home in which a child lived, leaving them practically nowhere to reside. Taken a step further, *being* within ten miles of a child was enough to get the offender arrested. Left with no choice, Steven, Rachel and Matt, along with hundreds of thousands of other offenders and their families pulled up stakes and headed to parts of the country that were miles away from humanity. If an offender needed hospitalization or medical help, it would be a danger going into any wellness facility because it would risk an arrest. Offenders who had spouses were forced to rely on their wives or husbands to do all the grocery shopping and errand running to survive. Many spouses ended up divorcing, as the non-offender side of the coupling couldn't take the heat of moving away from loved ones, especially their own children. Most single offenders found themselves relegated to living off the land in the woods or open spaces of Montana, Idaho, New Mexico or other wide-open areas. Steven, ever the innovator and computer wizard, moved to the Montana Hills southeast of Great Falls and stayed linked online with a secretly coded internet device, while Matt and Rachel moved to Idaho where thankfully, Rachel had family.

*

Steven was a survivor and managed to build his own shelter within the ground. Tree sap, bark, leaves and other items of nature's bounty served him well, as he was able to dig out and solidify a bunker roughly twenty-five feet long by twenty-five feet wide. He scrounged the land and found some wood here or some metal there, which served to make a very nice entrance and ceiling for his domicile. He kept it camouflaged so nobody happening by would ever know it was there. The chances for an encounter were slim, as Steven was deep within the woodlands.

He had hauled with him his electric devices, i.e. computers, phones, radios and over 5,000 lbs. of batteries to keep everything, including his minimal lighting, running strong. Upon entering the coppices, he ditched his vehicle deep in a thickly bushed area and camouflaged it so that he would have it if needed in the future: a future that looked bleak indeed.

Steven was an avid hunter but didn't have enough ammo to waste on shooting animals, so he conjured up traps made of branches, vines and patience. Baiting the trap with corn or any other canned vegetable; he'd trap small game such as mice, gophers and woodchucks. He managed to put together another device for larger game: He whittled out spikes from some of the stronger branches he'd collected, strung them together and squeezed them between trees where he thought deer and other animals ran. By building up three of four layers of these two-foot-by-two-foot square devices between numerous trees, no animal could get through without stabbing itself to death. His plan was successful in that the speed of the game worked against it. A rushing deer had no time to stop and couldn't see the traps, not that it made any difference to scared game. Within twenty or thirty feet of the stabbing, they dropped. Steven dragged the critters off and chopped them up into sizable meals. He didn't need to worry about eating, as his skill was far superior to that of which the government gave the offender credit.

Steven left his hometown of Cincinnati without a computer chip injection. He was in the wilderness by himself with arrest warrants on his head; but he didn't care. He had nothing to lose and knew something was amiss with the laws. He wanted no part of it. If the facility, or Brick Project in Northern Michigan proved to be a tool to further enhance the new laws regarding the offenders, he figured he'd rather run unrestricted. Even though having free reign in beautiful Northern Michigan wasn't the worst deal *(better than prison),* he thought to himself how he'd rather die than succumb to such a ridiculous plot hatched by Wisecroft. It was more a matter of principle. His thinking was that he'd served his time, honored his parole and should be free.

He also had to be very careful, as spy drones and the occasional Government workers would comb the open areas of the United States. Out of the nearly two million registered offenders, five hundred thousand ended up relegated to the harshness of nature. Out of that five hundred thousand, fifty thousand would die in the elements. Steven was determined *not* to be one of them.

*

Back in Washington D.C., President Wisecroft praised his law in the privacy of the oval office, telling advisors and cabinet members how well his plan was working well. His Vice President, Henry Jasper, however, gave him want to worry by voicing his opinion.

"You may think it's a great idea John but how many of the offenders that you've basically thrown out to pasture are either falsely accused or have a silly case of public urination on their record? I also have statistics that show the sex offender only has a seven percent recidivism rate. It's right here in black and white."

Wisecroft looked at the sheet of paper and dismissed it, tossing it aside and allowing it to cascade to the floor in its chaotic fashion. He always had an answer, reasoning his ideas by using age-old excuses.

"If a few innocent men have to go down for the good of this country, then so be it. I'm not going to worry myself over a lousy one-half percent of the sex offender population that pisses on a dumpster or claims to be innocent. When they die and meet their maker, all will be good with them and that's what counts. As for the statistics, they're just like presidential polls; unreliable and subjective."

Jasper couldn't believe the indifferent tone the president took. He tried to hit home by mentioning his own personal experience with the registry.

"The innocence percentage is a lot higher than half a percent and you know it John." Jasper's argument continued. "I have falsely accused family myself."

"That's why we took care of them Henry. They're living in Northern Vermont in the lap of luxury. They'll have it made per the deal we hammered out. Why are you being so condescending about this now? Maybe we should add them to the millions who are out there struggling."

Henry didn't know quite how to react. Yes, Wisecroft gave Henry's family members, two of them, one who'd been falsely accused and wrongfully convicted, very special provisions. He thought it would be stupid and selfish to ruin their lives over people he didn't know. To his great guilt and nervousness, he dropped the matter.

"Okay, let's move on to other matters Mr. President. I get the point and thank you for looking after my people."

With a nod of his head and a clap on the shoulder, Wisecroft led Jasper down the hallway to the war room where the much bigger plans were being discussed: Plans to begin the gathering of the offenders. It was shrewd strategy by Wisecroft to have all of the offenders leave the dense areas of the United States; it would make it much easier to track and capture them. Wisecroft hung the offenders' out to dry with his law.

*

Rachel and Matt begrudgingly did what they had to do. Rachel had two cousins who lived in the Saw Tooth National Forest, a thickly wooded, virtually uninhabitable area in Idaho. The two cousins, Rick and Jill, supported Matt and were disgusted with the laws Wisecroft was coming up with and implementing. It was bad enough Matt was on a sex offender registry. They gladly invited the couple to come and stay. Frankly, four more hands were a wonderful thing to help with the chores that needed doing around the cabin.

It was a modest two-story home, heated with firewood and housing two spare bedrooms. Rachel and Matt took the couple up on their offer to stay with them. It helped to lessen the amount of stress both were under, as nature and the great wide open had a tendency to sooth the inner-beast of fear. Matt, being a muscular man who enjoyed working, took to splitting logs and chopping down trees; he liked anything that offered physical challenges. Rick appreciated the efforts around the home. Rachel helped Jill with whatever needed done as far as shopping, keeping the inside of the house nice and cooking. Rachel still took to doing a few of the physically demanding jobs as well to keep herself in shape. Everyone got along well and the teamwork was a plus for all involved.

Rachel couldn't thank Jill enough for the hospitality and always tried giving her the spare cash her and Matt had on hand.

"We'd never take your money Rach. You're going to need it down the road."

"Please take it," Rachel would beg. "It won't help us at all out in the wilderness. We have to learn to live off the land."

Jill turned her down numerous times. Rachel, ever the obsessive personality, never stopped trying, hiding the money in tins around the house for the couple to find later.

The intensity between Matt and Rachel continued but that was par for their married course. They kept their personal life quiet and separate from the cousins by taking long nature walks together and making love in the woods whenever they had a chance. They enjoyed doing it outside, as it offered a completely new freedom within their relationship. The fact that the stress had alleviated made it much easier for the two to engage.

Rachel still spent much of her time in front of the computer looking after the dwindling advocate groups she'd formed. The members were thinning however; as the new laws forced them into free ranging within the open parts of the

U.S.A. Unbeknownst to Rachel, at least a hundred of her closest friends already went to jail for trivial matters. It was better that she didn't know, as it would've devastated her. She hoped against hope that all of her people were finding suitable conditions and would get back online with her soon.

Rachel was much like Max Schindler during the holocaust of World War II, trying to save as many sex offenders as Schindler had Jewish people. Rachel tried her best to hide the emotions but they often released in tears, anger and frustration. Matt would try to settle her down, rubbing her shoulders and lying with her on the bed as he stroked what he thought to be the most beautiful strawberry blond hair he'd ever seen, felt or smelled. He loved Rachel but he worried about them both.

"What's going to happen?" Was his purveying thought that he didn't share with his wife. Would he live, die, or perhaps face arrest for an insignificant reason and never see her again? Would she be okay? Would she make it through this crisis without going completely out of her mind? The questions filled his mind but he had no answers, only more questions.

*

Steven continued to live in the thick woods off an out-of-the-way trail. He didn't bother to check and see if he lived near kids because it didn't matter. If ever caught, he'd be sent to prison without question. He also thought to himself that the distinct possibility existed of being shot dead. There would be no recourse for the shooter because Steven wouldn't go alive and he'd be another dead offender. He didn't plan on that happening and figured if they did find him; it would be while he was out foraging. He always carried his gun with him in case a bear or other dangerous wildlife found him, but he would also use it if the government or N.V.A.C. vigilantes showed up. He would never go alive. They'd have to drag him away in a pine box. It wasn't only the outside that posed a danger.

As he continued his monitoring on the tricked out computers he had with him, he let Lowell and Parker know that he was alive and well and refused to allow the pair to continue to destroy the people who were unfortunate enough to be listed. He had some of the greatest arguments with Parker, as Lowell rarely returned his messages and texts.

PARKER: We'll find you, you son-of-a-bitch. You can't stay hidden forever."

SMITH: You don't want to find me Parker because if you do, I *will* kill you slowly.

PARKER: At least you can't unzip your pants and find little kids to rape you numbnut.

SMITH: You know not what you say Sal, but you'd better back out because it's going to get rough.

On and on they went, exchanging "pleasantries" and telling each other who would get the best of whom. Steven also figured many offenders had already died or been taken away. He'd found two dead men a few miles from his underground cavern. The elements had been too much for them. Being the stand-up man he claimed to be, he dug a hole and gave them at least some peace. He held a mini-service, just him standing over the makeshift grave. These instances would give him more of a temper even though he was already a hothead. He was also smart and tolerated no lip from anyone, especially Lowell or The Gal. The N.V.A.C. was enemy number one to him. For years, he'd tried to reason with them but it was impossible now that he'd taken up full-time for the advocacy. The struggle was monumental. He knew it was going to get worse as that bricked facility in Michigan loomed. He knew why Wisecroft had decided on

58

his new laws when it was getting close to completion, but tried to deny it in his mind.

"Maybe I'm wrong," Steven would think to himself, *"maybe the facility is for army exercise or a giant testing facility."*

No matter how much he tried to deflect the real reason it always came back to the same conclusion: the facility was to be a sex offender prison of a magnitude no one had any idea could exist. Still, he planned to evade capture. How he would avoid detection for years to come was another story entirely. He worked, studied, gathered ideas and thought. He wouldn't rest. He also continued his battles with Parker. The latest were due to her contempt for the sex offenders.

PARKER: "I hear some of your "friends" met their maker eh? Do you think it's by accident? Do you think they deserved it? I'll tell you right now THEY DID! I'm glad they're dead except that it keeps me from having to kill them myself. I hope they rot in hell like they deserve."

SMITH: "You abashing cunt. I would expect such stupid things to be said from someone living in Flor-i-DOH."

PARKER: What's the matter Steven? Cat got your tongue? HAHA. More will die; hopefully with *their* tongues

59

hanging out of their own mouths. How does that grab ya? They deserved it and you know it. Why don't you come out of hiding and face me? Are you "scared" to go nose-to-nose with your downfall? I'll find you. I'll make it my mission to go to the ends of the earth to find you and kill you myself."

SMITH: "Oh, I'm so scared Gal. I look forward to you finding me so I can personally take you out. You're a nemesis and a mistake in human evolution. Between you and Lowell, your mother's should have swallowed."

PARKER: "We'll meet and when we do, I have a nice surprise for you. If you survive long enough that is. Goodbye loser. I'll be seeing you...soon!"

Parker signed off while Steven seethed. He wanted her to stand down and end her reign of terror. Parker was frustrated because she couldn't get a location using her computer's GPS features. Steven was smart and she knew it. She, however, thought herself to be smarter. Lowell didn't care for Parker getting so personal with the advocates. He wanted his groups to exist with more class. He didn't mind offenders dying or imprisoned, he simply didn't want it to appear that he was condoning out-and-out murder. He insisted that she tone it down for the sake of the N.V.A.C. Parker was a loose cannon and he feared she could hurt the cause. She didn't exactly appreciate his stance.

*

Parker also had it out for Rachel. She constantly bombarded her with messages about her husband's crime of some sixteen years prior. What Parker didn't understand or care to find out were the facts surrounding the case. Parker especially, and certain others in the N.V.A.C. clan rarely used facts when it came to crimes of rape, incest and child molestation. Most never looked into whether it was a Romeo-Juliet case, or if it was true rape. If you were on the list, that was all they needed. Parker began referring to it as a "hit list." The ultimate goal, as it said in their flyer, was elimination of the sex offender, predator and pedophile. With the help of President Wisecroft, it would likely come to completion. Rachel never engaged with Parker, which made the N.V.A.C. co-captain angry. As hard as Parker would try, there would never be any comments or emails back to her. However, she knew where the couple hid and planned to get them, thanks to her friend, the man in the green truck. Despite the fact that Rachel wasn't on the registry, Parker wanted her eliminated. She was a pest in her eyes who was making it tougher on the N.V.A.C. The battle would heat up in the coming months, as many changes would begin to take place. It was turning into a much more serious situation than anyone originally believed. Deadly serious.

THE MAN IN THE GREEN TRUCK

Only Parker knew the man in the green truck. She hired him to tag Steven, Matt and Rachel and report to her every couple of days or when the three were moving. At this point, he was only able to track Matt and Rachel, as Steven was in a different place. He never spoke to anyone except Sal and he wouldn't relent in his assigned duties. The only thing that was known about him was that he lived somewhere in the Everglades of Florida, smoked three packs of Marlboros every day and drank whisky a pint at a time. He had apparently known Sal some years earlier and befriended her, which in itself was a difficult thing to do. He had the mannerisms and attitude she liked and they instantly hit it off. On more than a few occasions, he had defended her from people who wanted to hurt her.

No one knew if Sal and the man were having an affair or ever slept together, as neither ever spoke of personal issues between each other. He met and got along with Davis Lowell, but never spoke with him: Not one word. He simply nodded and smiled if he agreed with Davis and frowned if he didn't.

The latter was the experience for the rest of the N.V.A.C. members who had met him. He was polite and nodded but never spoke. No one knew his name and Sal never gave it up. He became known as the man in the green truck, in homage to the green GMC pickup he drove around in while wearing a cowboy hat. He smoked and occasionally took a belt of Jack Daniels, Jim Beam or whatever his whiskey of choice was for that particular day.

Not even Davis could yank any information out of Sal. As hard as he tried, she was stern in her silence.

"Don't worry about it Davis. He's just a person I know that helps when I need him. He'll be tracking those three offenders and letting me know their whereabouts."

This bugged Davis, but what could he do? He theorized that the man must have been CIA, FBI or someone on that level of importance. He also thought that he could be mafia, as they're famous for silence. Davis decided that silence was the better choice and clammed up about him.

The man in the green truck watched, smoked and drank. He kept in communication with Sal and reported only to her. He was on Matt and Rachel's tail, keeping a low profile and watching with a small pair of high-powered binoculars. The two headed west. He'd clue Sal into every move they made. He knew about Steven, who lived in Cincinnati, and kept the advocate on the back burner. He had no doubt that they'd all eventually meet down the line. The lowbrow attitude and quiet demeanor kept the man at a low stress level. With the amount he smoked and drank, any other level of stress would've probably killed him.

As mysterious and strange as the man seemed, it was a boon for the obsessive Sal, who could now keep track of her "prey" on more than one front.

A HITLER MENTALITY

Now that the offenders wore chips under their skin, an ankle bracelet and most had barcode scanners tattooed onto them, it was much easier to detect their whereabouts. If they stepped into any local business that had the chip scanner at the door (all businesses were *required* by federal law to install such equipment and most did) a buzzer went off indicating that an offender was present in the facility. After being spit on, screamed at and otherwise humiliated, security whisked them out of the store. Doctor's offices, hospitals, dentist offices and other buildings that were public were also equipped with the scanners. Offenders, if ill, found that the only way they could find viable treatment was to locate a trained professional that was also on the registry. Now that the laws had changed, they faced arrest and detention if found at any facility that was equipped with scanners because it meant they were undoubtedly within ten miles of a child. It proved to be extra difficult for the offenders after running

65

away from the denser areas of the U.S.A. It was a rare instance when they had the guts to show up at these locations, but it did happen periodically, especially those offenders who refused to have the chip installed under their skin. Care had to be used, as all of the nation's newspapers and magazines listed offender information with pictures. If caught, it would be jail for sure or even worse in some cases.

*

Because the media, newspapers and TV had made the offender a modern-day leper, some people began spitting at them in the street or ripping their clothes off so they were stark naked. The goal was to shame them. If the offender couldn't escape these mobs, he or she was injured and sometimes even killed. A twenty year-old woman who had sex with a fourteen-year-old boy was caught in the street in Dallas, Texas and *stoned to death* in front of a delirious crowd; cell phones and camera's documenting the attack. Despite the fact that she herself was a young woman, the media frenzy mixed with Wisecroft's propaganda sent the public into a livid fury. People took pictures and filmed her while she was bleeding from the head. Grown men were pulling up her skirt and taking pictures of her bare bottom and vagina as she lay dying. The sight was gruesome as the blood poured from her mouth, ears and nose. Death finally came, relieving her of the painful and harsh death. No one was implicated in the attack even though suspects could be recognized on the videos that went viral on social media sites. Wisecroft condemned the attack and announced it in a speech. Whether it was rhetoric or his real feeling didn't matter much as charges never came for the perpetrators. The few media outlets that did express outrage at the wasteful death found themselves fined and censured behind closed doors.

That wasn't the most violent attack. Men and women alike found themselves chained to the back of cars and dragged through the streets until their flesh literally ground off the bone. Male and female offenders alike were raped; teen-age registrants were raped and men were sodomized by the use of unspeakable means. The same people who were penalizing them for being registered sex offenders violated them in the most perverted ways possible. People pled for their lives.

"I was falsely accused!"

"I pissed in public, that's it!"

"My crime was being eighteen and having sex with a sixteen-year-old! I don't deserve this!"

None of the excuses mattered as the crowds seemingly foamed from their collective mouths. The police rarely stopped it unless they absolutely had to, even joining the fray in some locations (mainly south). In the middle of the country where most offenders fled, they were hunted like wild game, rewards given in hunting clubs for bagging the *non-compliant* offenders. It was no longer the "how I shot a deer" story in front of the water coolers, but "how I snagged a wayward offender." When the hunters would find them, they'd tie them up and then take pictures before turning them over to the authorities. Sometimes after documenting the proof of the offender's capture, they were humiliated before being turned over to police. The hunters celebrated with wild beer drinking parties and carousing over the offender's suffering.

These stories only scratched the surface. The media were no longer writing about offender harassment in fear of being castigated and tuned out, so they softened up the story by writing about how wonderful the public was in protecting the children of the USA. Soon the pervading opinion was that the bricked facility, if in fact built for the offenders, would actually protect them from further harm. The opinions of most people rarely wavered.

"They'll rape again if you don't lock them up forever."

"They can't be cured."

"If we don't stop them other children will suffer."

The offenders that were caught rarely ended up dead, but the humiliation was mentally taxing on the offender *and* their families. Children, spouses or significant others were left to their own emotional devices. Weeping, wailing and begging, according to non-offenders, were necessary in keeping the offenders in "check." Families of offenders were shunned as much as the offender themselves, so they had to befriend other offender families to have any camaraderie. After Wisecroft passed his laws, that all changed.

With few choices remaining, the family members had to stand aside and let their offender family member succumb to sure embarrassment. On occasion, offenders either hung or shot themselves, relieving their family of the shame, and themselves of the torment. Occasionally, they fought off the attackers for a while, only to weaken and get beat up in the end. Wives who stood before their men were slapped away, raped or both, and men who stood before their offender wives were beaten. Some vigilantes, raised within the compounds of an entirely different existence, occasionally took children away from these families, insisting that they were saving the youngsters from sure abuse.

President Wisecroft had fueled the attitude as he was slowly convincing the population that all the problems of the nation were attributable to the offenders. It wasn't much different from Hitler blaming the Jews for Germany's woes. Somebody(s) had to take the hit and with Wisecroft already having a reason to hate offenders, he let it all hang out in speeches across the United States. While on one hand

69

condemning the torture of offenders, his speeches actually
encouraged it.

*"My fellow Americans, we cannot live in the web of the
sex offender for another day. They must be stopped and dealt
with severely. As you know, we've passed the Wisecroft Act,
which requires all offenders to be micro-chipped for ease in
locating them and they have been required not to live within
ten miles of any child in this country."*

Part of the public agreed with it and contributed to the
violence while others ignored it. Some non-offenders went so
far as to start helping offenders in peril, but were always
accused of being pro-offender if caught, thus bringing on their
own brand of trouble: Everything from houses being
graphitized and even burned to the protectors being arrested
for "impeding the law." Most protectors went underground
and held a firm "hush-hush" rule with anyone they helped.

Cheers erupted as the masses bought Wisecroft's
speeches and propaganda. They listened closely and put the
blame for the country's economic crisis, joblessness and high
crime rates on the offender. Now that the two million or more
offenders had abandon everything they owned, the banks not
only helped themselves to what was inside their houses, but
also claimed some of the houses as their own due to

delinquent loan payments. Of course, they felt that this was helping the housing market and giving more "law-abiding" citizens a place to live. The offenders and their families had up and left. The attacks weren't subtle and always very effective.

"Soon, I will be making announcements on how all the offenders will ultimately be dealt with in the future. We have a plan here in America and it will be carried out. The House and Senate have approved my plan, agreeing with me that it's the best economic indicator in our country as for recovery. The sex offender is obsolete and will be eliminated from our cities, states and most importantly, our children! I urge all Americans to help us with the capture and imprisonment of all offenders. The Wisecroft Act now has a new law that all offenders be incarcerated pending my big announcement. If you are an offender, please report to your local police agencies for further instruction."

Most of the public, especially those in Michigan, figured that the large bricked facility surrounding the upper peninsula of Michigan was a large prison for all the offenders: Past, present and future. If that were to be the case, most would be pleased as they figured that their kids would be protected from abuse, rape and molestation. Even though the

71

facts showed that some ninety-six percent of abuse took place *within* the family and NON-sex offenders committed another ninety-three percent of the offenses, the people still thought that The Brick was the right answer. Most didn't listen to the statistics; they simply wanted the sex offender eliminated. Emotion ruled the decision-making process.

*

     Lowell and Parker were reveling in the idea, believing that a permanent end to the sex offender problem was just around the corner. They began sending out e-mails and having conversations on social media websites instructing people on what to do and how to find wayward offenders. They used propaganda and free speech to their advantage. Neither the police, ACLU or AFLCIO would dare get involved, as the country had moved to the brink of a Holocaustic attitude. Parker, of course, was still a big advocate of harassing offenders, but Lowell took a more conservative approach. The postings on the social networks were of a pitiless nature, with the occasional peaceful voice piping in. Parker, of course, was leading her troops.

     SAL PARKER: With The Wisecroft Act defined, I'm screwing with every sexual predator I can. Count on it. As far as condoning violence, I certainly *do* condone it. I will haunt every single person in the world who has ever harmed a child. I couldn't care less about their families or friends. The fact of the matter is that most predators re-offend. It has to stop. Will I kill them if I have to? Absolutely. May God have mercy on all their souls.

HUNG: I second that motion.

TOM: I'm with you.

JESSICA: I agree 100% with you Gal.

STEVE: The Advocates call you and N.V.A.C. "chickenshits", yet they all use fake names and anonymous pics. They're cowardly, desperate pieces of shit. I'm in.

RON: I have an idea; let's try to negotiate and talk it out in a calm manner. Violence begets violence. Let's show some class and be peaceful.

ROBERT: Count me in; we can jam some heavy metal while kicking brains and teeth out.

KRISTI: Count me in. I already have everything I need at my house. LOL. Hey Ron, go back home and be a little pussy. We don't need people like you throwing a wrench in the cause.

ANNA: I'm military trained so I'm a really great shot, and I agree with Kristi: Go away Ron!

RON: Really people? Violence is the only answer?

ARCHIE: I'm in and I have plenty of ammo! Sign me up. I think I'll add Ron to my "hitlist."

RON: If you can't be peaceful, I'm out. Nobody deserves that kind of treatment.

VAL: Good Ron. We don't want you here anyway. We don't enlist "pussies." You're probably an offender too.

Meanwhile, Lowell was at work on his side of the ledger, stirring up the masses for elimination against the offenders.

DAVIS LOWELL: Anyone that touches or implies anything sexual to a child should be "Bricked."

JILL: I hope the sick freaks are raped every day in prison. Hopefully, two-three times per day. Sick assholes.

DAVIS LOWELL: "The Brick" will be enough to rid our society of the offenders. We now have a solution to our problem. They can do whatever they want on the other side. They'll no longer be our problem.

Rachel tried in vain to get at least a murmur of doubt out of the N.V.A.C. and its members but she was only one against seemingly millions. The advocacy was broken apart and sent to different parts of the country, most without computer access. The odds were stacked against her.

RACHEL LYONS: I thought your N.V.A.C. group didn't advocate violence.

SAL PARKER: You're being watched Rachel, and so is your pervert husband. You've been warned.

LYONS: You're talking about extermination. You call the offenders sick freaks but that's what I'm seeing out of you and your cronies. Don't you have your own children to look after and raise?

75

PARKER: No more talk. Keep your head up.

The conversation continued, after Rachel was blocked.

PARKER: They're a waste of humanity. We'll castrate the males with a rusty hacksaw and sew the women's vaginas shut.

ZEEL: I'll beat them to death with my bare hands.

JEANA: We'll cut their dingdongs off with machetes.

DANIELLE: The Mother's will also get revenge. A Mother's wrath is the worst.

PATTY: Our safety depends on finding and killing these scumbags.

BAM: Damn right! Perverts get what they deserve.

MATEO: We'll take their families out too. No sense risking them having more perverts.

LARRY: You've all made my day...Thanx!

It went on day after day after week after month until the frenzy reached fever pitches. The next phase would involve the gathering and delivering of the offenders into The Brick, if that's what Wisecroft meant within his speeches. The assumption continued to be "yes" it would be for the offenders.

*

In Idaho, Rachel cried while Matt looked out the window in a glaze of disbelief. In the middle of Montana, Steven held his chin in his hands as he contemplated the future.

Matt, seeing his lovely Rachel carrying a look of defeat, took her in his arms. He held her with a strong, reassuring hold as she rested her head on his chest. Knowing that their time together may be limited, Matt led his beautiful bride to the bedroom. He held her, caressed her and loved her. He hadn't been intimate enough with Rachel and frankly, with the stress they were both under, it was no wonder. On this day however, Matt would make love to *his* Rachel all through the night. They laughed and giggled as if it was brand new to them. Rachel allowed Matt full access to her body, mind and heart. Matt did the same, taking his time to attend to the needs

77

of his beautiful woman. The two joined in a bond that could seemingly never be broken and looked into each other's eyes in a locked gaze. They whispered about love, planted soft kisses on each other's necks and ears and joined their wet tongues together in dances and moist twirls of sensuality. The orgasms they felt went beyond sex and lust; it reached into a zone of pure ecstasy and *want*. The pair hadn't smiled and frolicked in this way for months and the stress that poured out of them was, in itself, orgasmic. They didn't care how much noise they made in the throes of passion nor did they relent in their want of satisfying each other fully. When the light began to sneak into their room, they finally fell asleep in each other's arms. The cousins heard much of the festivities in the night but weren't at all cross over it. They knew that it could be a matter of time before Matt would be taken away. They smiled at each other, drank their coffee and kept their eyes peeled for any sign of trouble. It wouldn't take long before they'd be forced to sound the alarm.

*

Steven sat thinking. His mind swirled with thoughts and ideas. He was close (online) to Rachel and Matt when they were at their respective homes in Cincinnati and upstate New York. They'd never met, but through their advocacy efforts, they communicated daily and fought the same fight. The three were leading all the wayward and confused offenders in the assault on draconian laws and the many civil rights violations that had been a part of the war on the registry. The violations included not being allowed access to places where children congregated, including, but not limited to playgrounds, ice cream parlors and schools. The offender, although they had a measly recidivism rate, were the scarlet letter wearers of the 21st century. Even though there was no proof, pundits and media called the offenders "bus stop surfers," "playground watchers" and the "creepy people who waited around corners for your children to walk their way." Although there were a few ill offenders who did those things, the higher percentage of such abductions were committed by non-offenders. The government ignored those facts.

Now that Wisecroft had taken over, the fight was all for naught. The new President had persuaded the people to move in a different direction and there would be no turning back. The only thing that could possibly change the future would be Wisecroft's death or a new president taking over the reins who would change the nonsense back *at least* into its original pre-Wisecroft form. The chances were unlikely, and probably futile. Steven needed to re-focus his manner of thinking and figure out how he was going to live out his life as a free man. He had served his time and paid his penance but it wasn't good enough. According to the law, he needed to do more; he needed to do *forever*. He read of the assaults, humiliation and flat-out murders of the offenders that dared go near any populated areas. He knew Rachel and Matt were in Idaho and wanted to help protect them. He planned to contact them and figure out how he could get the two to Montana, mainly because he knew the couple's time in Idaho was ticking away. The couple was some 330 miles away from him, but Steven went to work plotting. It wouldn't be easy, as all would find out.

*

Prisoners around the country were in full riot mode against any offenders housed with them. Stabbings, throat slashing's and terrible beatings were the new rule inside the over-populated and understaffed penitentiaries. Instead of separating the offenders from general population, the guards let whatever happened happen. They simply cleaned up the messes and went on with their regular duty. The correction officers were just as negligent about the offenders as the government, and most recently, the public. Kids as young as nineteen were stabbed for doing nothing more than having sex with their sixteen-year-old girlfriends, but being imprisoned in spite of it. Some were back in prison on violations such as registering one day too late or being caught drinking while on parole or probation. Sal Parker made sure to get her messages to the inmates she knew inside the prisons. "Get all of the sex offenders" was her mantra. The lifers and people with little hope of ever leaving prison were the main culprits. Some offenders stayed in their cell and waited for the food to come to them. No more showers, no wandering the grounds and no talking with others. They had a safety at all cost mentality. They weren't required to leave their cells so they didn't. In some prisons, sadistic guards would unlock an offender's cell and allow the vermin to assault, badly injure or even kill them. They turned their heads and walked away. Out of the two million offenders in the United States, two hundred thousand took up space in the prisons. When the "holocaust" of sex offenders began, one million were either in prison or homeless on the streets looking for safety. In a matter of only a few short days since the Wisecroft law passed, havoc was taking its toll. The public, vigilantes and prisoners had so far injured or murdered thousands of offenders. Staggering were the numbers when you consider that Hitler's reign in Germany killed six *million* Jews total. Of course, in Germany, there were many more people helping eradicate the Jews while the armies in the U.S. thus far had only a small part in the offender siege. With armies assisting, the annihilation of a

81

group could take place much quicker. The military involvement would soon grow.

The madness that permeated U.S. soil was as scary as anyone had ever seen. It was scary for ordinary citizens who would never partake in such humiliating and hurtful practices, but not so scary for the vigilantes, especially Parker, who delighted in the abuse. Parker was continuing her torturous methods while Lowell sat in the background allowing everyone else in his vigilante groups to do his dirty work.

It would continue with terrorizing results.

CAPTURED

Steven contacted Rachel over the internet and told her he had a nice hideaway in Montana that would keep all three of them safe whether the situation blew over or not.

"Blows over?" Rachel sounded surprised and doubtful. "That could take ten, twelve, hell, even twenty years. Maybe it'll never blow over."

"Well I don't know what else to tell you. If you stay where you're at, they'll get Matt for sure. Is that the choice you want to make?"

As Steven typed, he mulled over his humble abode. Dirt, grass and artificial battery powered light were all he could muster. At least he felt safe.

"This is the deal Rachel. I have a nice spot in Montana. If you'd like to come, I'll help protect you and Matt. It isn't much and I'm not telling you exactly where it is but I will tell you to travel northeast. I'll find you as you approach."

Rachel agreed and told Steven to watch for them. After some hemming and hawing between her and Matt, a fight broke out.

"If we stay here Matt, we're sitting ducks. If we move, at least we have a shot. Why do you always insist on sitting on your hands and waiting? Christ Matt!"

"I'm scared Rachel. They're arresting and harassing offenders by the bucket load. I personally don't want to be a part of that group. I hate the stigma I have attached to me and I want it to be gone forever. Don't you get it? Why would they even come up with the "Wisecroft Law" if all they were going to do were start ganging up on us anyway? I don't see the point."

Rachel put her hands on her hips and dug her feet in for a good chewing out of her husband.

"They didn't make the law for any other reason than to make it easier to catch the offenders. The less dense the population, the better *for them*. I'll tell you right now that I'm going. If you want to stay here and be put on a kabob by a bunch of crazy fuckers, knock yourself out. Rick and Jill have a pair of four-wheelers and lots of gas. Do you want to man up or will you stay here and be taken, or worse? Remember, you're chipped, so they know where you are as we speak. We can remove the chip, make things more interesting and swing the advantage our way, but we have to get moving now!"

Little did either of them know that there was a watcher not far away: A man in a green truck.

Rachel went out back and baited a bunny with a carrot, something she did every day. When it hopped to her, she picked it up and gently placed it in a cage.

"Give me your knife Matt." Rachel ordered. "We're going to take care of this right now."

Matt handed her the blade with wide eyes, afraid of what she would do to the poor bunny. He was surprised when her plan was not to harm the cute, fuzzy creature, but to hurt *him*. She heated the blade with a lighter and took her husband by the wrist. She quickly cut a slice in his arm from the outer hand toward the elbow. Matt, feeling the electric pain, placed his other palm in his mouth as he pulled his arm back. He curled it into his midsection, snarled an expletive and walked to the garden butting up to the woods. Rachel gave him a minute or two of space before walking over and placing a hand on his shoulder. When he turned to look at her, a tear was running down his cheek.

"Rachel, I thought we lived in the best country in the world. It turns out it's just another cesspool on the earth. When people lose their fucking minds, bad things happen. I'm walking around with a bull's eye on my forehead."

"Yes, you are. But if we keep moving, we'll be a tougher target. Moving targets are much harder to spot and

85

catch. We have to do this honey. If we don't we could regret it. If the worst happens and you die, they might as well kill me with you because I'd die inside. Now don't worry. I was a cutter for years and I'm good at this.'

Matt took a long look at his girl. Her big, toothy smile and curly locks mixed with grease stains on her hands and cheek made him smile. She was the perfect match for Matt, not afraid to get dirt under her fingernails. He was finally convinced that he should at least try. He figured he owed her that much.

"Okay, finish what you were doing. I'll do it… for us."

His wife, as carefully as she could, finished cutting a slice that was four inches long, extending to the middle of his forearm. She had to search for the tiny chip, so she pulled out a reading glass and put on a latex glove. She stuck her index finger in the incision and carefully dug in a motion toward his wrist. Matt gritted in pain as her finger ran across his nerve and tendon. When Rachel was doing this dirty work, she was cringing, as seeing Matt's insides weren't the most pleasant sight. Her finger seemingly sent bolts of lightning through Matt's body. Finally, after what seemed like an eternity, she removed her finger in an upward motion at his outer wrist. On the end of her finger, as plain as day, stuck the chip. She was relieved that she found it on her first dig through his arm.

86

Matt quickly started wrapping up tightly in a large ace bandage to close the long wound. Rachel looked at him with a smile as she fed the bunny a carrot with the chip jammed into the end of it. The bunny gobbled up the treat. After he finished, she turned him loose. He hopped quickly into the thick woods, carrying with him Matt's "new" location, which would be permanent when the bunny finally stopped to expel the carrot. That would take twelve to sixteen hours, depending on the fuzzy guy's digestive speed.

After completing the difficult task and helping Matt get his arm well covered, she spoke. "Now I know you inside as well as out."

"Go text Steven and tell him we're coming." Matt insisted.

Rachel, thrilled with his decision, gave her man a kiss on the cheek and ran inside to text Steven the good news.

"Good." Steven stated. "Bear northeast. I won't miss you."

Matt and Rachel loaded up the four wheelers with as much gas as they could carry. Each was able to strap two five-gallon jugs to each machine. That would be more than enough for the some three-hundred plus mile jaunt. They would leave the next morning.

*

Sal "The Gal" had combed through Florida, went up into Alabama and continued in a northwest direction through Mississippi, Oklahoma and toward Colorado burning a swath of humiliated, harassed and even badly injured or dead sex offenders along the way. Now that she was close to Idaho, she was in constant communication with her friend in the green truck, whom was monitoring Rachel and Matt. Being mortal enemies with Rachel during the advocates' crusade to lighten sex offender laws, Sal wanted to take care of the pair herself. She stood only one hundred miles from where Rachel and Matt were staying. She had a device given to her by another friend that honed into Matt's personal microchip. Since Sal had friends in the police force, she was able to come to an agreement on "purchasing" the device. Thanks to a media and government that were becoming more and more one-sided in favor of the N.V.A.C., the police themselves had turned against the offenders. Helping the N.V.A.C. co-leader was considered an honor. The cop also made a cool five grand for his trouble.

Davis Lowell stayed on his home turf in Florida keeping the N.V.A.C. running from the comfort (and safety) of his own basement. He knew the hits were out on him and Sal but only cared about his own health. If Sal went down, he wouldn't have another member to match her tenacity, but he would have others willing to do the dirty work she was dedicated to accomplishing.

*

As Sal was closing in, she knew Rachel and Matt were completely oblivious to her arrival. She didn't want to blow it, so she would, with the three men she brought with her, come in during the night when everyone was asleep. That way she could make her collar and reap the reward of *killing* both Matt and Rachel at the same time. She didn't want to take them in or deliver them anywhere, as The Brick hadn't yet been opened; so slow torture, rape and odious evil would be her thrill of the catch.

Cutting up through the corner of Wyoming in the dead of night was no problem for the well-prepared N.V.A.C. group. Sal made sure they had two high energy 4x4's so the terrain would never present a challenge. They snuck up to within twenty miles of the house by four a.m., and readied for the kill. Sal went over all final instructions with the group.

"Okay. Matt Lyons is mine. You do whatever you want to Rachel; rape her, beat her, pee on her; but DO NOT kill her. That's my kill too. Understand?"

The three men nodded and off they went for the final stretch. As they reached the five-mile mark, Sal was not

89

amused, as the tracking device started moving erratically. It was headed northeast at a moderate clip, then southeast, then north, west, south and north again. The one consistent was that it didn't move far. Hoping that it was a minor glitch, the group headed down the driveway of Rick and Jill, where the signal emanated, their guns out and their mental torches glowing.

*

Rachel awoke at around three a.m. and thought she should wake Matt so they could get a head start under the cover of dark. After downing a quick pot of coffee, the two bid their wonderful cousins ado and headed out on the four wheelers. The advantage with the machines was two-fold: They could take any route they pleased and could easily hide whenever the situation called for it. It was three forty-five a.m. when they departed, some thirty minutes ahead of Sal's arrival.

The man in the green truck, having fallen into a drunken sleep, knew nothing of their departure.

After Rick and Jill bid the couple adieu, they sat down to their coffee, only to hear the roar of trucks getting close. They knew offender hunters had arrived, they just didn't know it was Sal leading the charge. The couple immediately ran upstairs and manned rifles that were set-up for just such an emergency. As Sal and her clan moved closer, it was obvious that they were there for a fight. Taking no chances, Rick was the first to open fire, hitting the driver of the first 4x4. A fatal throat hit sent the truck careening into a tree on the left side of the driveway. While the driver was killed, the passenger was left unhurt. He hopped out and found an adequate vantage point for returning fire. Upon seeing the lead truck veer, Sal cut hard right and stopped behind a bank of trees that shielded her and the man riding with her. The odds were better for Rick and Jill as it was two against three. What they didn't know was that Sal was a champion sharpshooter and relaxed in the knowledge that she would wait them out before returning her fire.

Eventually the survivor of the crashed truck made it to Sal and her protégé. She ordered the two men to serve as decoys so she could deduce directly from where the shots were coming. As she sent the first man across the driveway, Jill took a shot. Sal rolled to her right, lined Jill up in her sightlines and pulled the trigger. Hit between the eyes, Jill died instantly. Rick, in the room next to his wife, didn't know what had taken place. Jill had, however, injured the man that crossed the drive. He was down with a blown-out kneecap. Sal ordered her second man to make a beeline straight for the house. When he did this, Rick opened fire. Instead of firing back, Sal went around the opposite side and snuck inside through the kitchen door. As her minion exchanged gunfire with Rick, the most unfortunate situation occurred: Sal came from behind and put her knife across Rick's throat. He dropped the rifle.

"You and I are going to have a chat. You're going to be a big help."

Rick looked forward reserved and defeated. Sal explained the situation. "Your wife's dead, numbnuts. I shot her right between the eyebrows. If you don't want to join her, you'll answer all my questions."

Rick knew he had a problem. He also knew that his day of death had arrived.

The firing of guns woke the man in the green truck. He'd slept through the action and was curious as to what had occurred. He radioed Sal, who told him Matt and Rachel had departed. Knowing this, he slammed his truck in drive and arrived on the scene.

*

Matt and Rachel raced across the plains and through wooded areas with no hesitation. They drove through the rest of the night and into daylight. It was vital that they move fast and hard to reach Steven's "home" in a reasonable amount of

92

time. The good thing was that they could take back roads, trails and lonely paths as they drove toward their destination. Being three hundred and thirty miles away, it would take the pair a good ten hours or more to reach their friend. They had to stop for breaks along the way and re-fuel the four-wheelers, which averaged about one hundred miles per tank of gas. The tanks were five-gallon capacity, so they had plenty of fuel for the trek.

What the two didn't know was that behind them in Idaho, Sal was wreaking havoc on the people that had so kindly helped them. If they did know, they may have turned back to help. There was no way Rachel would ever allow her family to be hung out to dry.

On they rode, hoping to reach Steven fast. They had to take special care about their surroundings, as drones flew around the sky at an alarming rate. Matt knew that most offenders had opted for the great plains of the US, so it was no surprise that the planes hovered around so prominently. One mistake could prove costly, so the utmost in attention was paid. The two continued on their trek by using as many wooded areas as they could. There was the occasion when they had to cross expressways, but they stopped and looked carefully before moving forward. Rachel figured that by Matt not having the chip inside his arm, the advantage would go to them. Little did she know that the man in the green truck,

93

while a bit behind in his surveillance responsibilities, would do whatever it took to catch up.

*

The man in the green truck arrived to get the lowdown from Sal. He'd wait to see if Rick would answer her questions about the pair's whereabouts.

Sal tied Rick's hands behind his back and slung a rope from his wrists over an overhanging branch of a tree that overlooked the cabin's driveway. For added intimidation and cruelty, she had her minion drag Jill's corpse out and lean her up against the same tree so Rick could take a good long look at her while being interrogated. It was as cruel as it was sick but Sal couldn't have cared less. She wanted to know where Rachel and Matt had gone. Rachel's advocacy along with Matt's offense had her mouth watering. Out of all the offenders living between the four sides of what she believed to be the great country she called the U.S.A., those were two of the three she wanted to seize personally. The other was Steven Smith, another thorn in her side.

One of her goons pulled the rope hard, causing Rick's hands to rise from hips to shoulder blades, *behind his back.* The pain was immense as Rick shouted with a grunt.

"That's nothing old Ricky-boy." Sal pulled the front of Rick's hair, forcing him to look up. "The more you lie or avoid my questions, the more by man will pull on that rope until your arms rip off your shoulders like chicken legs off a carcass."

Rick looked up with a pained glance. This woman had just minutes earlier murdered his wife in cold blood. She was the love of his life. He would take incredible pain rather than telling the vigilante anything. He spit in her face. Sal gave the goon a thumbs up and he gave the rope another tug. This time Rick shouted. His hands rose above his shoulder blades. He could feel the muscles stretch and bluster against the unnatural movement. Sal spoke again. "You *are* going to talk. I won't relent until you tell me where Matt and Rachel went. If you say you don't know, I'll tug harder. If you smart-ass me, I'll tug harder. It's your choice pretty-boy."

"Okay, okay, I'll tell you. But on one condition."

"What's that?" A bored Sal asked.

"That you burn in Hell with the rest of your evil groups, you two-bit murderer. You're worse than any sex offender I've ever met. Go fuck yourself."

This time the yank of the rope easily broke Rick's arms. The crack of the bones echoed off the trees and back into his ears. The pain caused him to pass out.

"Well," Sal exclaimed, "this one's no good to me."

95

She pulled out her pistol and shot him in the side of the head.

The man with the green truck, who went snooping, came out from behind the house and caught Sal's attention. He pointed to the tracks of the four-wheelers headed towards the woods.

"They're moving northeast?" Sal asked.

The man nodded, tipped his hat and ran to his truck. He left without saying a word.

*

Steven was up in the tree hoping to see a sign of the couple. Along with wanting to protect them, he was feeling very lonely.

He had lived by himself for a long time and was growing restless with having no human presence to alleviate the unending quiet that the middle-of-nowhere served up each day. Divorced and on the run because of an encounter he had no knowledge of made him sad and depressed. An eleven year-old girl in his home state of Ohio had accused him of sexual assault. He was obviously set-up by his now ex-wife, who wanted the money Steven had stashed away in his accounts. Over the years, he had saved up some one hundred and fifty grand. A sex-crime rap gave his wife the exact

96

advantage she needed to wipe the accounts clean. She had saved traces of his sperm in which to do the dirty deed of inserting into the eleven year-old's vagina. She promised the family a twenty-thousand dollar reward for following her lead. Money spoke. The police were called and the DNA evidence was irrefutable. The courtroom was where Steven met his accuser for the first time. The family that accused him were longtime friends of his ex-wife. It was a plan that worked to perfection as he found himself tried and convicted in less than one day. The jury was out a grand total of forty-five minutes.

Steven spent five years in prison and five years on parole. He followed his detention and parole to the letter of the law. When it was time to get the chip implanted under The Wisecroft Law, he fled. He wouldn't lower himself another notch in the government's plot to rid the country of the offenders for good. Being a fighter caused him to break free and take his chances. Steven was a true advocate. He fought for the rights of offenders all over the United States. He wasn't about to give in to the totalitarianism he thought was developing under the president. He also smelled a rat with the building of the bricked facility in Michigan. When Wisecroft passed his act, he knew that was exactly what The Brick was for: Housing all the offenders of the USA. Steven also had a plan to get revenge on his sinister ex-wife. Revenge, being a dish better served cold, allowed time to soothe the emotional wounds. When his ex-wife least expected it, he would strike with a quickness reserved for an angry rattlesnake. That was a worry that had to simmer on the backburner, as a more vital situation lay just ahead of him.

Steven had waited patiently when he finally saw a cloud of dust in the farthest distance that his binoculars worked. It was Matt and Rachel racing toward him in a flurry. It had been only two days, yet the pair had covered the mileage needed to reach him.

The man in the green truck had also covered the ground and had caught up with the couple about one hundred miles earlier when they were forced to cross a main highway to keep their route intact. He'd made a call to Sal and Government officials about the location of the two and tailed them all the way to the Montana plains. He could only get within a mile of where they were, as the wooded area they approached made his sightlines nearly worthless. He was still able to see what transpired in the distance.

As Rachel and Matt roared toward the glare magnified by Steven, a police drone suddenly appeared overhead. It seemed to come out of nowhere. Matt gave Rachel a hand signal and they separated their paths to try to confuse the unmanned aircraft. The drone immediately veered right, staying on Matt's tail. In seconds, it was directly over him, about twenty feet above his head. A large net shot out from the underbelly of the plane and fell atop Matt with a swift whoosh. The weight of the net pushed him down on the handlebars of the machine and caused the four-wheeler to bind and stall. Rachel was racing hard for cover, which existed with a large clump of trees some fifty yards ahead. As she pushed the metal down and upped her speed, out from those trees came two jeeps with three men per vehicle. Thinking she was a dead duck, she veered hard left, almost rolling the machine over. She would try to outrace them on the harsh terrain even though the jeeps were much faster. Surprisingly, they never vacillated and kept a straight path, moving past her with a dusty cough of dirt.

Steven, sitting on his perch with his mouth agape, saw everything as it was transpiring. He knew right away that Matt was had, but hoped Rachel would continue her path towards him. He put the mirror down in fear of detection by the personnel in the jeeps. Rachel had stopped some one hundred yards away to see where the jeeps headed. That's when she saw the net over Matt. Steven prayed that she wouldn't try to be a hero and do something stupid. He clenched his hands tightly together and watched the proceedings through slitted eyes.

Rachel observed Matt surrounded by the men in the jeeps. They were all were carrying rifles and took aim at the ill-fated offender. Knowing there was nothing she could do

99

but at the same time crying inside her helmet, Rachel made the wise choice and gunned the four-wheeler in the opposite direction. Steven breathed a sigh of relief as he saw her continue her path toward him.

"Don't fucking move or I'll shoot." One of the men told Matt aloud.

He couldn't move, as the netting had completely ensnared him. He sat like a wild animal, harrowed and defeated. He knew exactly what the situation entailed.

After untangling Matt from the mesh prison, one of the men cuffed him and placed him in a jeep. He had questions for the wayward offender. "Where's your chip buddy?"

He tore Matt's sleeve up and saw the large bandage. He ripped the bandage off and saw the gash.

"Tsk, tsk. It looks like trouble for you."

Matt sat in stone silence, not wanting to add fuel to the fire.

"We let your friend go. We can't arrest non-offenders, now can we? We've been on your tails for two hundred miles and were able to identify both of you. Technology sucks for you, doesn't it? You're going to The Brick asshole. No more molesting children…ever."

No longer being able to resist, Matt spoke up. "Fuck you losers. You don't even know the whole story, do you?"

A sudden darkness engulfed his world.

100

Rachel kept moving forward. When the men loaded up Matt and drove away, Steven continued his glaring of the mirror. Within five minutes, she was almost under him. He lowered himself from the tree with his rope. Steven smiled, if half-hearted. Rachel pulled her helmet off and he saw the tears running down her face. He thought to himself how beautiful she was and how sadness had engulfed her. He walked up and greeted her with a hug.

"Nice to finally meet you Rachel."

"We have to help Matt." Was all she could convey.

"We will," Steven promised, "but I'm sure he'll end up in The Brick."

Rachel stood strong as she looked into Steven's welcoming eyes. She knew about The Brick but wasn't sure how serious the government was about actually housing offenders inside it. Now she had an idea.

Steven helped her stash the machine in the brush and invited her inside his underground home. It was a scorching 110 degrees outside but in the cave, the temperature dropped some thirty degrees. Rachel felt the relief but was still in a daze as to what had occurred only moments earlier. It would be up to Steven to help her make sense of it. He'd do everything he could to make her feel more comfortable.

Steven and Rachel were in an underground cave in the middle of *Nowhere*, Montana.

*

Sal the Gal, very disappointed in missing her target of Rachel and Matt, headed back to Florida, waiting for word from her friend in the green truck. He finally contacted her. He told her he'd spotted the two, but that Matt had been captured. He was too far away to know where Rachel went. He told her this in a text message.

Sal answered. "We have to get back to Florida. The president is going to make a huge announcement soon and I have to be with Lowell in Michigan to see it live. In the meantime, figure out where Rachel went and keep me posted."

The man signed off and took a walk to where he'd last seen Rachel. During his walk, he ran upon a car stashed in the brush. Surprised, he rummaged through the vehicle and found out that it was Steven's car. Curious and cautious, he searched the immediate area to no avail. Wherever Steven and Rachel were, he figured, was a good hiding spot. He slashed the tires of the car and made a mess under the hood. For good measure, he emptied the brake fluid and poked a hole in the gas tank. He left the vehicle undriveable. Upon returning to his truck, he stationed himself as close to the vehicle as he could in hopes of finding the two in the area. It wouldn't take long.

*

The Gal seethed. Rachel, Sal's archenemy in the advocacy-vigilante war, had slipped between her fingers. It wasn't close to over in her mind. She would continue her pursuit of her and her "pervert" husband later. She swore in her mind that she'd catch them and cut their throats… *slowly*. The two kills she had made on this day weren't satisfying. She wanted more. Her taste for blood had graduated to the outlandish. On her way back to Florida, she'd terrorize as many offenders as she could. The ultimate goal waited, however, and she kept that thought in the back of her mind.

Sal "The Gal" Parker was a murderer.

"WORDS BUILD BRIDGES INTO UNEXPLORED REGIONS."

-Quote by Adolph Hitler

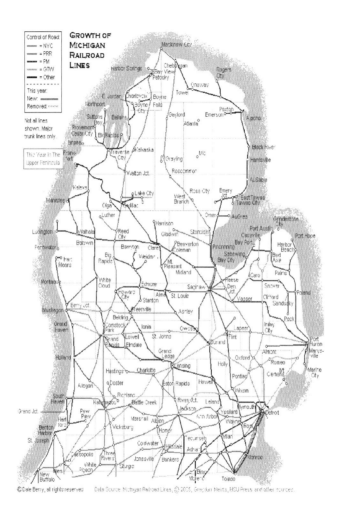

THE DEDICATION

When Matt awoke, he found himself in an unrecognizable place suffering from a nasty headache and a shiner under his left eye. Where he was, he had no idea, but he knew it wasn't good. Matt was sitting in jail somewhere while Rachel stewed with Steven at his underground shelter. Rachel pained over Matt's capture. She was mapping out what she'd have to do to get him back. The paper was blank, however, as she had no idea where he'd even been taken.

Steven tried working with her the best he could but Rachel was icy. At night, she slept fully clothed and well covered under her blankets so not to tempt Steven in any way. When it was bath time, she went to the small creek he'd pointed out to her and that was the only time she undressed. Always armed with her small caliber pistol, she wouldn't hesitate in shooting Steven if he attempted anything funny. She told him from the get-go that there would be no "extra-curricular" activities and she meant it. Rachel was not only loyal to Matt; she was also untrusting of others. Even though she'd been in almost constant communication with Steven for years, being alone with him in person was an entirely different situation. She knew he was lonely and hadn't had a girlfriend in a long time.

Steven would sneak down and watch her bathe, knowing she was probably aware of what he was up to, but he realized deep down in his heart that it was as close as he'd get to her. It wasn't that Steven was acting perverted or going out of his mind. It was pure loneliness as he'd been by himself for a very long time. Masturbation had lost its edge and Steven wanted the company of a woman, if for one night. Rachel made the situation clear to start and Steven begrudgingly respected her wishes. Fantasize he did though. While watching Rachel bathe, he pictured them making love outside under the beauty of nature. The smile on Steven's face was unmistakable. On this occasion, though, he wasn't fooling anyone.

As he daydreamed, Rachel snapped him back to reality. "If you have to watch me," Rachel sharply interrupted, "can you make it a little less obvious?"

Steven, shaken from his fantasy, adjusted the bulge in his pants. The ice that emanated off Rachel was undeniable. Red-faced, he made his way with Rachel back toward the shelter. It was an embarrassing moment for Steven, but didn't divert from the job they were both trying to do.

Despite the awkward moments, the two worked well together in the age of internet communication and devising plans according to what they'd heard and sensed. They both learned of the large bricked "prison" surrounding the entire U.P. of Michigan, but even though Steven figured it to be a prison for offenders, he couldn't say confidently. There were no specifics yet announced about the facility but the questions weren't far from being answered. President Wisecroft had publicized an unveiling of the large facility within two weeks' time. Steven and Rachel would be listening with baited breath. The fate of their plans depended on what Wisecroft would have to say.

Within their souls, Steven and Rachel knew what the announcement would entail, but they didn't want to commit *(admit)* to it. Too many funny things had been happening in that offenders were being captured at an alarming rate, despite having been equipped with computer chips and in the face of the Wisecroft Law that most offenders had been following to the "T." They saw, over the internet, offenders beaten in broad daylight. They also saw everyone turning their collective heads and walking the other way. Now with Matt captured and housed who knew where, Rachel could only sit back, blow out a huge breath and wonder how her husband was faring. *Too many funny happenings indeed.*

111

In the distance, the man in the green truck was watching intently. He didn't yet know where the hideout was, but he knew it was nearby. He gave Steven credit for effective sheltering. He watched, just as Sal had ordered. He also smoked and drank. He made it a point to be careful, though, as passing out and losing them again could spell real trouble for his livelihood *(life)*.

*

Matt sat in his cell with his face in his hands. He was naked but for his underwear. He looked out between the bars and saw a long, dimly lit hallway that led to nowhere. It was also very cold. There was no air conditioning or heat running, but a chilled dampness filled the air. He figured to be underground. His eye was swollen and his shoulders ached; most assuredly from the pummeling he took during his capture. When Matt turned around, he witnessed something that was far beyond his worst nightmare: There were at least fifty men and women standing before him clad only in their underwear and bras. Matt was in a large cell with a slew of captured offenders. Some were tremendously dirty, some lay on cots in the corners moaning and wailing, while others slowly stepped toward him, presumably to greet him and ask questions.

112

"Where did they capture you?" One offending male asked.

"Montana. I don't remember much. I was on a four-wheeler when a net came down on me. It was heavy and stalled my machine right away. Where were you captured?"

Matt was shocked when the man said "New Mexico."

"New Mexico? That's at least a thousand miles from where I was captured. Where are we? What time is it? What's the date?"

No one in the room responded. A couple of quickly shrugged shoulders were the extent of their answer. The man Matt was speaking with also shrugged his shoulders.

"I have no idea. Your guess is as good as ours."

Matt sat on an open part of a wooden bench and put his head back in his hands. He began to weep as silently as he could. It was too much to take in such a short time. Just when he was ready to shout, a woman approached him and brushed his hair back across his face.

"It's okay. We encourage crying here. Let it out. Some of us have been here for ninety days. We put a check mark on the wall every day when they serve, uh, what they call dinner. We're all here for each other."

Matt looked up and saw a pretty but downtrodden and tired-looking blond-haired woman standing before him in only her panties. He felt ashamed and looked down.

113

"It's okay. They caught me completely off guard. No bra that day, go figure. I guess it's my tough luck. Uh, where are you from sweetie?"

Matt didn't meet her eyes as she spoke. He didn't want her to think he was looking at her nude breasts.

"New York, originally. I moved to Idaho with my wife. We stayed with family. We were on our way to Montana when the police grabbed me. My wife was able to get away."

"Is your wife an offender too?"

"NO, why?"

"That's why she got away."

The woman looked at Matt with solemn eyes. He finally looked up, avoided her breasts, and asked her some questions. "What about you? What happened to get you placed here?"

"I was a teacher in Denver and had sex with one of my students years and years ago. I ended up marrying him after I left prison. That wasn't good enough, though. I'm still an offender in the eyes of the law. We finally divorced last year because he couldn't take another minute of the scrutiny. You know; interviews, TV, the whole shot. Being a teacher makes it double tough. We have the whole morality clause issue.

Matt put out his hand.

"I'm Matt."

114

"Hi Matt, I'm Mary."

Matt eyes wrenched wide open as he took a second look. Now he recognized her.

"You're that teacher in Colorado, yes, I remember, Mary..."

"Yep. That's me; and in my skivvies, sorry."

Mary spread her arms out to the left and right while shrugging.

Matt glanced at her a second time, again avoiding her breasts, and smiled as best he could before placing his head back into his hands.

*

Davis Lowell and Sal Parker were preparing for the flight to Mackinaw City, Michigan. President Wisecroft's staff had invited the N.V.A.C.'s leaders to be on hand for the grand unveiling of the bricked facility in Northern Michigan. The two knew it was to be a prison for offenders and they couldn't have been more thrilled about it.

"It's about time they did something useful to get rid of the pedo-freaks." Sal screeched.

"How many did you get on your trip to Idaho Gal?"

115

Lowell called her Gal often. It was his favorite way to identify her. The two were enjoying Pina Coladas next to Davis' pool.

"I'd say a good fifty. Scared 'em shitless. I let my aides have some fun too. Why not? They were screwed anyway. Har, har, har."

The laugh belonged to a heavy smoker, rife with a scratchy, rough texture. Davis figured her to die of lung cancer soon if she didn't quit the cigarettes.

"That's good Gal. How many did you kill?"

"Just two, but they weren't offenders. It was Rachel's cousins. They're as dead as doornails. They were shooting at us first. It was a pure self-defense measure."

Davis sat back and smiled sheepishly as the two clanked their glasses together. They then engaged in a heavy conversation that became somewhat argumentative and snippy.

"You know you don't get any special rewards for your hard work." The bald-headed, heavily tattooed Davis explained.

"Oh no?" Sal belched. "Who said I wanted anything?"

Davis pulled no punches in explaining that they had thankless jobs. "This work is underappreciated. I deserve

116

huge accolades but they don't come. People don't give me enough credit"

Sal put her drink to the side and went to work on Davis, who sat back in his chair and put his hands behind his head in a calm posture. He had no worries or concerns. Everything he'd been doing was going his way.

"What do you mean 'I'? You don't do shit except sit on your ass by the stupid pool drinking booze and taking credit for everything you DON'T do."

He brushed Sal off with a "sheesh", angering his partner.

"You can be a real asshole Davis. Do you know that?"

Sal splashed her drink in his face and left the premises while Davis chuckled.

"But I got the money Gal. Don't you forget where the money is Bitch!"

It was par for the course between the two egomaniacs.

*

The day finally arrived. President Wisecroft, Vice-President Jasper, and many other Heads of State gathered in Mackinaw City, Michigan for the grand opening of the concrete facility built around the entire Upper Peninsula of Michigan. It was a monumental day for Wisecroft. Jasper

117

wasn't as enthused, as he thought it to be the wrong strategy to deal with the sex offenders. Lawmakers and others within the "know" in D.C. all thought it not only effective but would lead to re-election as construction unions, bricklayers unions and electric companies paid handsomely for positive votes when the facility was introduced in Congress. Others present were Governors from other states including Wisconsin, Indiana and Ohio. V.I.P.'s from other states also showed up out of curiosity, but the Governor of Alaska came with a group of conservationists to demonstrate her contempt for such a monstrosity that destroyed the integrity of the beautiful Upper Peninsula of Michigan. She was glad Alaska hadn't been chosen as its destination.

Modern-day anti-offender advocates Davis Lowell and his right-hand woman Sal "The Gal" Parker were on hand along with others from Florida, the home state of the N.V.A.C. Many parents who had had children victimized were also present, as they'd been given advanced notice as to the facilities function. Other people, mostly from Michigan and surrounding states gathered 200,000 strong at the U.P. base of the Mackinaw Bridge to witness what was billed as the most historical modern-times event in the United States. Missing from the festivities were the Prime Minister of Canada, still fuming over the shot down helicopter of months earlier, and The president of Mexico, angry over what he perceived as more violations of human rights within the world, and fear that the facility would also house illegal immigrants. Steven and Rachel watched on the internet inside Steven's underground dwelling.

It was warm and sunny when the president took to the podium to speak. The time was 12:00 Noon on September 25, 2050. The waiting was over.

"My fellow Americans, I am honored to be here in beautiful Northern Michigan on a picturesque fall day such as this one. It's a historical day for our country and a day that will change forever how we view our laws.

Back before the election of 2044, I promised big changes in our country: Changes that would lead to a better life for all Americans from Maine to California and Washington to Florida. This is as big a conversion as one can possibly maneuver. You see behind me a structure that encloses 16,452 square miles of real estate. Allow me to speak briefly about the history of the Upper Peninsula of Michigan, and why it'll be an ideal spot for our plan.

The Upper Peninsula of Michigan is the northern of the two major landmasses that make up the U.S. State of Michigan. It's been commonly referred to as the Upper Peninsula, the U.P. or Upper Michigan. It is also known as the land "above the Bridge." The peninsula is bounded on the

119

north by Lake Superior, on the east by The St. Mary's River, on the southeast by Lake Michigan and Lake Huron, and on the southwest by Wisconsin. By the way, hello Mr. Governor."

The Governor of Wisconsin nodded.

"Based on geographical differences, the peninsula is sometimes divided into the Western Upper Peninsula ("WUP") and Eastern Upper Peninsula ("EUP"). The Upper Peninsula contains 29% of the land area of Michigan. Ordered by size, the peninsula's largest cities are Marquette, Ste. Sault Marie, Escanaba, Menominee, Iron Mountain and Houghton. The land and climate are not very suitable for agriculture because of the long harsh winters. The economy has been based on logging, mining and tourism. Most mines have closed since the "golden age" from 1890 to 1920. The land is heavily forested and logging was a major industry. That's a basic cover of what the Upper Peninsula of Michigan encompasses.

We as a country have decided that it is time to make a change that would benefit all citizens of our great country and Michigan's U.P. was the best place to encompass such change. The structure surrounding the U.P. is all brick and barbed wire. It's the heaviest and most sound of any brick manufactured here in the United States. The walls all the way around are fifteen feet high and fifteen feet thick. The brick is supported with tons and tons of re-rod to give it lasting stability. The barbed and straight wire that you see along the top rises another thirty feet and is electrified. The structure has been designed to last thousands of years. That's enough time to serve the purpose of which we are using the facility."

Wisecroft had charts and maps demonstrating his points and they were visually transferred to a large screen behind him to give all the attendees an equal look. The crowd buzzed and moaned as they waited for the real answer: Why was it built?

"Back many years ago, ladies and gentlemen, I witnessed a most heinous act. I saw some of my family members savagely raped, beaten and murdered before my very eyes."

A loud and amplified backwash of moaning could be heard from the throng.

"I made it a mission of mine to put the rapists, child abusers and pedophiles away where they belonged. With our jails overflowing and our sex offender registry having reached

121

two million plus, we had to resort to measures that were more drastic. Ladies and gentlemen of the United States of America, I give you "The Brick Project." The largest population control facility in the entire world."

The cheers were loud and appreciative. The walls loomed beyond the crowd. The people ohhed and ahhed over the size of the project.

*"This facility will be fed by railroads lines from Detroit and Chicago. Offenders throughout the United States, no matter what the charge and no matter when the crime, will be housed in the bricked facility. As I speak, the U.S. Army, Marines and Navy along with local and State Police have begun the copious task of gathering all the offenders for temporary housing in F.E.M.A. facilities we have stationed all across the country. After being gathered, checked-in, tattooed and housed, the offenders will wait there until the time comes for transport to this wonderful new facility. Let me be clear in my explanation that this is **not** a penalty but a protective measure for the offenders themselves. They'll be housed in this beautiful facility in Northern Michigan that will serve as their home until death. They'll be protected from a population that is violent and hateful toward them. We as a nation are actually doing this group a favor.*

122

There is available housing, transportation and acreage for crops in the U.P. We, as a nation, will make drop-offs of food and water once monthly to help them stock their stores, farms and any other facilities they choose to stock. The main cities in the U.P. will be for these people to enjoy and grow as they see fit. With over two million offenders nationwide, there will be plenty of room for them to exist without threat from the outside world.

There will be no air traffic allowed within a radius of one hundred miles around the perimeter of the facility. Anyone trying to scale the walls will be dealt with severely. I cannot emphasis enough that this is for the safety of the offenders as well as the safety of your children.

The facility has been equipped with electric power for the fencing you see by installing fourteen power stations along the entire outer perimeter of the U.P. These power stations also double as guard stations in an effort to keep the American Taxpayer's costs down. This facility is state of the art and will be a major boon for lowering incarceration costs within our country. Drummond Island will serve as the central headquarters of management."

The crowd was in a state of sheer bedlam, happy that the child molesters, rapists and other modern-day lepers would be banished from their sights forever. It wasn't everyone who

123

enjoyed this day as families of offenders and the offenders themselves sunk their collective heads in disappointment. Davis and Sal stood off to the side looking very professional but inside they were as thrilled as they had ever felt. It was a dream come true for the vigilante pair and they wanted more. It was fine that they were putting these offenders away for good but they wanted to help capture as many as possible and have them sent away. Sal wanted more blood. Along with their thinking was the fact that they were already planning on hunting down any absconding offenders. They listened as Wisecroft finished.

"It is my hope that all children will be spared the pain of abuse. It is my hope that sexual abuse and sexual crime will become non-existent. It is my hope for a better America for the citizens to live in. Thank you and may God bless you."

President Wisecroft walked over to a table where a one-by-one foot layer of brick stood. On the brick it was chiseled **ESTABLISHED 2050**. A ribbon surrounded the table and a bottle of champagne sat next to the chunk of brick. After the obligatory photo ops, Wisecroft lifted the bottle and smashed it against the brick, thus commemorating the facility. The chunk of brick was the final piece to be placed at the entrance, which was located two thousand feet beyond the end of the Mackinaw Bridge. The construction was designed to give at least two thousand feet of land around the entire facility. That made plenty of room for guard stations, supervision of the facility from the outside and the ability for tourists to drive next to the enormously long and impressive structure, *along with taking the popular shortcut to Wisconsin.* It was a monumental day in US history, according to Wisecroft. As Wisecroft walked over to place the brick, a number of parents were invited for a special commemoration of their own. In many different areas around the entrance, they were allowed to nail dolls up onto the brick wall with their deceased or abused children's names on them. It was an epic and healing occasion for the parents as well as the president, who also nailed a doll to The Brick.

*

Steven and Rachel diligently worked on supplying more facts to as many people as possible. They were providing much of the same information they shared at the town hall meetings, which were largely ineffective. They sent out mass e-mails explaining that the majority, or ninety-six percent of all sex crime came from within the family. They tried to explain how low the recidivism rate was for offenders released back into society. It was approximately seven

125

percent. The only replies they received were from disgruntled people who disagreed with the figures, even though they had no proof to refute them. They also heard from vigilantes, who didn't care much about stats, only about incarceration or death. A few others expressed a desire to flag the location of Steven's e-mails and make a capture of their own. A very small percentage actually agreed and wanted the bricked facility destroyed.

The ordeal was taking its toll on Rachel, as she teared up when thinking of her beloved Matt and what he must've been going through. Steven attempted to comfort her but was always rejected and pushed away. Rachel felt that even accepting a hug from a good-natured friend was cheating. She would have no part of it. Besides, she also figured, he doesn't need the torture of feeling her breasts against his chest. Steven became frustrated to the point of slowing his dialogue with her to a near standstill. He didn't attempt to start a conversation and when she did, he was short and to the point. Many times, it was a nod of the head one way or the other. Shoulder shrugs also became prevalent. The tension between the two was building up and Steven knew it would eventually reach a breaking point. He was also dealing with his own masculine feelings and want of a woman's companionship. Her femininity fascinated him. Rachel was pretty, always smelled good and had that aura he found irresistible. He disciplined himself to stay away from her despite his urges. The day of reckoning though, was fast approaching and they both knew it.

*

In the meantime, a bricked facility was opened, a husband, Matthew was *who knew where,* and the vigilantes were planning their next strategies' and ideas. Soon all hell would break loose and it would take an army to stop it. A very small pocket of resistance existed on the offender's side. The situation looked bleak. No Superman or other cartoon character would come to save the day and no miracles were about to hatch. The world had changed and now the United States had changed along with it.

Wisecroft was already plotting and planning his next victimization campaign. He wanted guns taken away from the public and he hated lazy people who he felt were weighing down the government initiative. Welfare was at an all-time high, food stamps had sharply increased and unemployment was being paid at a ridiculous rate. Pornography was also an evil that Wisecroft insisted to be a boon for offenders, so he was devising his plan for the riddance of all smut within the country.

As angry as the president became over these "messes" within society, he was just as giddy about fixing them. He was becoming something of a tyrant who spent an unsettling amount of time reading and highlighting "*Mein Kampf*" by Adolph Hitler.

"If the U.S. is to survive another day," he thought, "It'll be by my iron fist."

The offenders were only the first of many changes coming. The lazy, fat, beer-swilling, television watching, fast-food eating public had no clue. Soon their worlds would be turned upside down.

WE THE

SHEEPLE

GATHER THE SHEEPLE

"Davis, I need snipers, lots of snipers. I want snipers stationed at all the Michigan borders; although I don't think the Wisconsin border will be as much trouble because the only Brick entrance is Mackinaw City. Can you do this for me?"

Sal made these requests with stern seriousness. She wanted shooters to pick off sex offenders that *were headed* to the bricked facility. Davis was slightly offended at The Gal's bloodthirsty instinct.

"I don't think so Gal. I'm not sure I dig your methods all that well."

Sal looked at Davis with a hint of surprise along with a condescending glare. She was shocked to hear him actually wanting to spare people who were convicted of sex offenses. Davis ignored her evil eye and continued speaking.

"We'll do it this way; I want you to gather teams of watchers and send them out east to west from St. Louis to Los Angeles and St. Louis to Seattle. I also want them headed up toward Maine and down toward South Carolina. Since the

131

offenders have been forced to live in open areas because of all the new laws, we'll force them toward the F.E.M.A. facilities. It'll make more sense doing it this way. We'll flush them out. Any offenders you find who are absconding, you capture or lead the police to them. DO NOT KILL THEM! Your teams will all be given chip monitors so they can hunt down those lowlifes and get them busted."

"But Davis, I thought we wanted to kill these guys. I was under the impression that we wanted to get *rid* of them. Are you turning yellow on me?"

Davis ruffled his brows in an angry matter-of-fact leer. He was the boss and didn't appreciate Sal's apparent power trip.

"Sal, Most of the offenders will be on trains and buses headed to F.E.M.A. Camps. We want to help the authorities, not hinder ourselves. Any offenders already on their way to those places are off limits, unless they escape. If that happens, then their asses belong to us. That's final Sal. Don't make me worry about your attitude. I'm starting to wonder if you get off on killing."

The Gal sneered menacingly and asked Davis if she could say something, *if he was finished.* He agreed and she spoke in no uncertain terms. "You best be careful Davis. If it leaks out that you're being a pussy about these offenders, you may get called out."

"You let me worry about me Sal. I'm the boss and you shouldn't forget that. You get busy doing what I ordered you to do. If you don't like my orders, then get out. Nobody's holding you back. *You fucking bitch.*"

Sal fed Davis one last menacing glare and while leaving the room, spoke condescendingly. "Yep. You're right Davis: You're the boss."

Davis knew the pair was faltering. He had to do something to show his power and command the respect of the N.V.A.C. He would in due time.

*

The idea intrigues me...

Steven thought up a way to try to help the offenders who wanted to remain free. For days, he'd thought about the quote "Keep your friends close but keep your enemies closer." He was going to try to infiltrate Sal's circle and get the inside scoop about the woman herself. He wasn't sure it'd work but he had to try. He shared his thoughts with Rachel.

"What if I could actually get on the inside Rachel? What if I could get close to Sal and find out what they're planning?"

133

"You'll have to do it online because they know what you look like and they'll kill you. They've had you on their "A" list for years."

"I understand that. We do have small pockets of people all over the country who are also in hiding that may want to help."

"We don't want a gun war, Steven." Rachel said with composure. "So you'd have to think of a peaceful way."

"I know that. Do you really think I'm fucking stupid Rachel? What do you take me for, an idiot?"

Steven began to develop an angry look in his eyes as he stared Rachel down, waiting for an answer.

"Oh I see." Rachel nodded. "You're going to play the 'women don't know shit' card. I see it Steven. You jerk. You're different in person then you were online."

Steven was astounded and irritated. He didn't like being told what or how he was, especially by a woman, no less a woman that was taking up space with him and in his mind not being very nice. He had a dash of bigotry inside that was leaking through like blood through a white shirt. Rachel stood with her hands on her hips, bobbing her head in an "I dare you" manner. Steven, deciding not to escalate the fracas, did the smart thing and took the high road, stepping out of his lair and into the soft sun of a Montana morning.

"It's too bad," he muttered to himself. "I'm a good guy. I don't deserve to be talked down to like a child."

In reality, two things made Steven react the way he did: He very much wanted to have sex with Rachel, but she was married. The second point ruined the first: Rachel was married to the man she loved and that was the final word in her *and* Steven's mind.

Rachel, unfazed, took over the computer and continued typing. She had to warn as many offenders as she could about the facts laid out by President Wisecroft earlier in the day. She messaged her advocates profusely. Steven's tantrum didn't hinder her for one second. As far as she was concerned, he could stay gone. Rachel had a focus and Steven wasn't going to alter it. She wanted Matt back and wanted to protect people she knew and loved. Knowing there wasn't anything anyone could do about Matt until finding out where he was; she thought hard. *"If I can find out when and from where Matt is being transported to The Brick, I could try to intercept him before he arrived at the facility."*

Her thinking was logical, as once Matt was inside, it would be impossible to get him out. She kept working, and messaging when she suddenly heard commotion outside of the den. It sounded like a drone.

Steven was outside and a drone was flying low: A bad combination.

...but it'll never work.

*

The country itself had been divided into four sections for Government purposes: West, Midwest, East and South. F.E.M.A. camps were speckled about each region but one camp in each of the four areas served as the final step before transporting offenders north to The Brick: Chicago in the west, Detroit in the Midwest, Buffalo in the east and Cincinnati in the south. Those four cities were everyone's last stops before being railroaded into the facility that loomed in Northern Michigan.

The gathering and placement of the offenders eventually fell into the hands of the Army and the Marines. They had a clever way of making sure the offenders were available for transport: By threatening to burn down the houses where the offenders were staying, if they were inaccessible. It would prove a useful tactic unless entire families up and left. Nonetheless, if a full family did abandon their home it was usually burned to the ground for good measure. The expensive houses were spared for the banks and lenders. If offenders ran when the military arrived, they were tasered and loaded onto the bus or in very rare cases, shot dead

136

in front of everyone to serve as an example. The gathering tactics depended on who was in charge. Davis Lowell was given charge to a handful of units in the self-proclaimed *vigilante sector (Florida, Alabama, Mississippi, Georgia and Louisiana)*. Lowell ordered his ranks to taze first, and then shoot only if absolutely necessary. He gave Sal her orders. She went about her task with a murderous eye and a craw in her side because of him. She stationed herself in the midwest and worked her way north with her gang of helpers. She captured or assisted in the capture of over one thousand offenders in a one-week span. As she drove north, she energetically pushed offenders north ahead of her. Whenever the buses passed that were loaded with offenders destined for The Brick, her and the group saluted and spit at the windows. It was a celebration of sorts, an exuberance displayed by the capture and virtual elimination of the offenders. She wanted to kill them, but abstained.

Meanwhile, in other cities all across the U.S., the displays were even nastier and crueler then the first wave weeks earlier. Offenders were dragged from their houses at all hours, stripped naked, placed in vehicles; usually pick-up trucks, and driven around town with placards around their necks that said "Pervert", "Creep", "Baby-Raper" or any other number of nasty titles and terms. The offender had eggs thrown at them or in extreme cases, feces, urine and spit. The

137

public themselves were getting in on the act, beating offenders when they were spotted in public. In locations where offenders were hiding, such as the plains and southwest, many were giving themselves up and getting on the buses. Overall, it was a nightmarish separation of families as offender's children; children who the laws were supposed to *protect,* cried at the sight of their mom or dad being humiliated and taken away. It would most assuredly result in years of therapy to repair the mental damage done, if repair were even possible.

"Protect all the children, except those that belong to the offenders" seemed to be the public's mantra. At least that's how they acted.

Drones hummed along the countryside, nets tossed on offenders as they were captured and if lucky, placed in the buses. The unlucky ones were toyed with violently during their apprehension. Captured female offenders were often raped before placement on the buses for transport. It was *beyond* an all-out assault by the military branches in an effort to do the president's will. Crimes that would result in Court Martial during wartime were routinely waved off during the collection of the offenders.

The ugliest display of societal brainwashing had been infiltrated on the people by the words of one man. John Wisecroft, often harking back to the Hitler novel sitting on his desk, was an expert at intimidation, propaganda and taking advantage of a lazy country. His plans were working well, yet there was more to come: More than anyone could ever fathom.

*

Steven found himself in trouble as his temper tantrum caused him to flee the underground space he shared with Rachel. As suddenly as his anger had turned on him, a drone screamed overhead with Steven in its sights. The powerful, thick netting was mechanically lowered as he ran toward the trees as fast as his feet would take him. He huffed and puffed as the drone closed in. Undoubtedly, the trees for which he headed would be loaded with hunters. Steven suddenly heard a blast from the left. The drone careened in the air and veered hard to the right. He slowed his pace and eventually came to a stop. He watched as the drone, smoke pouring from its tail, struggled for altitude. A second later, it landed rightwing first on the ground one hundred yards beyond him. The explosion was powerful as the gasoline, combined with the friction of the earth, caused enough spark to trigger ignition. To his left, he heard the call of Rachel. He saw her standing with a sawed-off shotgun, courtesy of his weapon arsenal.

"Come on asshole, get back here. HURRY!" Rachel yelled.

The hunters were filing out of the woods; three of them; toward Steven. He dashed into the trees with Rachel. The hunters followed; looks of scorn upon their faces. As the hunters crossed into the brush, they stopped, completely perplexed by the fact that the two had seemingly disappeared into thin air. As they walked perilously close to the entrance of the burrow, Steven and Rachel sat in the far corner quietly pacing their breathing. They could hear and even feel the footsteps directly above them. The hunters lingered for what seemed like forever before finally leaving the area. Steven and Rachel exhaled a relieved breath as the threat was narrowly averted.

Rachel blasted Steven with a thorough chewing out. "The next time you have one of your stupid tantrums and dash out of here, I'm not helping you. They almost had you and then what? You could, *at best,* end up on a bus. At worst? Well, you know."

Steven had nothing to say. He sat with his forehead in his hands, trying to catch his breath and slow the adrenaline flowing through him at an alarming rate. His heart was beating high in his chest as he considered his good fortune. He promised Rachel that he'd never be that careless again.

"I should hope not." She tersely chastised.

"Well it's partly your fault," he tried to rationalize. "If you hadn't pissed me off, none of that would've happened. That almost exposed our position."

"Listen Mr. Smith; you get that little temper problem in check. I've seen it all over the internet and now I'm seeing it in real life. You, and *only you*, damn near blew our cover. If you want me to hang any longer, I need to clear up a few things with you. Number one; don't think for one second that there will be any sex. That's never going to happen. Number two; check that volatility at pride's door. We can't have emotional outbursts if you're going to be on my team and number three; I'm finding my husband with or without your help. I hope you're listening because I don't repeat myself."

Steven looked at Rachel with disparagement along with the demeanor of an eight-year-old child. He nodded reluctantly in agreement. The two shook and an understanding was graciously reached. Steven dropped the hope for sex out of his mind and relented to working with Rachel. He had worked his advocacy on his own for so long that it was an uncomfortable change to be sharing the duties with anyone, let alone a female. He wasn't used to being selfless with his attitude. He had shared an apartment with a friend, but this was far different. The chemistry with Rachel lacked smoothness. He knew his insolence had to change.

141

The man in the green truck watched with both amusement and concern. He tipped his flask and lit another cigarette. He was glad the drone missed the two because he wanted Sal to have the honor of catching the pair. He'd report his findings to her later. He was still confused about how and where they disappeared. He was too far away to know, so he simply sat back and continued to wait until there was more movement. His radio was the only company he could find, along with Jack and the Marlboro Man.

*

The Gal was acting out her deepest fantasy of leading a charge of N.V.A.C. members capturing offenders. She swore to herself she'd torture and deliver to authorities as many as possible before the buses and trains rolled out of the areas she proclaimed to be cleaning up. She was still feeling empty, as Steven, Matt and Rachel remained out in the world somewhere, presumably alive. If she could get her hands on those two and finish them herself, all else would be mere child's play. She continued her impromptu conversations online with the pair.

SAL PARKER: You know I'm on your asses. I will take great pleasure in seeing the life drain out of you before

142

my eyes. You two think you have this all figured out. I have news; I'll get you…soon. And I know you two are together.

STEVEN SMITH: You have to find us first Sal and that's not going to happen in your lifetime. If you don't kill yourself drinking or run into the wrong person who does take you out, it'll be mine, not your, pleasure taking you down. It'll be slow and long Gal. Lots of pain.

SAL PARKER: Oh, don't worry about that you little numb-nut. I already have a bead on you. It's only a matter of time.

RACHEL LYONS: You don't scare us Sal. I know your game. All talk and no action. Finding us would be your biggest mistake.

SAL PARKER: How's your hubby doing Rachel? Oh, you wouldn't know now would you? He's all locked up nice and tidy in a jail in Denver.

Sal didn't realize it, but she goofed by telling Rachel where Matt was being held. Steve and Rachel played it cool, acting as if they didn't notice. Rachel responded.

143

RACHEL LYONS: Screw you Sal. I'll get him back. You won't stop that you cold, ruthless bitch.

SAL PARKER: Tsk, Tsk Rachel. Temper getting the best of you? Oh, I forgot to tell you; Auntie and Uncle are both dead. I shot her between the eyes, and we tortured him before a bullet to the brain finished 'em off.

RACHEL LYONS: You're a liar Sal. You don't even know them.

SAL PARKER: Really Rachel? Let me see here: Rick and Jill. Does that ring a bell? I've got their ID's in my hot little hands. OH, just so you know I'm on the level, Rick had a tattoo of a surfer on his left bicep. Rather nice. Jill? She had a blue birdie on her left breast. It was just above her cute little tittie. How charming.

Rachel backed away from the screen, knowing Sal was telling her things she couldn't possibly know. She brought her hands to her face and began sobbing. It soon turned into an all-out cry.

SAL PARKER: Hello? What's the matter Rachel? Cat got your tongue?

Steven looked at Rachel with a hint of sorrow and then took over the keypad.

STEVEN SMITH: You're a dead woman Gal. Be forewarned. DEAD. We'll fucking kill you with our bare hands.

SAL PARKER: Oh my sweet little Stevie. He that promiseth too much. You tell your honey I said to have a great rest of the day and I'll be seeing you kids…soon.

Sal signed off with Steven left to try to comfort Rachel. She allowed him to rub the back of her neck as the tears spilled to the dirt floor below.

"We'll get her Rachel. I promise."

"Oh, I know. I'm going to be the one who kills her though. She'll die by the sword she lives by; I'll see to it personally.

The one positive about the conversation was that they know knew Matt's whereabouts. Though the two still had to come up with a plan to spring him before he reached Northern Michigan, at least they had an idea of his whereabouts. It would take everything they had: Stamina, patience and smarts. They figured they had what it took. They'd soon find out just how much effort it would be to carry out their plans.

Nothing worth a hill of beans was ever easy.

We've only just begun…

MATT'S JOURNEY I

Sitting in a cold cell wearing only underpants, waiting to see what might happen and not knowing where you were was difficult. The *most* difficult part? Wondering if you'd live or die. Matt speculated about his mortality. He'd seen many people dragged out of their cells kicking and screaming as if their lives would end. The cell that he was in fit ten but housed fifty, everyone elbow to elbow. The food: Mush, bread and one bucket of water to share amongst all of the cellmates had a deplorable odor. They shared one toilet and it was wide open, so they did their deeds in front of one another. There were no blankets or pillows, and the cell was a filthy, stinking mess. It was a wonder disease and famine weren't festering everywhere they stepped, sat or lay. The men allowed the women to sleep on the bunks while they took up the space on the floor. It was colder lying on icy concrete, but men were still chivalrous, even in such extreme conditions. Matt woke up shivering every morning and never found any warmth or comfort during the daytime. People huddled together to keep warm: Men and women together if necessary. The cockroaches, spiders and other nasty insects crawling around added to the distress. The *mostly-male* guards were awful, making passes at the females on a regular basis, with some females removed from the cell and forced to pose for nude pictures or worse. Mary, the blonde-haired woman, was one of the most popular choices based on her natural beauty. The cellmates weren't offered showers and the cells themselves began stinking of body odor and feces. Overall, it was the worst of the worst. The jail resembled third world conditions.

Matt was a perfect gentleman, trying to comfort other inmates and boosting the morale as best he could. Some three weeks after his jailing, the cell began to slowly empty due to sickness. Anxiousness, unsanitary conditions and simple movement of prisoners contributed to the thinning. Matt took on a leadership role and helped people with whatever he could, be it a pep talk, kindness or encouragement. It was all he could really give, as the conditions allowed little else. He helped dole out the rations, comfort the sick and assist in first aid within the cell. They all did their best to do what comes natural to the human condition: Surviving.

The day came when they were called out one-by-one to be marked (tattooed) with a scan bar and handed jail smocks. They were simply a thin shirt and pants, but helped to warm

148

them and allow for physical coverage. They all discarded their underwear and bras, saving them to use as tourniquets. That idea, however, was quickly squashed as the guards collected all of the discards and burned them. Matt began to wonder if they'd face execution or extermination. Even so, he maintained his composure for the good of the weaker inmates and began giving his pep talks regularly.

"I know it's tough people, but we have to stick together through this difficult time. We aren't going to be murdered. I believe they're getting ready to ship us off to that facility in Michigan that they've talked about so often on TV and in the papers."

"But how can you be sure?" One of the frightened inmates asked. "What if this is like the concentration camps of 1940's Germany?"

"It's not," Matt assured. "We live in a free country. Those days are long since passed. We need to think positive, not worry about the 'what ifs.'"

He knew he was lying and hated it, but he needed to keep the spirits up as much as possible. He started inventing games for them to play. Charades, guess the word and other "get your mind off the situation" competitions. He began leading them in song, at least until the guards came and told them to shut it down. They also exercised as much as possible, as it was good for the mental strengthening of the

149

human spirit, while also combating anxiety and depression. Matt's activities gave them something of which to look forward. The inmates began adoring him and appreciated his positive attitude.

A few days later, a number of guards approached the cell. There must have been twenty or thirty. The cell door was open and the inmates were ordered to come out in a straight line, single file. Led down a long corridor and into a large shower area, they stripped naked as ordered and went inside. Some of the inmates cried and wept aloud as they figured the gas would come on and that would be it for their lives. The history books scared them, as they couldn't help but wonder if it was repeating itself. They were wrong. The showers came on and the inmates, supplied with soap, shampoo and other hygiene products, washed up enthusiastically. Toothbrushes, deodorant, razors and combs completed the cleanup. It was a welcome and uplifting relief for the inmates as they finally had the opportunity to freshen up after many weeks of incarceration. The healthy inmates helped the weaker folks who couldn't help themselves. Human compassion again ruled the day. Everyone had an hour before the water cut off. From there it was onto the next step: A humiliating step.

*

Sal and her cohorts continued across the Midwest states toward Michigan helping to capture and *occasionally* kill the sex offenders as they found them. The point came, however, when the government ordered the N.V.A.C. and other groups to cease and desist any killing of offenders. The Brick needed prisoners and the private sector that was running the facility were losing cash as their number of prisoners dwindled.

The privatization of the prisoners combined with the building of The Brick was a lucrative deal indeed. Signed by Wisecroft, the company, called W.I.P.E. (We Insure Prisoner Essentials) now had a huge stake in both the regular prisons, which housed murderers, arsonists and thieves among others. And of course, The Brick, which was to house sex offenders. By lobbying Congress and schmoozing with lawmakers, the company was able to grab a ten-million dollar yearly stake; mostly supplied by taxes and other earmarked funds. In exchange, the lawmakers themselves were all but assured re-election and success in the form of a big paycheck themselves. As the money continued to roll in for W.I.P.E., the Government of the United States had opened F.E.M.A. Camps all over the country, thus insuring another funnel of money coming their way. Government workers went into these old, closed down railroad facilities to clean them up, which

151

included installing prison (security) bars, painting and connecting electrical equipment used for not only lighting, but also easy control of the facilities gates, entrances and cells.

As disappointed as Sal was with the new rule of no touching offenders, she still managed to pick off a few more as she made her way north. She would excuse the slaughtering as self-defense.

"They were going to hurt me, so I hurt them first."

She always got away with it unscathed.

It didn't matter to her whether the offenders were men, women or even teen-agers. It also didn't matter what they were charged with as she simply wanted to see them all put away forever and for good. To her, the bricked facility served as a separation between the riff-raff and the good (whatever that meant) people of the US. She didn't have a problem with murderers or arsonists as she figured in her mind that they were either killing offenders or assisting in burning their houses down. To her, it was all a win-win. Lowell also contacted her and told her no more pillaging, as disappointing as it was for her to hear. To him, it was as much a moneymaking deal as it was for the government. As self-proclaimed Bounty Hunters, there was much cash to be made from the capture and delivery of wayward offenders. He was more satisfied with that then shooting an offender between the eyes, as he could brag about the one or two hundred large he'd make as he led the offender to the promised land of life behind The Brick.

*

For Steven and Rachel, the time had come to leave the domicile built for hiding and face the real world in their search for Rachel's husband. They also hoped to free as many offenders as possible en route to Michigan, the place they figured Matt would end up. They had to leave many of the amenities behind, such as computers, batteries and food because it created too much weight. They did manage to take two secured cell phones, a laptop and the few batteries that they could carry. Steven was not surprised, to find his car destroyed. He figured the military men or hunters did it, but had no idea about the man in the green truck, who was watching intently between swigs from his flask. Steven siphoned the remaining gas from his car to fill the empty jugs so they'd have fuel for the trip.

They had the one four-wheeler, so it would be cramped as they made their way east. They knew that trains and buses would be carrying offenders from far and wide, so they planned to spring as many as they could on the route, *if possible*. Steven had two high-powered rifles in case they were needed while on the run. They would also take back roads and trails to avoid easy pickings by drones and hunters alike. A spotting by drones would mean almost sure capture for Steven while sightings by hunters would bring humiliation or death. It was a chance he had to take for the good of the cause as they both saw it. They also had to move because Sal would most assuredly be on their tails. To stay one-step ahead of her would be of the utmost importance as she would not only kill the pair but also torture them relentlessly. It would be tough, as the man in the green truck would follow them closely, reporting to Sal regularly. The odds were firmly stacked against them.

Sal, through that very man in the green truck, heard about Steven's near miss in Montana and now had a good feel for where her archenemies were hiding. She immediately called Lowell and told him she wanted to head that way. He understood her desire to be the person who caught the pair and okayed her deviation from the plan. He re-emphasized his warning to her against any more killing. She agreed not to harm any others while behind her back her fingers stayed firmly crossed. She gave all her minions their orders and set out with two burly men with which to track down the pair. In her mind, they needed to die because they were a hindrance to her cause of having all offenders locked up for good. Despite the new law in which all offenders were to be shipped to The Brick, it wasn't good enough for her. A Histrionic Personality

Disorder combined with a dash of Bi-Polar Personality caused her to go to great lengths to make other people's lives a living Hell, especially if they didn't agree with her theories and ideas. She hadn't been back from Idaho for too long when it was time for her to turn around and go back towards Montana. This angered the woman and made her even more determined to find, torture and kill her adversaries.

For starters, she headed to Cincinnati and decided to pay a visit to Steven's old domicile. She wanted to get a feel for him, having never met him, by seeing what he'd left behind in his haste to leave town. It was easy for her to locate the apartment, as she had kept lists of addresses on certain Registered Offenders and he was on the top of that list. She arrived at his abode and didn't bother knocking. She simply had her goons break the door down. Inside they found Steven's friend and former roommate Casper, who *wasn't* a sex offender. That mattered little to Sal, as she hated offenders along with those who helped them.

"Who the fuck are you and what the fuck are you doing?" Asked Casper. "You busted my door you jerks."

The Gal gave a nod and one of the brutes slapped Casper hard to the floor. He managed to crawl up on his couch, where she pulled up a chair to have a chat with him.

"I want to know all about your butt-buddy Steven. Where'd he go and what's he up to?"

155

"I ain't tellin' you nothin' bitch. Who the fuck are you anyway?"

Sal gave a nod and the big man gave Casper another smack in the side of his head, causing his ears to ring with a cicada-like tone.

"The name's Sal Parker, but people call me "The Gal." I don't appreciate your mouth and I'll have one of my guys hit you every time you act like an asshole. Okay?"

Casper's eye widened as it dawned on him that it was the nasty Gal he was warned about by Steven.

"Oh my God. You're that bitch Steven always talked to me about. You're one crazy, fucked up lady."

Casper noticed that Sal had an army-like jacket on with patches that read, "Save a child, kill a pedophile," "Hang 'em high," "Don't save any lead" and a Nazi swastika sewn on the upper right of her jacket's chest. He knew he was in trouble and had to make a decision on whether to talk or keep quiet.

"Just point me to where Steven slept and conversed on the net," the Gal insisted with tenacity. "It's no big deal. I just want to look at his stuff."

After contemplating her request for a measly five seconds, he made the ultimate decision.

"Go screw yourself you mad whore. We live in a free country and you have no right barging in here like some kind of fuckin' Calamity Jane. You and your dicks get out right now!"

Another smack in the head followed, only this one twice as hard as the last.

"We can make this easy and I'll split in no time," Sal said, "or we can make this hard and hang out a while. It's all up to you."

Casper hocked a huge loogy that landed just over Sal's nose and under her eye. She nodded to her thugs and this time a full-scale beating took place. They beat Casper senseless, after which they laid him on the couch, bloody, bruised and moaning.

"Are you ready to talk now?" Sal inquired curiously as she finished wiping the snot off her face.

Casper, bleeding from his nose, lip and mouth, decided he'd been roughed up enough and nodded yes.

"Good, now point me to where all his stuff is."

Casper shakily stood before leading Sal down the hallway, goons holding him up by both shoulders. He opened a closet door and grabbed a broomstick. He then poked upward at the closet's ceiling, knocking open a trap door that spilled down toward him. Coming with it were papers, a knife and a few other miscellaneous items. Sal picked up some of the stuff and went through it. She found nothing of any consequence.

157

"This is it?" she asked. "That's all he has?"

"That's it. At least all I know about. Oh, wait. Check that room at the end of the hall. It was where Steven slept."

Sal nodded and the goons barged through the door. This time it was a mistake, as two full-sized Doberman Pinschers, saliva dripping from their teeth, sprung to attack.

"OH SHIT!"

The goons had no time to shoot as the dogs were on them instantly. The teeth sinking into the men's forearms burned with pain as they tried punching, kicking and slapping the maddened canines. It was no use as they simple became angrier with each hit and bit harder. The dogs were going for the men's throats in an effort to rip their jugular veins out of their respective necks. The growling and strength of the dogs were incredible.

While her goons fought with the dogs, The Gal pulled out a handgun and pressed it against Casper's temple. The shot blew brain matter and skull bits onto the wall next to him. He fell in a dead heap. The two bodyguards continued their losing battle when Sal began shooting down the hall. The shots startled the dogs, who retreated into the bedroom. One of the bloodied goons managed to reach up and pull the door shut.

158

"Get up, you stupid fucks and let's get out of here."
Sal was aggravated. She was beginning to show true signs of
insanity.

*

Following the showers, Matt and his cellmates; men
and women alike, were marched down a hallway, still naked,
to a door with a small square window. The sunlight shone
through the square. This was the first light in many days or
even months for the prisoners. A guard, **Officer Dannon** on
his badge and nametag, stood at the door and announced the
plan.

"You will all walk, single file and with your hands to
your sides, to the waiting train at the end of the fenced path.
You will stop at the table in front of your assigned boxcar for
registration and sizing for scrubs. Once you register and get
your uniform, you will file onto the car. Move to the rear and
fill toward the front. Is that understood?"

Nobody spoke until a medium sized woman raised her
hand. Dannon pointed to her and she spoke.

"Why do we have to wait until we get to the table to
get clothes? Why are you doing these things to us? You're
humiliating everyone here."

"I don't make the rules lady." Dannon attested. "And I didn't rape anyone either, so deal with it."

A chuckle was heard between Dannon and the officers standing in a line watching the prisoners. The small woman couldn't let it go. She spoke again.

"Shame on you and your government. Shame on everyone here in the country that allows this Hitler-esque shit to happen. Has everyone gone mad?"

Dannon nodded to an officer who was nearest the woman. The guard walked over and pulled the woman out of the line. She led her to a room across the hall with no windows. Before reaching the room, the small-framed woman protested in vain.

"Are we going to keep letting this happen to us? When are we going to fight back? I was accused of raping a student at my school where I taught. I didn't do it. The kid had it out for me and now I stand naked before everyone? What are we going to do about it?"

Nobody said a word. They simply looked straight ahead or down at their feet as the woman was taken into the room and the door slammed behind her. Dannon opened the steel door and told everyone to get moving.

"LET'S MARCH!"

Single-file they walked out. They had to walk down a fenced path for a good 100 yards to reach the tables by the train. On the outside of the fence were hundreds of anti-sex offender protesters frothing at the mouth. The walk began for the naked prisoners. The crowd began shouting.

"Look at him there, the tiny-dicked one."

"How do you like it pervs? Now you get a taste of your own medicine."

"Nice ass mama! C'mere and offend me!"

The prisoners concentrated straight ahead and kept up their gait, humiliated all the same. There was no sense in confrontation because they knew they'd lose and end up wherever they took the woman earlier. The crowd threw eggs, tomatoes and started spitting. The prisoners were under an attack of the nastiest elements. Someone actually reached in their pants and threw human feces, hitting a woman in the side of the head. Despite the tears of embarrassment, they marched forward, eventually reaching the registration area. They did as asked, were finally given clothes and filed onto the boxcar for a trip to who knew where.

Matthew was in front of the line and now in the rear of the boxcar. He sat with his elbow on the knee and a fist on his chin, scanning the area around him. He'd been captured in Montana but now found himself, according to the sign on the boxcar, in Colorado.

"Where are they taking us next?" He whispered to himself. *"The Brick? Another jail?"*

161

Matt began to weep when he peered through a crack in the wall and saw a door open just to the right of the boxcar. Out came two guards; one was the female officer who took the mouthy female prisoner away. They were carrying a stretcher with a person covered *under* a blanket, which was pulled over the face. Matt assumed the victim dead. As the guards walked with the stretcher, the victim's arm fell out. Matt saw the tattoo and his worst thought had been realized; it was the female prisoner they had taken into that room just minutes earlier.

"They murdered her." He thought to himself. *"In cold blood."*

Matt felt his heartbeat rise and his spirits sink. He wasn't sure where the next stop would be, but he knew wherever it was wouldn't be good.

He thought to himself that history was repeating itself. It caused him to conjure up an even scarier thought.

"Those that don't learn from the past are condemned to repeat it."

The statement couldn't have been more accurate.

...a kiss for luck and were on our way.

"THE MORE WE DO TO YOU, THE LESS YOU SEEM TO BELIEVE WERE DOING IT." - Dr. Josef Mengele

F.E.M.A.

Railroad companies across America vied to become one of the companies hired by the government to haul the offenders to their destinations. A rich contract worth millions landed in the hands of SSX, West Pacific, Beltway Railroad Chicago, Virginia Southern Rail, Midwest Southern and R&A. The first stop was to be the F.E.M.A. camps stationed from coast-to-coast. From the F.E.M.A. camps, the offenders would be delivered to Chicago, Detroit, Cincinnati or Buffalo where their final rides to The Brick would originate.

All of the railroad companies were freight companies, not commercial passenger, so the offenders were loaded into boxcars and hauled from destination to destination. It was much like Germany *circa* World War II in that it delivered the Jewish to concentration camps all over middle Europe.

F.E.M.A. (Federal Emergency Management Agency) Camps existed across the country in six regions: Northwest, west, southwest, south, midwest and east. Red, Yellow and

165

Green evaluation lists were used to rate the severity of the offenses and who'd be going to The Brick the soonest. Offenders had to travel from jail-to-jail-to-camp until they reached their eventual destination in Northern Michigan. The offenders were treated like cattle or other goods in that the railways didn't care about anything other than getting their "goods" to the destinations they were assigned, thus getting paid. With some two million offenders in the country, it was a profitable venture. There would also be new offenders as time passed, turning the hauling of people to F.E.M.A. camps into a major business. Railroad stock skyrocketed and people bought up the resources in record numbers. The economy was improving and of course, it was *all due* to the eradication of the offenders, at least according to Wisecroft.

A Detroit newspaper reporter, Michelle Henneman, even wrote an article about how lucrative sex offenders were for privatization, and especially The Brick:

Sex Offenders Rewarding for Private Prison

Detroit- Locking up sex offenders has grown lucrative for the privatization industries such as busing and railroads. The Associated Press has been running a study to find out just how much capital is being gained by having these private companies do all the legwork to

166

gather and deliver sex offenders to the bricked facility in Northern Michigan.

It found a complex, mutually beneficial relationship between C.E.O.s in the corrections department, the railroad companies and sex offender policy-makers regarding the hauling, housing, and feeding of the offenders.

The growth is far from over, as the United States Government expects the sex offender hauling trade to last for years and beyond. F.E.M.A. Camps are also sharing in the pot of revenue by holding offenders until their time comes to be hauled to Michigan is determined. An extensive government program hired painters, construction workers and guards, all privatized, to improve and overlook the F.E.M.A. Camps on the taxpayer's dime.

Federal contracts make up 43% of its total revenue, in part thanks to rising sex offender detention and the building of the bricked facility.

B.L.O., which cites the sex offender as its largest client, saw its income jump from 16.9 million to 78.6 million in the last quarter.

At the same time, the business has spent some forty-five million on campaign donations and lobbyists at the state and federal levels in the last five years while The Brick was under construction.

The shift toward privatization happened quietly. While Congress' successful efforts to overhaul sex offender laws drew headlines and sparked massive demonstrations, lawmakers' negotiations to boost detention dollars received far less attention.

B.L.O., which manages most private F.E.M.A. Camps, insist they aren't trying to influence sex offender policy to make more money, and their lobbying and campaign donations have been legal.

"As a matter of long-standing corporate policy, B.L.O. does not lobby on issues that would determine for a sex offender's incarceration." Said B.L.O. spokesperson Seth Olin.

The company has a website dedicated to debunking such theories.

B.L.O., which was a part of the Huntandwhack security firm for years, declined any further comment.

The F.E.M.A. Camps are in cities and remote areas, from a Denver suburb to an industrial area flanking Newark, New Jersey. In fact, chain-link fences and razor wire surround one of N.J.'s airports.

The total average daily cost to taxpayers to detain sex offenders is about $200. That's up from $80 just one year ago. B.L.O. declined to furnish details.

This reporter's findings? It's a millionaires business, and they're living off profits from the taxpayers of the United States.

-Michelle Henneman, Detroit Free Press

Five days after the release of this article, another report was released. This one was much sadder and sent a solid message to all newspapers around the country.

DETROIT REPORTER FOUND DEAD

Detroit- Michelle Henneman, 27, was found dead in her home Saturday, an apparent suicide the cause of death. A friend found Michelle hanging from a noose, unconscious and pale, when she looked in on her. She called 911 and upon arrival EMT's worked on Ms. Henneman for almost sixty minutes. Henneman was pronounced dead at the scene. The only comments from local police were that she died of a self-inflicted nature and that no foul play appeared to be evident.

-A.P. Newswire, Detroit Free Press

A message had been sent and the media across the country took it very seriously.

*

Matt started his first train ride in Colorado, destined for a F.E.M.A. camp in the Midwest. Chicago, Detroit, Buffalo or Cincinnati waited as a stepping-stone before a final ride on R&R railroad to The Brick. Matt and his "cell" mates, who had no idea where they were going, were given clothing, loaded onto the boxcar with the others from the jail and sent out on the cross-country trip. Upon entering the car, they had to sit on hay bales or the floor, whichever they preferred, and it was ghastly hot. The offenders had water supplied to them, so that helped alleviate the discomfort. As the train left the pick-up point and gained momentum, there was more relief with the breeze that shot through the car. There were four boxcars connected to the engine of Matt's train, three still empty, as they would stop along the route to pick up more offenders in other cities. The officials running the train made the cars roomy for the offenders: Not necessarily for their personal comfort, but so that there would be a constant flow of train traffic for at least a year and beyond. Matt and his group had room to stretch and even lie down if they became too

170

tired. It was by no means humane in Matt's eyes, but he knew it could've been much worse.

Matt, as always, took it upon himself to look after the other offenders in his group; mainly the weaker individuals that would have a much tougher time traveling like hobos jumping railcars. He made sure everyone had enough water and organized the older folk's hay-softened rest areas so they could relax during the ride. The age of the offenders ranged from 12 to 90 across the country, but Matt had no one in his group younger than 20 or over 55. Despite the age, he watched closely for exhaustion, symptoms of heatstroke and other dangerous conditions. The railways wanted to get the offenders to their next destination alive, so there were medical personnel available for emergencies. Dead offenders did them no good as they lost money when they lost bodies.

*

The U.S. Government officials were the only people that knew the routes from jails or prisons to camps and kept it a secret for as long as they could. Eventually the public would figure it out, but by then it wouldn't matter, as Americans would be on to other, more pressing issues standing before them, such as which movie star was overdosing or what gossip was being shared among the elite. Within six months to a year, the offender would become an afterthought. Until then, however, the light would shine brightly on the perceived verrucae of society. President Wisecroft was happy. His approval rating from the time he dedicated the facility shot up from forty percent to an all-time Presidential high of eighty-nine percent. He'd be a sure winner for the next election, if there was one, as his plan was to press Congress for an elimination of term limits, citing national emergencies and natural change. Until then, he'd concentrate on seeing his Brick program through. He hoped to announce within a year the collection of all *existing* offenders. He'd also announce many other new laws and rules that would send the public into the worst downward spiral in American history.

*

V.P. Henry Jasper rued the Brick. He went along with it when in the president's company, but secretly hated the idea of a single group of men and women treated as all of society's problems. He knew it was a sure-fire way for Wisecroft to garner support, but he hated the pure stink that came with it. The stink of people railroaded into F.E.M.A. camps struck a nerve, as the camps were strictly for wartime emergencies. He knew better than to approach Wisecroft with any further complaints, as it would surely cost him respect and a voice in other matters. It could also put his family in peril.

After thinking the situation over, Jasper came up with an idea that could possibly spell an end to the problem of the bricked facility. The idea was devilish, murderous and over-sensationalized in his mind. He was seriously considering hatching a plot to have Wisecroft assassinated. He knew that if the president died, he'd take over the country. His first order of business would be attempting to pass a bill to have the bricked structure demolished. Jasper felt enough guilt with having family members on the registry, but the fact that they were living in nice houses, out of harm's way, kept him up at night. He ultimately didn't feel that the government was being fair with the offenders. However, he figured, while housing them within a bricked facility was bad, it was better than jail. It was of no matter to him, though, as it still stung, and he was worried that Wisecroft was leaning toward tyranny. On top of all his worries, he'd fished, hunted and toured the U.P. of Michigan and loved it. From the history of Lake Superior to the beauty of the Keweenaw Peninsula, he felt that the waste was too much. To imagine that all the "Yoopers" were now living in Wisconsin and Minnesota on the Government dime also made him cringe. He wasn't mad at the people themselves, as they had no choice; he was mad at his own government for passing such an obtrusive law. He

knew even more severe laws were to come. He remembered
Wisecroft mentioning the "Obsolete" population, such as
welfare recipients, the unemployed or unemployable and
especially the poor. He wanted to eliminate them from the
scene so the U.S. could grow even bigger as a world power.

Henry Jasper kept his wits about him, but knew that he
may have to resort to other, more radical measures to stop
Wisecroft: Radical as in the death of a President.

*

The group wasn't comfortable on the long train ride.
They hadn't stopped in hours, so the offenders resorted to
urinating in empty water bottles. If a number two called, they
went into a corner of the boxcar and covered the mess with
hay when finished. It was nasty, but necessary considering the
circumstances.

In the quieter moments, Matt longed for Rachel in a
way that he'd never felt before. He wanted to hold her close
and kiss her lovely lips. He longed to feel her small but perky
breasts against his chest. He stared straight ahead as his
daydream continued. The feelings were a mixture of
emotions. He reminisced and smiled, wept and scowled. It
was good to think of her, as it was his only way of coping. He
missed her loving personality, but wasn't missing the

174

obsessiveness that drove him mad. She could be as determined as a stubborn mule to the point where he'd have to get loud to get his points across, or just to get her to stop for a few minutes so they could be intimate. It had become a full-time job for Rachel, and Matt resented that part of her. He still loved her deeply, and forgave her for the Hell she brought upon herself. A Hell he shared with her.

His dreaming continued until a loud screeching of iron on iron rousted him alert. The train was trying to slow as the cars slowly swayed back and forth. He wasn't sure what was going on, so he had everyone gather in the ends of the boxcar and hunker down, just in case. His fear turned out to be unwarranted as the train eventually screeched to a complete halt. He heard people outside talking and boxcar doors opening. The sounds came closer and closer until they finally reached their car. The door slid open and everyone put their hands in front of their faces, blinded by a bright sunshine.

Armed military personnel guarded the railcar, as they fed the offenders baloney and cheese sandwiches and allowed them to get out and do their business in the bushes with an armed guard escorting them. The conditions weren't very good, but did in a pinch. The group was tired and hungry. Matt wondered where they were, as all he could see were flat plains as far as he looked.

"Are we still in Colorado? Or maybe Kansas?"

175

Matt figured they'd been traveling a good eight hours, so he figured his guess to be close to accurate.

"You're in Kansas headed to Michigan. You people are one of the lucky trains headed straight for the F.E.M.A. camp in Detroit."

Matt mulled over the word that stung him like an angry scorpion.

"I'm not sure how 'lucky' you think that makes us. You're lucky you're not going." Matt pointed at the official, "I'm not too sure you'd dig it."

The soldier smiled sheepishly and then spoke, as Matt looked him in the eye.

"I didn't rape anybody, so I can't say I have to worry about it, now do I pervert?"

Against better judgment, Matt kept up the argument. Mary, the woman he spoke to in jail, tried to pull him back by the arm, but Matt had no part of it. He wanted to speak and frustration led his words.

"You know not everyone here committed rape sir. Some people were falsely accused; some were Romeo-Juliet cases. A little common sense goes a long way."

"Common sense huh?" The soldier was simmering a few words away from heated. "You fuckin' rapists and child molesters always think it's everyone else's fault. When are

176

you people going to grow a backbone and take some of the heat you deserve?"

Matt mulled him over with the evil eye and said the words that broke the camel's back.

"I'll bet you stuffed your fingers into little Suzy stink-crotch when you were a kid. That makes you a sex offender too...*Officer.*"

The soldier grabbed Matt by the collar, throwing him onto the hard, dusty ground. The cellmates all took a deep breath.

"Did you call me a sex offender boy? We're just trying to get your sorry asses up to The Brick. A little respect would go a long way. I have the right mind to leave you out here with two broken legs asshole. You'd deserve that more than going to a fucking facility that protects you from the public that wants to draw and quarter you."

The soldier butted Matt in the lower lip with his rifle, causing an instant burst of blood to fly in the air and onto the ground several feet away. Another soldier came by and kicked Matt squarely in the ribs. Now Matt was holding his stomach and spitting up blood as Mary intervened.

"Please stop. You're hurting him."

"Yeah? Well then, teach him some manners. You shit-ass offenders are the scum of the earth. Hey Josh, help me get this loser back up on the train."

177

The two soldiers picked Matt up by the seat of his pants and tossed him back into the boxcar. He landed awkward and let out a yelp upon impact. The soldier had one more word of advice for the rest of the inmates.

"Keep your fucking mouths shut, slime bags, or the same will happen to you. Shut this fucking boxcar."

The door slid fast and slammed with a loud metal-on-metal snap. All the prisoners, especially Matt, learned a lesson about the attitude of the soldiers, as if the dead inmate back in Colorado wasn't enough.

Mary sat with Matt and pressed a wet cloth against his broken lip. She tried to tell him what a stupid move he'd made. He lay with a moan and closed his eyes, not wanting to speak. The train jerked and coughed before again moving down the tracks.

*

Rachel missed Matt as much, if not more, than he did her. She wept often but carried a toughened outer demeanor. She knew tracking down Matt would be the biggest uphill challenge she ever faced. If anyone had the resolve or the pep to do it, it was Rachel.

She knew because of Sal's mistake that Matt was in Colorado headed presumably for Michigan. Even if he stopped somewhere else in-between, she'd head off his route by getting ahead of him. As was the old-fashioned train robbers of yesteryear, they had to have a plan not much different from Bonnie and Clyde, save for the murder, bank robberies and the fatal ending those two outlaws met. The first problem would be getting someone to tell her about where Matt's bus, train or whatever vehicle he was riding in was located. Secondly, she'd need a plan to stop the vehicle. With Steven's help, that seemed like the easier maneuver. After bucking million-to-one odds on those fronts, she'd still need to find Matt after locating *and* stopping whatever vehicle he was riding. The thought was far too overwhelming for her. She lit a cigarette, cozied in her space and shut her brain down. She thanked Steven for his care and assistance and laid her head back against the backpack she had with her. If the impossible were to happen, she'd need all the rest she could muster.

*

Sal was thinking much in the same line as Rachel. She was also going to pursue the transport of which Matt was traveling. She would use the same strategy she used on-line with Rachel; she would let her know, *on accident* of course, exactly where Matt was and where the train was headed. This way, she would draw Steven and Rachel right into her trap. She fully intended on intercepting everyone through the help of the man in the green truck. Lowell supplied her with the information about Matt being in Colorado, but knew nothing more. Unbeknownst to anybody at that point, Matt was headed for the F.E.M.A. camp in Detroit. The minute Sal could get the information she'd try to contact Rachel and set her up for the fall. Of course, the best laid plans of mice and men often fell apart before the eyes of a genius. Not to be deterred, she would see it through. Sal was as stubborn as the day was long and wouldn't take no for an answer under any circumstance...not even short of murder.

The only problem Sal sensed were the occasional sounds she was hearing. At times, she swore she heard her mother call out to her; but after looking around, saw nothing. She shook it off as a case of nerves.

"Sally. My Sally, where are you?"

*

As the hours passed, Matt and his mates heard and felt the train stop four times. They could hear people and train doors sliding open and shut. Presumably, they were picking up more passengers for the trip to Detroit. All the prisoners assumed Detroit because the guard had mentioned it before pummeling Matt.

Motion sickness, heartbreak, anxiety and grief were regular passengers on the ride along with the people in the boxcars. Matt, a broken lip to his credit, did all he could to assist, cheer-up and aide anyone afflicted. The train would pick up speed and the cars would continuously rock back and forth, sending everyone into a kind of seasick feeling. Sleep never came easy and nobody was much in the mood for talking. Every now and then, someone would tell a story or share their life experiences, but few listened intently. The stress was thick and the fear was in the forefront even though no one mentioned it aloud. The boxcar would get hot during the day, but cool off nicely in the evening. The only way to know day from night was by looking through a small crack in one of the corners that allowed light inside.

On they went, never reaching a destination of any kind. Some wondered how long it would take, while others simply didn't care. Matt and Mary would sit and have long conversations during the evenings, sharing stories of their loves, lives and what they had in common.

"I couldn't stay away from him Matt. He was only thirteen but he was like a man. I had to have him. I had to be close to him. I don't consider myself a pedophile, but I guess that's exactly what I *used* to be."

181

"Why didn't you wait until he was old enough to be legal in the eyes of the law? Was it really worth all of this?"

Mary contemplated Matt, glanced at the beam of moonlight shining through a crack and reached a surprising conclusion.

"We were caught in a car together three times before they finally put me in jail. I know if I were a man, I would've been nailed on the first shot. The laws are crazy. When you love someone, you love them. I'm 37, he's 25 and we loved each other until the divorce. If I had it to do over again, I'd probably do the same thing."

Matt was disagreeing with her logic, but didn't say so. He had enough problems of his own without judging someone else's. Mary wanted to know more about Matt and his situation. He shared his story.

"When I was eight or nine, my mom molested me almost every day. She sucked on my penis, played with it and made me touch her private parts. She said it was okay, that this is what kids did for their parents. I didn't know the difference, so I did it. I didn't like it at all. The smell, the feeling, the *wet*; it didn't seem right. What was I supposed to do?"

A tear dripped out from Matt's eye as he recounted the torment that was now haunting his adult life. The train rocked left and right, Matt occasionally having to push himself to one side so he'd avoid losing his balance. He fought off the a of nausea.

"Being told it was okay made it okay, in my mind. When I turned twelve, I thought it would be okay to *help* my six-year-old sister, so I touched her, put my mouth on her and other stuff. My sister tells my mom what I did and what does Mom do? She calls the fucking cops. I'm arrested at twelve and led away in handcuffs while my sis and mom stand on the porch watching me go."

Matt now had tears running down his cheeks. Mary listened intently as he continued his tragic tale.

"I'm taken to the police station, interrogated, intimidated, screamed at and then put in a cell. Sure, I admitted everything because my mom said it was what we did to help family. I didn't know. I would've never hurt my sister. I love her. I didn't mean anything and I live with this pain every day."

"So what did your mom do Matt?"

"That bitch testified *against* me in court. She told the jury I had problems and would touch her when she slept. The lies that came from that woman's mouth were horrifying, although now I know she was protecting herself from any prosecution. She didn't want the rap for any of the shit she was doing to me. No one believed me at all. They shrugged me off as an incorrigible little snot-nosed brat with a bad attitude. It hurt a lot when the Judge threw the book at me. I had to stay in Juvenile Hall until I was eighteen, and then I served three years in prison, until I was twenty-one. Now here I am, on a train bound for Hell."

"Where's your mom now?"

"Dead, I hope."

There wasn't much else Mary could say. Matt stared straight ahead and had the firm look of defeat on his face. Of all the tests Matt had faced in life, this was the most frustrating and challenging. Matt and Mary fell asleep leaning on the wall of the train.

*

"LET'S GO! EVERYONE UP! LET'S GO!"

The guards were yelling as the train was at a standstill. The doors were sliding open up in front of their car. Matt figured they were on another break, which was good, as the offenders needed a breath of fresh air. The guards finally reached their door. The latch moved slightly and then stopped. A rush of breath whooshed through the car. In the next moment, the door latch again moved, this time it went up all the way and the door began sliding open. The sunlight hit their eyes and blinded them instantly as they covered their lids with the palms of their hands.

184

"LET'S GO PEOPLE. GET OUT AND LINE UP. MOVE IT!"

Slowly, the world started to focus in. Matt at first saw only a negative of his surroundings, which included lots of movement and feet scurrying across floors. When the sunlight finally reasoned with his eyes, he saw it. It was a spectacle to be sure, but one that was both awesome and fearsome at the same time. Finally, after a solid ten minutes, it all came into complete focus. Matt had reached the F.E.M.A. camp in Detroit. The facility stood before him in all its prison-like glory. It was yet another step on his journey. A journey that held more terror, hatred and bias then any he had ever traveled. It was only the beginning. Much more lay ahead for him and his cellmates.

To the right, the city of Detroit and to his left, another dungeon into Hell. Matt shuddered as if he'd taken a shot of 190 proof whiskey. His breath choked and his brain spun out of control. It all lay before him in its unbridled glory. What was next, nobody knew for sure.

*

"They're going to Detroit Gal," Lowell informed his second in command. "That's the word on the wire. I hear

185

they roughed Matt up on the trip. His mouth got the better of him."

"I'm going to kill him. Please don't tell me not too. If I can get my hands on his wife, she's dead too."

"I told you to do what you needed to do Gal. I'm not going to stop you on this one, but you've been killing others Sal and I specifically told you not to do that. Oh, by the way, that talk we had the other night? I think we should talk again without arguing. It doesn't bode well for others in the N.V.A.C. who look up to me as a leader."

Sal cringed as Lowell shared the last bit of information with her. She was getting tired of his constant protection of his own reputation while at the same time hanging people out to dry. Ultimately, she didn't care about the killing, the talk she had with Lowell or the stomping out of his presence that followed.

"Forget it Davis. I wouldn't want to hurt your precious reputation now would I? I'm signing off; I have creeps to catch...*uhh, kill*."

"Sal, wait a second."

It was too late; she was gone. Davis felt a slight twinge in his stomach. He felt he shouldn't have said anything to her about the argument, at least not yet. He didn't regret telling her to stop killing. Despite the 110-degree heat in Southern Florida, Davis suddenly felt like he was in an

186

icebox somewhere in the north. The cold chill of Sal "The Gal" Parker blew over him. He knew she was a dangerous woman. The seeds of unrest had been growing in his mind. He finally reached a conclusion he'd been struggling with for a long time.

"I need to get rid of her." He thought. "Would she have the balls to hurt me? Yes, I think she would."

Davis picked up the phone and whispered orders to a minion on the other end. He wanted Sal dead.

"You got it boss. She'll never bother you again."

Davis smiled seductively as he placed the phone back in the cradle. He knew she was a loose cannon, and loose cannons tended to get in the way with their over-the-top antics. He felt better about his decision and settled down with his favorite drink, a pina colada. The air heated back up to its familiar swampy warmth.

Meanwhile, Sal's mind whirled with thought. She didn't want the trio getting past her, yet at the same time she felt a hint of consternation from Davis. She had a decision to make and wanted to do the right thing at both ends of the spectrum. After much thought, she decided to head back to Florida to iron out any rough feelings she and Davis may have been harboring. She figured she could catch up with the advocates immediately after she dealt with the problem. Sal figured Matt to be stuck at the F.E.M.A. camp for at least a

187

week or two. She ordered her two brutes to pack up the truck and told them to keep their eyes peeled for any sign of trouble. It was chilly in Cincinnati but she'd soon find herself back in the conversant and comfortable warmth of home.

Sal felt an ominous tone as the group headed back down I-75. The feeling began to overwhelm her as they reached Georgia. By the time they passed Atlanta, Sal felt morosely tight. She decided that the group would roost there overnight and drive the rest of the trip in the morning. It would be one of the longest nights of her life.

*

Davis was watching Sal's movement on the same type of device he'd supplied her to track down the advocates. He'd had it wired into the underneath of the vehicle. Seeing now that she had re-routed from Cincinnati back towards Florida, he called his minion and told him to stand-by for further action. Later in the night, when he saw that the vehicle had shut down south of Atlanta, he made one final call to spring the plan into action.

Davis and Sal weren't seeing eye-to-eye and enough was enough. Her radical ways had rubbed him wrong. Not for much longer though. Soon he'd be free of her nuisances and could concentrate more on his role in the capturing and

188

delivering of the offenders to The Brick. For each offender he and his group delivered, there was a nice payout. He wanted the money and the security. With Sal around, he could have neither. A very important showdown was about to take place and it would be felt by everyone involved.

Davis was afraid of "The Gal."

THE F.E.M.A. LISTS

Red List - They are the worst of the offenders. These people will be the first group of people, free and imprisoned, prepped for shipment to The Brick. The F.E.M.A. facilities will keep these "high risk" offenders isolated among themselves within the facility. They will be re-evaluated upon arrival at the F.E.M.A. camps and watched closely. It is possible that some Red List offenders will not survive the F.E.M.A. camp preparation. All care will be used to assist in the delivery of said "red list" F.E.M.A. members in an effort to get them to The Brick safely and with minimal harm.

Yellow List - These are enemies of the government along with being second tier offenders. They're also followers and supporters of the *Red List* offenders. These people will be evaluated **after** the initial phase of *Red List* offenders for The Brick is in place, and will be taken to various detention centers for re-educated before shipment to The Brick. Various mind-

191

control techniques will used. Some may not survive the techniques employed by the government. All care will be used at the F.E.M.A. camps to insure delivery tom The Brick with minimal harm.

Green List - These citizens are the mildest of the offenders, or lowest risk, and know nothing about the government programs and don't want to know. They're considered minimal threats, and will be instructed as to how to behave and will be the last to be shipped to The Brick. They will face only minimum security within the F.E.M.A. facilities and will be allowed family visitation until they are shipped out.

MATT'S JOURNEY II

When Matt finally came to his senses, He saw what lay before him and the other prisoners in his group. The level of intricacy startled him. He stood in a line on the train platform with prisoners to his right and left as far down as he could see. When the guards were convinced that the train was empty, a loud, piercing whistle blew that was the signal for the train to move out. The guards wore earplugs to protect themselves from the high-pitched noise while the prisoners covered their ears and squeezed their faces into a grimace. After the train moved out, guards, male and female, took up space on the platform approximately fifty feet apart. Each guard spoke to a certain amount of offenders.

"You *will* enter through the rotating gate, one at a time. After you enter, you *will* be taken to a shower area where you *will* strip and get into the shower. I don't care if the water is white hot or ice cold, you *will* get under the water and soak yourselves. You *will* be taking turns as a group. You *will* stay

193

in line and you *will* stay quiet or else you *will* be dealt with severely."

Matt listened closely as the guards continued reciting their rules using their drill sergeant-like banter.

"After the shower, you *will* be led out single file and powered with a substance that sterilizes and dries your skin. You *will* be given new scrubs. Put them on and walk forward into your holding cell."

As the guards continued, Matt finally lost interest and started looking around the complex. Large floodlights lined the edge of the roof. On each corner of the roof were guard shacks where armed guards stood and watched. Looking behind him, he noticed that he was actually inside the facility. The train had been allowed in through a large automated gate that apparently ran on motion sensors. The gates opened only wide enough for the train to roll in, as there was a mere ten inches of room on each side. There was no way anyone could squeeze through and attempt to escape. The worst of it, according to Matt, was that it wasn't considered a jail, but protection for the offenders. This caused him to cringe and have an ominous thought.

"Why am I being held prisoner? What have I done that deserves this kind of treatment? I served my time and I did my penance, yet here I am, here we are, waiting to see what happens next. Our own government is kidnapping us.

The government has taken over and the people are allowing it to happen. We're in prison: A prison for the scourge of society. I'm wearing a tattoo and a Scarlet letter. I'm considered the problem with the U.S. This is wrong and illegal. This is moral retardation. It's Martial Law. What's next? Where do we go from here?"

"Are you fucking listening to me boy?"

The guard spotted Matt daydreaming and approached him with anger.

"Wake the fuck up pervert. I'm telling you about your new home and you couldn't give a fuck less. Do I need to take you to the side and give you special treatment fuck-face? Are you going to be a pain in my ass? Answer me pervert!"

Matt stared straight forward and kept a straight face. After a good chewing out, the guard went back to his spiel. Matt was surprised he wasn't clobbered.

"That son-of-a-bitch. If I weren't standing her with guns pointed at my head and face, I'd beat his ass. He's a pervert too. He made out with his girlfriend when they were fourteen or fifteen years old. He just wasn't caught. He's also perverting justice and freedom. All of these people are perverted. That guard watches porn and jacks off, that female guard dresses up as a leather bound mistress and kicks men in the nuts, that guard over there probably out-and-out molests children. Not only are these people perverts, they're also

195

hypocrites. The whole nation's based on hypocrisy. It's a crime in itself."

"Alright perverts, it's your turn; single file through the rotating gates. Not one word, just go through and don't make this a pain in the ass."

Matt was about halfway in his line. Everyone walked slowly and headed toward the gates that allowed them in, but didn't let anyone out. He saw Mary some ten people ahead of him and hoped she was okay. He hoped all his people were okay, but the mixing of prisoners was unmistakable when the train emptied. None of the guards, government officials, lawmakers or public cared about these "obsolete" people except to get them out of the picture.

As they crossed through the rotating gate, Matt noticed a number count kept electronically on a large illuminated wallboard. It struck him that the number of people going through probably correlated exactly with the amount of money that changed hands in the greedy corporate world. The next sight was even more startling, as on the large wall above his head was another electronic message: This one illuminated a list of names underneath red, yellow and green signs. Upon closer inspection he noticed that red was for people going to The Brick the quickest, yellow for those on the fence and green for those who would stay in the camp the longest. The green list was very short, while the red list had to scroll

196

constantly to record every name that was coming to the Detroit F.E.M.A. Camp in preparation for their trip to The Brick. He couldn't believe how many people were registered, as two million didn't seem like such a big number when simply spoken, and this was only one of four main F.E.M.A. facilities. Matt startled as he saw his name scroll under the red list. Nausea rushed through his stomach. As he watched, he saw so many other offenders' names on the scroll that it moved him. They were all scheduled to come through the Detroit camp. He had no idea who was going from the other facilities to The Brick and he didn't care. Everyone was an equal in this unfortunate and scary equation. His unsettled stomach finally stretched back into shape as his turn for the showers was nearing. More thoughts crossed through his confused and angst filled mind.

"What in God's name is going on in this world? I see, feel and hear all the things that could possibly go wrong now before my stunned eyes. What person or persons could possibly come up with such a scheme to get rid of law-abiding citizens? I have to control my actions and myself so I don't end up on a stretcher like the woman at the jail. It's tough but I can do it. Rachel's coming. I know she is. She won't give up until she finds me. I love you Rachel. I hope you hear me because I'm thinking of you. Please come Rachel; I need you.

*

"I love you Matt and I'm coming. I'll be there as fast as I can."

Rachel was missing her man as she sat next to a serene river with Steven a few feet away. The two had reached Iowa, headed east. She still had no idea how they were going to spring Matt from the hellhole in which he now lived. Luckily, for her and Steven, Sal had headed south to settle her score with Davis and they'd have time to make some headway in their pursuit. It was good that they didn't know Sal's whereabouts, as it kept them on their toes thinking she may be around every corner they approached. Steven was opening the laptop once every four hours so he could communicate not only with other advocates, but perhaps get a bead on Matt or Sal. It was tough as no one had any definitive answers. Some said Matt was in Detroit, some said Chicago, while others said he was headed straight for The Brick. As for Sal, many advocates were angered at her murderous ways and wanted revenge bad enough to taste it. Steven calmed the clan but would never stand in the way of her possible, or probable, *he hoped*, slaying by an advocate crazy enough to do it.

Trying to keep her own focus, Rachel grilled Steven with question after question and insisted that he open the laptop every five or so miles. Steven finally told her to relax.

198

"I can only carry so many powered batteries Rachel. We have to conserve and play it cool. We'll eventually find out what's happening. Now please try to calm yourself. You need all the energy you can muster."

"It's not your wife or girlfriend being treated *who knows how* Steven. You'd think different if it were your loved one headed for that fucking Brick."

"Rachel; I'm alone! I've been alone for five years. I have nobody. My mom and dad are dead and I don't have brothers or sisters. I come from a shit town in Fuck You, Alabama and I'm trying to help you find YOUR loved one. Back off or I'll go my own way and you can do this yourself. I don't need the headache."

Heeding Steven's warning, Rachel quietly nodded her head in agreement. She was being selfish and knew it. She loved her man like no other, but needed to cut Steven a bit of slack. He was, after all, doing this out of the goodness of his heart. She figured it was time to stop being cold and join him as a team, not look at him as a potential rapist.

"Okay Steven. It's time for a truce. I'm sorry I've been such a bitch and I promise to get on the same page with you. Let's work together."

Steven shook her outstretched hand in agreement.

"I know it's hard Rachel, but it's hard for everyone."

199

He looked at his laptop one last time before shutting it down for the moment.

"I think he's in Detroit, but no matter, we have to get to him before he reaches The Brick. I think our best strategy is to figure out when he's being shipped north and intercept him en route."

"Agreed," Rachel nodded. "Let's move toward Northern Michigan."

*

Having had enough of Davis' conservative attitude, Sal headed to Florida to confront him and get the problem straightened out. She and her goons stopped at a motel outside of Atlanta for rest before heading the rest of the way the following morning. As she lay in bed thinking over the problem her and Davis shared, she came to feel at ease with the fact that the two would talk it out as they always had and would reach a mutual understanding. The two went back years, with Sal backing up the N.V.A.C. leader. When Davis started the group, she was the most vocal and enthusiastic about it. She lobbied hard for assistance and people to join the push, and always gave Davis a nod and a proud pat on the back for all of his accomplishments. Lately, the pair had been getting nasty with one another. It didn't bother Sal, as she

200

liked being somewhat argumentative with the leader of a group she supported so surreptitiously.

"What's a nasty word or a quick fuck you between close friends," was her thinking whenever it popped into her mind. She never thought it would go too much further than arguing status. When Davis criticized her on the phone, it caught her off guard. This was another of the subjects she'd broach when meeting Davis. She figured after the meeting, she'd head back up to Detroit to finish the business of finding the advocates.

Her two goons took turns staying up so they could keep an eye out. Sal slept in her own room and nodded off quickly. She slept for two hours when she heard a loud BANG that rattled her awake. Startled, she gathered her pistol from under the pillow and headed tepidly toward the door. Carefully looking through the peephole, she saw nothing but the amber glow of the light that always shines at night outside any motel room. Being ever so vigilant, she picked up the cellphone and buzzed a signal to her two guards. There was no return signal from either of them. Now feeling her skin crawl, along with the aggravation stewing within her, she knew she'd have to investigate further.

The bang she heard was unmistakable. She was concerned that her two goons might be sleeping at the same time, a huge no-no in Sal's world. She dressed and quietly

201

opened the door to her room. Walking out into the glow of the light was dangerous, so she'd have to dash quickly for the safety of the darkness that called from a small corridor between rooms. That protection sat twenty feet away.

The humidity had thickened and the night air was sultry and still. Despite the fact that it was two A.M. in Atlanta, the warmth was unmistakable. Combined with the stress of worrying about her minions, the heat felt much hotter to Sal. The sweat had beaded on her forehead and the perspiration under her arms ran down her side in a ticklish stream. Slowly perusing her surroundings, there was no movement that she could detect, so she headed out of the room with a vigilance she'd come to expect from herself. She reached the perceived safety of the dark nook between her room and that of her two goons. It was then that she heard another muffled bang and saw a quick flash of light bounce off of the walkway in front of her. There was no doubt in her mind that something had gone terribly wrong. She kept her eyes peeled as the door to her goons room swung open and a large man clad in a ski mask exited. He made his first (last) grave mistake and headed for her room. She had him right where she wanted him. Sal was now the pursuer. Everything was perfect and she would soon spring into action.

*

The showers were crowded but Matt did what he had to do and filed in with the other prisoners. At least another one hundred people cramped into the room. Everyone was naked and butted up against each another. It was uncomfortable and degrading, which led to Matt's next line of thinking.

"This is the new Nazi Germany. We're being herded like cattle for the slaughter. This is the kind of stuff I read about in tenth grade history class but never thought had a remote chance of happening in America. Now it's happening. How am I going to get out of this? How am I going to get back to Rachel and my "normal" life? I'm scared down to the deepest recesses of my being but I have to stay strong. If I freak out, they'll just get rid of me. I have to do what they say and think like a sane man. Am I still sane, though? Do I still have the faculties blessed to me when I was born? How bad will The Brick be? Can I survive it? Can all of the people with me survive? God, please give me the strength to persevere and get through this mess. Please, I beg you."

The guard interrupted Matt's train of thought.

"The showers are coming on. Get cleaned up fast. We have people behind you."

The guard's orders rang loud as Matt snapped into the present. The showers started up; very cold; and the people washed as best and quickly as they could. Matt couldn't believe the day had come where he was standing naked with hundreds of other naked strangers while guards stood to the side and ogled. He noticed two women removed from the shower lines by a pair of guards, presumably, in his mind, to be raped. It sickened him as they slapped the women's nude bottoms as they went by crying. Those guards, in Matt's mind, were about to commit the same atrocities that had condemned many of the prisoners. It reminded him of *The 120 days of Sodom* by Marquis De Sade. He never in a million years thought when he read that book; it could actually happen in real life. The hypocrisy reeked as the day continued.

Once the shower was complete, each prisoner was escorted out one at a time into a separate room. It was there that they were powdered with a sterilization formula. The line moved quickly as it took but two seconds per prisoner. Matt, powdered and given scrubs, was finally able to dress. As he continued in the line, he noticed the women were led to the left and men to the right. They were separating the sexes. It surprised Matt as he figured all would be together again in The Brick, so why separate now?

"More degradation from the powers that are in charge." He thought.

Finally, after three and a half hours, Matt was led into a cell with twenty other men. There were ten cots and the room was about thirty-by-thirty in area. It would have to do until the trip to The Brick.

Matt's friend Mary found herself herded into the women's area, which was more hostile than the men's section. The guards were mostly male and ogled the women with unclean longing. It was a sick sight as the women worried about not only their mental, but now physical health. There weren't as many females on the registry, so the cells weren't as crowded. Mary considered herself lucky that she hadn't *yet* been selected for "special treatment" by any of the guards. Despite that, she knew it could happen at any given moment. The *only* redeeming quality is that the facility was warm. Mary listened as the other five women sharing the cell talked about the process they had been through thus far.

"We don't deserve this kind of treatment. I don't care what we *did* or *didn't* do, it's just not fair."

Another woman spoke. "I know. Now they feel like they can just take women out and rape them. What in the hell is going on here and why aren't we doing anything to stop it? They have the wrong idea with these jails."

Mary was listening intently when she decided to join the conversation and make a point that would be well taken by the group.

"It doesn't matter what we say, what we do or what we believe. The Government has us in their talons and they aren't letting go. We have to make the best of this… unless you'd rather die."

Some expressed their collective will to see the situation through while others wished for death to take them. Either way, Mary was trying to convince everyone that the reality of the situation wasn't going to change unless individuals brought the change on for themselves by thinking positively.

"We're heading to The Brick, whether we like it or not." Mary pointed out. "We have to stand strong and make the best of it. We'll have a whole Upper Peninsula of Michigan to make our own; let's make it the best it can be for the good of our new mankind."

Matt was preaching the same message on the men's side of the camp. The determined and proficient man had a gift for pep talks and positive emotion.

"It can only get better guys. Our situation isn't the worst. In Germany, the Jewish people were exterminated. At least we aren't facing that horror."

"Yeah? Well I lost my family." One man said.

"I miss my kids," said another. "I can't stand that the Government has decided that this is the best course of action to deal with offenders."

Matt contemplated each opinion and tried to ease the men with the best advice he could think up.

206

"I miss my family and my wife too. I miss being free and I miss the way it used to be, but it's different now. The public's afraid of us and the Government has used propaganda to get the people to side with them. We have to accept what we've been given and soldier forward. I'm not sure what else I can say."

The prisoners around Matt nodded their heads. The answer eluded all of them like an unsolvable riddle. They had to make the best of it and by doing so would be better off. Never an easy sell, Matt kept at it every day. He considered himself the advocate he never was on the outside. He wished he'd been more attentive to Rachel's battle. Keeping up the morale of the other prisoners was hard, considering he was fighting to keep his own optimism up. He often daydreamed.

"Every day, I wake up and place my feet on the floor and that's it. There's nothing more to look forward to, unless you count that shit they call food; privatized food at that. There's no visitors, no kindness expressed by guards, no recreation and no games. There aren't even any books or magazines to read. The human spirit is strong, but this is testing me to the extreme. Can I hold onto my sanity? Can I make it to The Brick without completely losing my mind? Will Rachel find me and get me out of this mess. What is there? I think I'll go back to sleep."

207

Depression crept into Matt's mind. It was also wreaking havoc with the other prisoners. What had started as high anxiety had now crept to a slow crawl. Matt had pertinent questions: *Would* he stay sane? *Would* Rachel find him? *Would* he lose his collective mind and end up shot or worse? Time would tell. Matt fell asleep.

*

Rachel prayed for her man before bedtime every night. Steven prayed for the ability to remain free and beat the vigilantes, government and president at their own games. It was an uphill climb for the two that were actually free; if freedom was only considered not being in a F.E.M.A. Camp or behind The Brick. Rachel's man was in such a place and she felt powerless to help him. Steven was determined and obnoxious, a great combination for someone trying to preserve their own self-worth. The two had reached a point of relying on each other. Steven was now able to hug and comfort Rachel when she was sad, while Rachel could tolerate and even reason with Steven during one of his temper tantrums. Trusting and helping each other was of the utmost importance if the goal; rescuing Matt; were to come true.

Steven stayed in touch with his people while Rachel continued her internet saturation. It was the best line of defense in a world that had turned its back. Both of the advocates needed to continue spreading the word while they persisted in not engaging with The Gal or any other of her group.

The two continued their movement toward The Brick. They had left Iowa, reached Illinois overnight and decided to rest up there. Traveling during the day meant almost sure capture. They always traveled down dirt paths and through woods, Steven relying on his compass and sense of direction to keep their travel in the right direction. The time had come to stop and wait: To listen and learn. Soon the traveling would become more treacherous than either of them would ever imagine. They were closing in on Chicago: One of the largest of the F.E.M.A. Camps. Care had to used when approaching, especially if they found out that Matt was taking up residence in that facility. They both knew breaking him out would be virtually impossible, but they could at least try to follow the train into Northern Michigan and take their chances with derailment, or whatever they could do to stop the locomotive. The ultimate plan was to intercept the train, disrupt its travel and spring Matt. Whether any of their ploys would work was a completely different story. It was still the chance they had to take. Steven had everything to lose and nothing to gain except the satisfaction of stymieing at least one group headed to The Brick. If captured, they'd attempt to

209

load him up like the rest and haul him to that awful idea in the north. Of course, he concluded in his own mind that he'd rather die before going there. It was his way. He was stubborn and very independent. Rachel would die…for her man. She had built a deep trust for Steven and appreciated all he was doing to assist in her own personal venture, even though he could get extremely touchy. Heroes were rare, but Rachel thought Steven to be just that: A hero. He was beginning to get a bit snotty with her lately, but she shrugged it off as stress.

Many things would have to happen and many breaks would have to go their way, but the two thought they had what it took to do the deed and set Matt free. Soon their resolve, will and compassion would be put to the ultimate test, a test that would involve life or death.

THE WRATH OF SAL

Stalking silently toward her room, Sal knew she had the intruder right where she wanted him. At first wondering whom the man was and what he wanted with her, she eventually surmised him to be an advocate gone crazy. Was he one of Steven's cronies? She didn't know the answer but intended to find out in mere seconds. As she neared the room with the pistol cocked and ready, Sal crept with the care of a stealth Navy Seal on active duty. When she slightly nodded her head in the door, it appeared that the man was going through her things on the desk. She slithered up behind him and in a moment of pure glory for her, pressed the muzzle against the back of his neck.

"If you move, I'll splatter your brains all over this room and I don't give one shit about the mess."

The man slowly raised his hands until they were just above his earlobes. He said nothing and didn't move a muscle.

"Who sent you here?" Sal asked. "Are you an advocate?"

No answer came from the man. Sal knew she'd have to resort to measures that were more drastic in order to get her question answered. She pulled out her knife and dropped to the floor, quickly slicing both of the man's Achilles tendons in mere seconds. He tumbled forward with a grunt and landed hard, clutching his calves. Sal quickly relieved him of the gun he'd brandished, as it had slid a few inches away. She marveled at the huge man lying on the floor before her. It was at that exact moment when Sal "The Gal" Parker felt invincible.

*

The more Henry Jasper thought about having the president offed, the sicker he became. The mere thought sent shivers down his slender spine. If he didn't want to follow closely behind in death or end up imprisoned for life, he would have to use the utmost care in his planning and implementation of the excursion. After all, he had taken an oath to protect the country and serve loyally under Wisecroft. To make matters even more complicated, he had gotten to know many in his boss's family. Despite these facts, Jasper continued to disagree with the president's policy of walling the offenders into The Brick. The U.P., in his opinion, was one of the most beautiful and serene settings in the entire U.S. and needed to be preserved. He had taken care in not exposing his opinion when the law was being passed through Congress and the House. What could possibly make a man disagree with gathering and walling off the offenders? Henry Jasper had reasons: Reasons that made sense in his mind.

Henry's father, Mitchell Jasper, was a hard-working coalminer in West Virginia. Henry looked up to his father as being a great provider and a humble man. It was when the young woman accused Mitchell of rape that Henry decided a career in politics, not earth mining, was in order. The young woman, twenty-one years of age, accused Mitchell of taking her in the back room of the trailer and raping her repeatedly. The story didn't make sense to eighteen year-old Henry because the trailer was often occupied with members of the management team and Mitchell was usually a mile or two down under the ground.

"Besides," Henry thought, *"the woman was a stone-cold bitch. She spent a lot of time running men down with her sharp tongue and accused them all of being out for the same thing; a piece of tail."*

The woman said it was late at night when he entered the trailer to claim his paycheck for the week. Mitchell insisted that the trailer was completely empty and that his check was on the desk. When he walked to the back of the trailer and caught the young woman masturbating in the restroom with the door open, the only thing she could do to save face was to accuse Mitchell himself of raping her. Mitchell's story was simple.

"I heard moanin' in the back of the trailer so I walked over and saw Ms. Harris a sittin' on the can with a finger stuck up her coochie."

The jury heard "I walked to the toilet and raped Ms. Harris."

Needless to say, his story didn't fly, as they convicted Henry's father of rape, sodomy and other less severe, but just as harmful, violations. The minor charges meant nothing in comparison to the damaging convictions he faced. Mitchell spent only ten years in prison, as when Henry reached Washington D.C. in his mid-thirties, he pulled strings and had his father released.

It wasn't one year later when Henry's brother Todd was next in line for an accusation. This time Henry believed the woman.

Henry had studied the facts of his father's case hard and concluded that he was a fall guy for an embarrassed and man-hating secretary. His brother Todd's case was given the same extensive look by Henry, and he came to the agreement in his mind that Todd had committed the crime. The problem

214

lied in that Todd was his brother. Henry again lobbied with the hard hitters in D.C. and the sentence was evacuated after Todd served only three years of a thirty-year sentence for forcing a ten-year-old girl to perform oral sex on him. The family of the little girl never knew he was released, as the backlash would've been politically damaging. It sickened Henry, and he met with Todd to make his feelings clear and concise. As he spoke to his brother, he rammed his index finger hard into his chest.

"I believe you did it you sick fuck, but I'll give you one get out of jail free card. Next time, I'll make sure they triple your sentence and stick you in with the worst of the worst, *under* the fucking jail."

Todd could only nod and move on. He was lucky and knew it. He also knew Henry would keep his word if he screwed up again. Todd stayed clean for the upcoming years before Wisecroft took office and Henry ran as his V.P. It was then that the idea of The Brick came forward and Henry had to figure out what to do for his loved ones, who were still listed as offenders despite their sentence commutations. They had families; his mom and dad still lived and were together, while Todd married and had two kids.

Henry was torn. He knew his father to be innocent and his brother was guilty, but blood proved thicker than water and both avoided The Brick because of his own tenacity amid

215

private meetings with Wisecroft. The two agreed that Henry's father and brother move to a chalet in Vermont with their families, far away from the population. Wisecroft would also see that their names were removed from the registry forever. The president did warn Henry that any other mistakes from the pair would see them sent straight to The Brick with no questions asked.

This made Henry think hard about all of the others in the U.S.A. that were sent to the facility. How many, like his father, were innocent and simply railroaded by over-zealous prosecutorial teams in whatever town they lived? This was a good question and tormented the V.P. into terrible stomachaches and eventually, ulcers. It was very difficult, as he also knew many offenders were cold-blooded rapists and pedophiles.

"They all say they didn't do it," Henry thought, "but how do we really know for sure?"

*

"One digit at a time." Sal warned. "I'll start with the fingers, move to the toes, and then the tongue, ears and you know what."

The large man was rendered immobile by the very angry Sal and she wanted answers. The threat didn't strike a nerve. The man stayed quiet as Sal began the torture.

"You tell me who sent you, or I'm taking the index finger."

No sound came from the man. Sal reached down and swiftly cut off the finger, along with part of the thumb, from the man's left hand, much like separating the leg and thigh from a cooked chicken. A low growl was the only sound he uttered. After taking two more fingers, she figured out that this man was much tougher than she could've imagined. Sal decided to use a different approach. She found and pulled her handcuffs out of her knapsack, cuffed the man's hands firmly behind his back and rolled him over. She opened his buckle on his pants, unzipped his fly and pulled the pants down to his knees. There was still no sound from the man as Sal cut off his underpants with her knife, exposing his penis. When she picked up his unit and put a pair of pliers around it, his eyes widened.

"This is the deal creep." Sal screeched with an angry tone. "You'll tell me what's up or I'm taking your pecker as a memento of this occasion."

This time she had his attention. The man spoke in a deep, slow and slightly fearful monotone.

217

"Don't do that. I'll talk. It was Davis, Davis Lowell. He sent me here to off you."

Sal was disappointed, but not surprised.

"That's more like it big guy. I thought the threat of your dick on a plaque would make you squeal. Where's Davis now?"

"That's all I'm telling you bitch. You're going to kill me anyway. I know your kind. I know how you think. Trust me though; it'll come back around to you. You'll pay for your deeds just like I'm doing now."

Sal, slightly taken aback, listened to the man and looked at his face. Despite two severed Achilles tendons and half of his hand cut off, he was smiling. The smile was as sinister as it was real. Sal shuddered as she spoke. She was shaken, which was extremely rare for the toughened woman. She quickly recovered and told the man how she felt in no uncertain terms. "I don't care about you. I don't care what you did with your life. I have a cause to follow. I have a job that needs done. I'm not spooked by the likes of you."

"Suit yourself Gal, but I've been doing this for twenty years. I'm a killer, a hunter and a loyal member of the N.V.A.C. I knew, however, that my day would come. I have no regrets. Trust me though, you're day is coming. You'll be the one on the bottom knowing deep down that soon you'll die. It'll be at the hands of someone you never expect. Trust me Sal. It *is* coming."

Sal surveyed the man for a moment longer as anger and hatred filled her emotional crevasse. Without another word, she pulled out her pistol and shot him between the eyes. He died with that same sinister smile on his face. It was unsettling for Sal as she kept hearing the same thing in her head.

"It is coming Sal. It is coming."

"Well, maybe it is." Sal thought. *"But not before Davis gets his."*

Sal packed up and prepared to head for Florida and Davis Lowell. A tear creased her eye as she felt violated and let down. It was at that moment that the goon's phone rang. Sal picked it up and listened.

"Hey, are you there? Hey, it's Davis Lowell. Did you get her yet?"

Angry and disenchanted, Sal's fist squeezed closed as she spoke.

"No, Davis. He missed me, but I'm coming to get you; you son-of-a-bitch."

The phone clicked silent on the other end.

*

Davis sat near his pool drinking whiskey sours while he contemplated life after Sal. She had been his right hand person for some time, but change, in his mind, was always inevitable. He thought back to the good times they had together when Sal had been less sinister and maniacal. She used to actually dress *somewhat* like a woman, with nice jeans, a feminine blouse and earrings. She had now ascended into a military style look with short, slick-backed hair, a shirt with an N.V.A.C. patch on it and combat boots. She carried heat and was proud of it. Her mood swings were now legendary. One minute she was a nice, soft-spoken woman, while the next would find her in a sweaty delirium of hate. For Davis, he could handle it no longer. He was desperately trying to win favor with the higher ups in government and didn't need a blasphemous tone ruining his chances for success. He sent one of his best to hunt her down and kill her quickly because he didn't want her to suffer, as he had a soft spot for her.

The worst part of the coupling, Davis thought, was that he and Sal had been having nasty arguments off and on for the prior six months. It was a series of weak moments for Davis and he lived to regret the words every time it crossed his mind. How he could have found himself trapped into a power struggle with Sal was beyond him.

"Of all the stupid decisions; of all the idiotic things I could've done; letting Sal think she was more than what she really was has to be on the top of the list."

Penalizing himself was nothing new for Davis. He was a pro at second-guessing his choices and had proved it by ordering a hit on Sal and then going over it in his mind repeatedly. After a couple of nights contemplating the decision, he had to make the call to the goon sent to do the bidding.

"Did you get her? This is Davis. Did you get her yet?"

When Sal spoke, making her announcement before slamming the phone shut, Davis felt the creep of ice water shooting through every vein in his body. The adrenaline flowed instantly and his heart thumped with a force meant for marathon runners.

"Oh shit. Now I've really done it."

Davis called his other goons in and explained to them what had happened. He told them to prepare for her arrival and kill her when they so much as sniffed her presence. The second call Davis made was to his big shot friends in D.C. who he thought had his back. He was wrong. They wanted nothing to do with his feud and told him that they *actually didn't care* if he was dead. Another shot of adrenaline went through his body, but this time it mixed with the bitter flavor of disappointment. He had the audacity to believe that the U.S. Government favored him and his cause when in fact they had total control from the get-go. They used Davis as a sort of pawn to help gather offenders but now had the situation well in hand. There was really no further use for Davis.

*

The Gal made her way down the freeway with a heart full of hurt and anger, but was not too far-gone emotionally to realize that going straight to Davis would be suicide. She had to come up with a strategy that would be keener and make her less visible to the N.V.A.C. leader. While she mulled on Davis, she also made room in her mind for Rachel and Matt, along with that cursed Steven. When she was finished with her business in Florida, she'd have to turn back around and catch up to the pair wherever they happened to be hiding out. Matt was the least of her concerns, as he was headed straight for The Brick. Sal had to make sure she intercepted the two conniving pests before they had a chance to get out of her reach. She felt excitement in her body and ate it up. She felt like a cat ready to spring into action. The feeling of anticipation coupled with the knowledge that she was going to kill Davis and track down Steven and Rachel gave Sal a rush she couldn't explain.

222

Ever since Sal was ten-years-old, she loved killing. She captured frogs and squeezed the life out of them using her father's vice-grip in the garage. She also captured kittens, puppies, snakes and other small animals. She learned how to torture and hurt in the most painful and prolonged of ways. Beating the life out of a kitten while it held its paw in the air gave her a rush that was unmatched. At the tender ages of twelve, thirteen and fourteen, Sal was becoming sexually excited with the thought and act of killing. She began masturbating to pictures of dead bodies, videos featuring death and other very dark images. Her dad was never concerned. Her mom was devastated and worried about her Sally

"Kid's will be kids." Dad would say.

"Don't do that Sally. That's bad." Mom begged

"Oh well, they have to control the pet population somehow." Dad reasoned

The parental inadequacies were evident.

Sal went on murdering and maiming small game. It was when she turned sixteen that she had her first taste of human murder.

A friend of Sal; Jennie, went with her down to the swamps in the back of their neighborhood to smoke cigarettes and kill small game. They found toads, mice and snakes to torture and kill. All was great fun until Sal looked over at her friend and asked her what it would be like to die. "Do you think there's something else after we leave here?"

Jennie didn't say much except to shrug her shoulders in an "I really don't care" manner.

"Would you like to find out Jennie?"

Jennie looked at Sal with a leer and an answer. "No. Not really. You ask weird questions. What's the matter with you?"

"I don't know. I was just wondering."

As Jennie's attention ventured elsewhere, Sal bent over and found a moderately sized stone. When Jennie turned around to offer further comment, Sal swung the stone violently, striking her friend directly on the left temple. She fell in a heap.

"You're half-way there Jennie. Let's finish the job."

Sal bent down, grabbed the back of the unconscious Jennie's hair and placed her face into the soft, boggy mud. The tussle was minimal as Sal held tightly while pushing her knees against the back of Jennie's neck. Soon the struggle stopped. Sal listened for a heartbeat, felt for a pulse and found none. She stood over her victim, feeling an orgasmic buzz within her like nothing she'd ever experienced. The rush ran from her toes, up her middle and all the way to her head. It was pure adrenaline and Sal loved it. A killer was born.

Sal went home and told her parents that Jennie had fallen in the swamp, hit her head and seemed to be in trouble. The police were called and extensively interviewed Sal. After a week, the death was ruled an accident and that was it. Sal's sweet "I'm so innocent" attitude won out over the facts. She knew that day that she was a natural born killer and wanted more.

A loudly honking horn shook Sal out of her daydream. She was traveling down the wrong lane and the lights of another vehicle shined straight into her eyes. She swerved hard and avoided a huge catastrophe. She'd nearly struck another car. After regaining control of her truck and realizing how close she came to a huge accident, *she laughed.* It appeared as though Sal was slipping between reality and imagination.

Pull the trigger...

*

Davis waited. His hands shook slightly and the sweat beaded across his forehead. He knew he'd crossed the wrong person and regretted his move of trying to have her whacked. Davis legitimately feared for his life. It was ten p.m. and he knew it was a matter of time before Sal's arrival. Davis smoked his last joint of the day and laid his head on the

225

pillow, confident that his goons would protect him from the killer heading toward him.

As Sal sailed down I-75, getting ever so close to Davis' home, she prepared for a gunfight. She knew he'd have his guards stationed around the house. She knew exactly where Davis slept, as she'd been in his bedroom with him on many occasions, which was fodder for the rumor mill, as the two had never even once had sex. Because he was an OCD personality, she had no doubt he'd sleep in the same spot as always. The big advantage Sal had was that she knew where every entrance to the house was and if Davis or his goons made the tiniest mistake, she'd take full advantage. It'd be much easier than she originally thought to infiltrate his abode.

After a long eight hours on the road, Sal reached her destination. She was on the mark as the goons had failed in one very important facet; they didn't cover anyone coming from *above* the house. Sal grabbed her climbing gear and headed for the trees that stood around the perimeter of the property. She launched a hooked rope and snagged a branch on her first try. She began her climb and prowl strategy.

Davis had a tough time falling asleep. His heart raced with negative anticipation and his mind never stopped thinking of all the possibilities set before him. It took two hours before he finally slumbered. His dreams were intense and woke him once, but he was able to stay asleep on his second try.

While Davis drifted between sleep and the "in-between," Sal carefully scaled a tree, making an effort to stay as silent as she could. She was dressed in black and wore a black facemask, making herself invisible to the amateur hit men that waited below. She slunk across the roof, careful to step on areas that felt secure and sure-footed. The last thing she wanted, obviously, was to slide off the roof and land ten feet down among the goons that lurked, which would spell sure death. Sal was treading above a lion's den, hoping she would keep her wits. Despite the occasional slip or two, she was successful as she reached Davis' window. She peered inside and saw that he appeared to be sleeping soundly. As cautiously as she could, she pushed the window up and slipped inside. Sal surprised herself with the grace she had come to learn through her years of hunting. She approached Davis' bed and bent down. Sal again had the advantage.

"Psst. I'm home Davis. Wakey-wakey."

Davis reared up quickly and began to reach under his pillow for the gun that he'd hidden. Sal, way too experienced for such fodder, met him with a gun barrel sticking directly in his face. She warned him not to move another muscle. The freeze response was resounding, as Davis felt paralyzed at the appearance of Sal. His awareness tripled and the sweat beaded around his brow. In his mind, it would only be a matter of moments before death's nasty claw grabbed him, taking him to another world he knew nothing about. He wasn't ready to go.

"Oh, hi Sal. What are you doing he...?"

"Don't bullshit me Davis. Your goon told me everything *before* I answered his phone and I'm as pissed as I've ever been. How dare you try to have me whacked? I've bent over backward for your fucking group and this is the thanks I get. How dare you take our conversations and render them moot. I'm as hurt as I've ever been in my life."

Davis had to think quickly if he was to keep his life. He put his hands up in a defensive measure, hoping Sal would see his contrition.

"Easy Sal. I didn't try to have you whacked. I just wanted you to realize how easy it could be to *get killed* in this business. I only want the best for you. Call it training."

Sal felt the twinge of a tear attempting to escape her eye and run down her cheek, but she held fast and firm. No tear would present itself in such a sensitive situation.

"I don't believe you Davis. I'm not one of those stupid wenches that eat up everything you say as gospel. We have a score to settle here. You tried to whack me out and failed. Now it's my turn to repay the favor, and I won't mess it up like you did."

As he was trying to distract her with his talk, he'd been inching his hand under the pillow behind him. Sal was far too quick and experienced to be had in such an embarrassing way. She placed the barrel of the gun against Davis' forehead and issued a final warning.

"Move one more inch and I splat your brains all over the pillow."

Sal reached under and grabbed the pistol, thus disarming Davis and taking the full advantage in the standoff.

"I'll tell you what Davis. If you admit that you sent that goon to whack me, then I'll let bygones be bygones and we'll start from scratch. Is that a deal?"

Davis mulled over the request and answered.

"Okay Gal. It was me. I'm sorry. I wanted to teach you a lesson about listening to me. I wanted you out of the way so we could move forward as a group. Since it failed, you win. Let's iron this out and move forward, OK?"

Sal burned, feeling a sullen torch deep inside her spirit. She felt betrayed and used, hurt and discarded.

"You're right Davis. Let's start new."

Davis smiled as the Sal pulled the trigger. The .45 caliber slug ripped through his forehead and into his brain, exiting at the back of his head.

"There Davis. We're even now."

Sal stood up, replaced her gun into its holster and smiled.

"Now I'm the leader of N.V.A.C. No if, ands or buts."

...Now you're dead.

NVAC Leader Murdered

By the Ft. Lauderdale Sun- Sentinel

Davis Lowell, the leader of the famed anti-sex offender group, the National Vigilante Action Committee, was found in his home dead of a gunshot wound. It appears that the leader was shot in the head execution style. There are no leads or clues as to who or why Lowell was shot, but the police will interview members of the N.V.A.C. in the coming days. Number one on the suspect list is Sal "The Gal" Parker, the second in command, or right-hand woman, of Davis Lowell. Police said it doesn't appear as if she's a suspect at this point because she was said to have been out of town during the murder. Her alibi has been confirmed.

The N.V.A.C. is a recognized network that dedicates themselves to being a watchdog group against registered sex offenders. Lowell founded and headed the group. Since the inception of The Wisecroft Law and subsequent removal of offenders to The Brick in the U.P. of Northern Michigan, Lowell had been instrumental in the gathering and apprehension of said offenders.

Brothers, sisters and members of his coalition survive Davis Lowell. Funeral arrangements are pending. Davis was 45.

SHAUN WEBB

"THE GREAT MASSES OF THE
PEOPLE WILL MORE EASILY FALL
VICTIM TO A BIG LIE THAN TO A
SMALL ONE."

-Adolf Hitler

SHAUN WEBB

THE POLITICAL MACHINE

Since the inception and passing of the Wisecroft Law and the barring of sex offenders from society, prosecutors all across the great United States were taking the time to send every possible person to The Brick in hopes of gaining political clout for upcoming elections. "Railroading" or doing whatever it took to convict people, offenders or not, was the new goal of the lawyers and judges, (even though the practice had been in existence since Adam met Eve). The courts didn't care. If sending a few innocent men and women to The Brick was the cost of getting the offenders off the streets, then so be it. Judges were excusing obvious errors in the trials across America. Appeals courts were of no help, simply upholding the lawlessness with one or two sentence statements that spelled doom for the appellant. Congressional representatives, Senators and most everyone in Washington D.C. also turned their backs on the problem, allowing the disgrace to continue. Letters from disgruntled families were tossed into the trashcan unread, while protesters were quickly admonished and

235

punished for allowing their voices to be heard. The public wanted rid of the problematic offenders and the majority thus ruled. During this obvious breaching of customary US laws, the real sex offenders were being put away, but it was the innocent, falsely accused non-offenders and their families who suffered the fallout of public panic.

Newspapers across the US were also filtering their reporting techniques drastically, firing anyone who attempted to publish articles condemning the poor treatment of offenders along with the courts "wild west" attitude. Lawsuits for wrongful discharge were always dismissed when the courts heard that the reporter was trying to protect the offenders. Some of the best and most revered columnists were fired and some Americans missed their candid views. They couldn't get past the fact that a columnist had actually had the audacity to raise a fist for the offender's rights. Some reporters even ended up dead or missing.

It was much the same on television. News personalities that were popular among the people were fired for expressing their negative views on The Brick. Political ads, run mostly during the voting seasons, were now being aired every day of every week. The ads chastised the offender for making the United States one giant ghetto, destroying cities, killing the economy and worst of all, raping the children. The citizens bought it and voted in all of the anti-

236

offender politicians they could. They tended to base their vote on that one issue, much like abortion back in the late 1900's and early 2000's. Still disguising itself as a democracy, the United States' Government was hugely successful at spreading the propaganda among the states and getting exactly what they wanted. A new type of leadership was forming: Rapidly.

What used to be freedom was now approaching tyranny, but the citizens didn't recognize it, to Wisecroft's delight. What used to be a country that gave any and everyone a chance to prosper had become a cesspool of corruption and all-out totalitarianism. President Wisecroft's approval ratings continued to soar, and more than a few new ideas crossed his mind. He shared them with advisors including Henry Jasper, who was getting more and more disgruntled as the days passed.

"I want an abolishment of presidential term limits. There is no reason why I shouldn't continue to lead the people, especially given how popular I've become."

Congressional representatives and were actually giving the idea consideration. Jasper spoke at length about the history and tradition of the U.S.A.

"We can't just up and change something which has worked since 1776. What kind of country are we becoming? I support Mr. Wisecroft on most of his ideas, but I can't grasp or support this one. A changing of the guard every four to eight years keeps things fresh and alive. It gives the people a new perspective of which to consider. It's exactly what our ancestors from the 1700's wanted in the years 2050 and beyond.

Wisecroft liked Jasper, but bristled when he expressed an opinion that directly conflicted with his own. The two argued and disagreed often, with the president always holding the trump card.

"Why are you so goddamned hostile about my ideas Henry? The people want it; Congress wants it; why don't you want it?"

"With all due respect Mr. President, I'm beginning to get frightened by your political ideas and shenanigans. You're going against everything on which this country has stood for over 300 years. Something has to give sir, and so far, it's not been you."

Wisecroft obviously hated what Jasper would tell him and always brought out THE threat.

"You keep on messing with my agenda Jasper. Perhaps a trip to The Brick for your family is the medicine you need to start paying closer attention to the ideas I bring forward for the people."

"You always bring that up sir. You know I hold those people dear. I don't understand why you wave them over my head every time I disagree."

"Because I can Henry. If you keep chanting and chirping about my policies, I'll see that your worst nightmare comes true."

Jasper stared at Wisecroft with disdain. No matter what he said or did, if it didn't agree with Wisecroft's agenda, he was threatened. The arguments always ended there.

"Fine sir. I have nothing more to say."

"That's what I thought Henry. Now go be a good V.P. and cater to the people that elected us."

The steam billowed within Henry's heart and he knew that if he didn't at least try to do something radical, the tyranny, which was overtaking society, could easily become permanent. He was planning in his mind what to do to derail Wisecroft's continuing abuse of his political power. Knowing he couldn't handle an assassination of the world's most powerful man by himself, he talked to an old pal of his, Rene Duchard, a retired C.I.A. hit man, about the possibility of orchestrating the plan of all plans. Finding Duchard was the easy part, as he was lounging on the beaches in the Bahamas, but getting him to agree to such a radical idea proved a bit tougher.

Jasper flew Duchard into Dover, Delaware under the guise of an old visit from a friend. He planned to meet with him in a top-secret location outside of Washington. Jasper sent a car to pick up the reclusive man and had him driven to

239

an old underground warehouse in Woodbridge, Virginia. The
man driving Duchard knew nothing of the plan and Jasper also
kept a firm lid on any kind of idea being accidently leaked.
Only one man knew of the plot: Henry Jasper. Soon it would
be two.

*

As Henry headed to the private warehouse to meet
with Duchard, Wisecroft was busy plotting his own further
plans to infiltrate the American people's minds. This time it
involved the use of the internet and the pornography business.
Convinced that Pornography was causing much of the sex
offenses throughout the country, Wisecroft set up a meeting in
D.C. with the highest of the high on the porn industry ladder.

Pornography in the United States was, in 2050, as in
the previous seventy-five years, the highest grossing industry
in the land. American citizens, to watch people having all
kinds of sex, spent some twenty billion dollars a year. It
didn't matter what the acts involved, it only mattered to
Wisecroft that the porn industry, which collected the said
twenty billion a year, be destroyed. In Wisecroft's mind, the
child porn industry was a direct relative of adult porn. He
figured that if you stopped one, you stopped it all. He would
go for the throats of the big boys.

240

Wisecroft also shared a plan with his advisors to monitor the internet activity of every American citizen, thus not only censoring what people looked at, but further filling the coffers by sending more people to The Brick. By making it illegal to not only download, but also simply look at porn, he figured he'd snag at least another one million Americans. There would also be new, harsher laws against terrorist activity, social network banter, and any other outlet that encouraged free speech. Wisecroft wanted complete control of the internet.

The first meeting involved all of the pornography moguls. A special dinner and conference, scheduled at the White House with the thirty top Porn executives attending, was also planned. The conference and dinner were disguised as a profit sharing plan by Wisecroft when in reality it was *actually* a speech to inform the executives that their industry was about to die an ugly death.

After the executives finished their dinner, they were politely led into a large conference room. The wooden table centering the room measured fifty feet long by twenty-five feet wide. It was a dark mahogany with nary a scratch on it. As the pornography dignitaries seated themselves, President Wisecroft entered from another part of the room. He had two large bodyguards flanking him while a plexi-glass shield separated his chair from the rest of the parties. It was strictly

241

for security, but seemed unnerving all the same. When Wisecroft took his chair, the meeting came to order.

"Gentlemen," Wisecroft welcomed, "you are all under arrest."

A team of Special Forces barged in through the same door the porn execs had entered. They had machine guns and stood blocking any exit out of the room.

"I'm holding here a piece of paper that says pornography in the United States is officially declared illegal. You will be the examples of my clean-up process." Wisecroft smiled widely.

One of the executives stood up to argue, but was quickly struck down with a guard's butted rifle.

"Please take these vermin to the local F.E.M.A. facility," Wisecroft ordered, "and then to The Brick."

As quickly as he'd entered the room, he left. He had done the job he promised to do and the reverberations spread all over the country the next day. Video stores were ordered to have all X-rated material destroyed. The internet blocking of all X-rated material had begun. Through governmental entities, such as the F.B.I. and other departments across the U.S., porn was wiped clean within a week's time, save for the black market. The Conservative Christians cheered the decision and held porn-burning parties in the streets all over the U.S. In California and other known pornography hotspots where dirty movies were shot, raids were carried out. Actors, actresses and directors were all arrested and booked for their trips to F.E.M.A. Camps. The stock market dropped significantly the first few days after the arrests, but recovered nicely, as there were other, cleaner alternatives to replace it. Porn stocks were never big with traders to begin with, so the economy didn't take a serious hit.

Anyone known to be in possession of porn-related material was arrested. Television ads warned that possessing the illegal material would result in more arrests. The minority of Americans applauded the action, while the majority loathed it, but eventually accepted it as necessary to protect the children. A watchful eye was open and looking over the United States, just waiting for individuals who made mistakes that would result in their incarceration at The Brick. The watchful eye was known as "Bigger Brother."

It was another notch in Wisecroft's widening political belt. His plan continued to go well, as the United States' trip into tyranny continued.

*

Rene Duchard was an imposing figure of 6'5" and at least two-hundred and fifty solid pounds of muscle. He worked for the C.I.A. for twenty years before retiring at the

243

peak age of forty. Now fifty, Duchard still owned the prowess and ability taught to him while working for the government. He was one of the best when it came to carrying out assassinations and Jasper was as close to him as anyone was allowed to be. When they finally met in the warehouse, Jasper and Duchard embraced with a friendly hug. That was the extent of the happy feelings as Jasper went right to the point and told Duchard what he wanted. Duchard was less than impressed. "Are you fucking crazy Henry? What kind of asinine plan is that? You'll get us fucking killed."

"You see from your lofty beach house exactly what's going on in this country Rene. Why would you be okay with that?" Henry was wide-eyed, but calm in his explanation. "We can't let this country slip any further toward tyranny or it'll be better to move to the Middle East."

Rene leered at Jasper with apprehension along with a touch of agreement. He knew the country was falling INTO absolute power under Wisecroft, but wondered why the American people hadn't protested. He asked Henry, who explained. "Because the American people are fat, lazy slugs who want to sit in their houses, watch idiotic reality TV and eat artery clogging fast food. They don't have the gumption to resist. Only a quarter of them go to the polls, and out of that, seventy-five percent are fundamentalists. The taxes being saved by not having so many people in prison is trickling back to the American people, *for now*, and they're eating it up."

Duchard knew that to be true and knew Wisecroft's family had been brutally attacked before the president's eyes. That explained The Brick, the crackdown on porn and everything else that could contribute to sex offenses.

"He's taken it all personally huh Henry? Wisecroft has made it his own personal vendetta. His propaganda program has effectively rendered the average American hypnotized."

"Yes. If we don't stop him, it'll go further. It'll drag this country to its knees. Other countries are licking their lips waiting for us to weaken to a state of North Korean proportions. They know our people will offer no resistance, even though we have a formidable military. I see terrible catastrophes in this country's future."

After stepping out to have a smoke, Duchard returned to the room.

"Okay. So what do you have in mind?"

*

All across the country, the fundamentalist groups continued burning books, pornography and other jargon they considered blasphemous or damaging. The Conservative Christians headed the ranks, doing the same. Large protests

245

against porn, abortion and other "sins against humanity" were being carried out while the rest of America sat in their recliners wondering where the next glass of lemonade was going to come from and who was going to serve it. The people who didn't vote, didn't watch the news and didn't care were the ones that the government counted on the most. They saw their paychecks rise and fell in love with Wisecroft.

For thousands of years in countries everywhere, people spoke up, and many died, to fight oppressive government. From China to the Middle East and Korea to Russia, the power belonged to the people. The governments embarrassed themselves all over the world with scenes of shootings, tanks running over protesters, and oppression that hadn't been accepted by the citizens. In the United States, circa 2050, the people were more concerned with the tiny square of land they had in their tiny neighborhoods. The citizens of America had become docile, overweight and sedentary. Getting up to find another beer in the refrigerator was as much exercise as many of them exerted. Where people used to fight toe-to-toe over politics, they no longer cared. Where people went to the parks and moved around (exercised), most now sat in their domiciles waiting for their lives to play out. President Wisecroft counted on those lazy, entitled people to inflict his will. It was working all too well. Oh, some protested, but not nearly enough. The protesters needed thousands to get their points

246

across, but only a few hundred showed up. The government didn't care about such paltry crowds, as they couldn't come close to making a dent in the opinion of the Americans who fell flat in the face of tyranny, totalitarianism and what some called close to a dictatorship.

2050 in America was looking much like the 1930's and 40's in Germany. It was a new time, a new attitude and a new regime. Wisecroft was pulling all the strings and would soon garner enough power to stay President longer than the Constitution allowed. He continued reading and learning from Hitler's *Mein Kampf* every day. As dangerous as he was, nobody cared to stop him: Nobody except the one man that had the inside scoop: And the ear of an assassin.

*

"It has to be subtle." Duchard insisted. "We can't just go out shooting guns off and creating a big scene."

Having been involved in his share of executions, assassinations and other espionage, Duchard knew the ins and outs of killing. Having listened to Jasper's reasoning behind offing President Wisecroft, Duchard seemingly agreed, but insisted on being very careful.

"The presidential security is by far the best in the world. I was head of the C.I.A. during Tomlinson's reign as

247

president and I learned all there was to know. If you even
breathed funny, they'd kill you. If so much of a whisper of
our plan gets out, then we're dead men. I'll also know that it
was you, Henry, who spilled the beans. If that happens, I'll
get to you before they do and inflict legendary pain. Are we
straight on that?"

Henry gulped. He knew Duchard meant business.
That's why he'd looked him up. He wanted the job done right
and needed a well-trained killer to carry it out.

"Yes, I do understand. Not a word of this goes
anywhere, ever. I know better than to put my mouth ahead of
my brain."

Duchard, whittling at a branch he'd picked up outside,
looked into Henry's eyes. Looking back at Duchard, Henry
saw death and pain staring back at him. It was the deep-rooted
seed of red-eyed anger, hate and loneliness. The rage and
hostility was as dark and ominous as Duchard's rich five-
o'clock shadow. Jasper had to wonder to himself if he'd
already taken this idea too far. He thought hard to himself.

*"What if it doesn't work? What if word somehow slips
out?"*

The "what ifs" rained down upon him like an
avalanche of Rocky Mountain snow. He felt the cold ice
water running through his thickened arteries. His mouth felt
dry and cottony, while his heart rate, usually a solid seventy-

248

five, had reached an uncomfortable one hundred and ten. Sweat beaded from his forehead and his palms felt like tingling appendages about to fall from his wrists and crash like glass on the floor. Henry pulled out his handkerchief and began patting his brow.

"You nervous, Henry?" Duchard comically quizzed.

"Yes, I am as a matter of fact. This is only the most dangerous and life-changing mission I've ever been a part of; save for The Brick project."

"Don't be nervous. It'll be easier than you think. It'll happen so fast you won't *know* what to think. Here this second and "poof", gone the next."

Duchard had gathered a handful of dust off the floor. He blew it out of the palm of his hand directly at Jasper.

"I'm glad to hear that. When are you going to do it?"

Duchard looked at Henry with a surprised look of contempt.

"Moi? No Henry. *You're* going to do it."

Henry's eyes opened wide. He looked at Duchard as if he was kidding, crazy or both.

"Don't say a word Henry. It'll be just fine. You'll see."

A plot was born. Henry Jasper and Rene Duchard had hatched it. There would be no turning back if Jasper wanted change. This was going to be his only chance for it.

249

A MORE

PERFECT

UNION?

"FREEDOM IS NEVER VOLUNTARILY GIVEN BY THE OPPRESSOR; IT MUST BE DEMANDED BY THE OPPRESSED."

-Martin Luther king Jr.

MATT'S JOURNEY III

The rain splashed about the city as Matt stared out of the barred window that the government said was for the offender's protection. He could see the skyline of Detroit, wishing he could figure out a way to escape and find his beloved Rachel. He knew she was close; he could feel it within his soul. If she could find him and get him out of the mess, she surely would. Matt found that his clutch on the bars was becoming so painful it hurt to release. The tension built up inside him until it reached a maddening crescendo. He wanted to be free. He had served his time and followed all the rules, yet this was his reward. He rued the day he was born an American. The country that he thought to be a free democracy had drastically changed. The United States as he knew it no longer existed.

Lying on his cot, Matt neared sleep when he heard his name.

"Lyons. I'm looking for Matt Lyons."

SHAUN WEBB

Matt looked up and saw a female nurse standing at the cell gate. The fact that the facility was clean and livable didn't make up for the reality that he felt like a lab rat: There to be observed and ogled over. There was no freedom at the camp. It wasn't the "family center" that the government made it out to be in public forums.

"I'm Lyons. What do you want?"

"Come with me Lyons. It's time for your physical."

"Well, what if I don't want a physical? What if I ask you to leave me alone?"

"Then, Mr. Lyons, I'll get a couple of the guards to pull your ass out of the cell and we'll force you to get a physical. How would that be? Any better?"

Matt didn't have to think for long. He shared the cell with a few other men; all of them real and rightly convicted pedophiles. They nodded their collective approval that he followed directions. He reluctantly followed the nurse out of the cell. The gate slammed shut behind him.

The nurse led Matt down the hallway where they stopped at another cell and extracted one of its prisoners. On to another cell, another and yet another until there was a group consisting of Matt and nine other men. They were hustled down a long corridor and into an outside courtyard area. The nurse, with the nametag reading *Lisa* across the front, ordered all ten men to strip naked. Matt and the others looked at each other as if she were nuts.

"I said take off your fucking clothes now! Everything, including underwear. I want ten buck-naked men in front of me within thirty seconds or we'll bring the dogs in and they'll shred your fucking clothes off."

To the far left side of the outdoor courtyard, Matt saw three guards: One with a Doberman pinscher and the other two with German Shepherds. The men all stripped down, and quickly. Nurse Lisa spoke.

"You guys, it turns out, are the troublemakers of the whole operation. You ten are the ones that speak the loudest against everything we're trying to accomplish as a country. Certain higher ups have had enough of your talk. I'm here to see that you learn to keep your mouths shut. The nurse walked down the line, pulled each man out one at a time and whispered in his ear. Each man, upon hearing what she had to say, cringed and a couple almost burst out in tears. She finally reached Matt. She attempted to shake his resolve.

"Your little girlfriend, Mary? Right now, as we stand here together, four guards are raping her so severely that she's bleeding from her rectum."

"You're a fucking lying bitch."

"Oh really? Let's just see about that."

Nurse Lisa pulled out a cell phone and thumbed through the face. She tilted the phone toward Matt and there it was: Mary enduring a savage rape while being recorded. Matt felt sick to his stomach.

"You perverts." Matt shook as he spoke. "You fucking perverts!"

"Would you like to know something else Matt? Your wife Rachel is deader than a doornail. Seems after they caught you they killed her. Tough break, huh son?"

Matt lost his temper as his vision faded to a purple-black hue.

"Why you fucking bitch!"

Matt reached out to grab Nurse Lisa, but she was prepared with a small shock device. She hit Matt on the neck and down he went. She stood over him and chuckled. The other nine men stood silent and stared straight ahead.

"You're the fucking perverts and you get everything you deserve. You'll find out we aren't too keen on child molesters."

Matt, slightly shaken, regained his composure and spoke.

"So you people rape, torture and humiliate to get your points across? You're worse than any sex offender I've ever been around."

258

Lisa reared back and gave Matt a boot square to the diaphragm. He felt the pain as it sucked the breath out of him.

"Everybody get on your knees." Nurse Lisa ordered. "Let's go!"

She strode along the line of men, taking pictures of the naked men as she did so. She wore latex gloves and grabbed a couple of the men as she walked by, causing them to come out of line toward her. She continued her terrible psychological assault, cutting the men down and telling them lies about loved ones.

"You guys are going to keep your mouths shut during your stay at our beautiful little camp. The next time we hear anything out of you, the penalty will be worse; we'll start killing more of your loved ones on the *outside*. If we find that you simply can't shut up, we'll sew your fucking mouths shut. Get it? Good!"

After two hours of agony, Nurse Lisa led them back to their respective living quarters. A few of the men went straight to their cots and wept, while a few others went straight to the shower. Matt walked into his cell, sat on his cot and stared straight ahead, more determined than ever to find a way to get even with the people that were hurting him, his friends and his family. One of the men asked Matt what happened.

"No comment...right now."

Matt laid down and shut his eyes.

"We need a car Steven. It'll make everything easier."

Rachel was tired of traveling by four-wheeler and
knew, of course, that they could cover more ground quicker
with a vehicle. Steven, at first against the idea because they'd
have to steal said vehicle, agreed and figured the faster travel
would make finding and springing Matt much more
achievable. Steven also had an ace in the hole; he knew an
advocate outside of Chicago who may give him and Rachel
some refuge during their trip.

A surprising number of people across the United States
were taking in offenders, falsely accused *and* guilty, and
hiding them from the government. Of course, if caught, it
would be curtains for them along with the offenders they were
harboring. It was of the highest importance that they keep a
low profile to avoid such detection. Although a few were
caught, many went undetected. The people Steven had in
mind were harboring some one hundred on-the-run offenders
in Tinley Park, Illinois. Tinley Park, about thirty miles outside
of Chicago, was out of the way enough to make avoiding
being spotted an easier proposition. Steven made a phone call
and the arrangements were set. He and Rachel would shack

up with the group for a few days while they tried to figure out exactly where Matt was being held.

*

The man in the green truck was in hot pursuit. After finally catching up with the pair, there was no way he would let them out of his sights again. He figured he was lucky to find them after they left the hideout in Montana. Tempting faith twice would be unwise. The man still had his flask full and drank while he drove. It was no big deal, as he easily kept up with the four-wheeler.

He was proud to be helping Sal and the N.V.A.C. round up the offenders and get them off the streets. He'd never had any experiences with them, so didn't have an opinion one way or the other as to the capturing and bricking of said offenders. He was as blind to Wisecroft and his laws as most other Americans. He didn't see the broad scope of what the president was trying to do and never gave it a second thought. He figured that as long as the majority of the public were for it, it must be a good idea.

Unfortunately, he was no different than the lazy Americans who sat on the couch, managed to collect a paycheck, unemployment, welfare or even all three. Sal was paying him a modest fee to track Steven and Rachel, thus satisfying both his wallet and his drinking problem. He saw no harm in what he was doing, as long as no one was getting physically hurt.

He didn't know Sal as well as he'd thought.

*

Rachel agreed with Steven and they went about the task of stealing a car for their drive from Northeast Iowa to just outside the city of Chicago. They happened upon a bar at ten o'clock at night; a perfect time for a theft, as the patrons usually partied until closing hour arrived at two. They went for a black 1999 Ford Ranger, as the owner was probably drunk and had nothing much else to do *except* drink. Steven knew enough about how to hotwire a car, but needed no assistance as he found the hidden key behind the rear quarter panel of the truck. Like taking candy from a baby, they drove away with what they hoped would be an easy ride to Tinley Park.

During the ride, Rachel was all over the radio dial listening for information about The Brick and anything else that had to do with the new laws Wisecroft had adopted. To her chagrin, there was very little, as the United States and its people were simply doing what they did and ignoring the events of only weeks earlier.

"Nobody gives a shit Steven. This country doesn't even care."

Steven chuckled. "It's all yesterday's news. This public is definitely a what-have-you-done-for-me-lately type of people."

Still, Rachel soldiered on, doing her best to find and hear what she could. By what must have been pure luck, she stumbled onto a station that broadcast train route updates, F.E.M.A. news and The Brick. It was faded into almost nothingness, but she did manage to catch a few tidbits and call letters from the station that would come in handy while they rested and laid low in Tinley Park. The station played much like a weather report, repeating itself until new information surfaced.

"This is station WBRK, THE BRICK. Trains are en route to Detroit and Chicago F.E.M.A. camps via St. Louis, Cincinnati, Baltimore and Denver. The total number of sex offenders in custody at F.E.M.A. camps totals five hundred thousand, six-hundred and twenty. Trains are expected to arrive before midnight.

Trains are en route to The Brick in Mackinaw City, Michigan from Detroit, Chicago, Buffalo and Cincinnati."

The message repeated itself for the next two hours until Steven told Rachel to shut it down.

"But we need to listen. Something important could come up."

"If it does, we'll hear about it later. I can't take the same two-minute message for another second. It's not going to tell us where Matt is anyway. He may be on his way to The Brick or already there for all we know."

That comment stuck in Rachel's craw, as Steven was being insensitive and uncaring again, in her mind.

"God forbid we're too late. Please don't suggest such things." Rachel fretted. "We have to find him Steven."

"If he's findable, we'll find him Rachel. We have to take this one-step at a time. I'm sure we'll get some information at the place we're going. They have much more technology than we do. And I'm only being realistic Rachel."

"I hope you're right. And please keep your realism to yourself when it comes to Matt."

"If I'm not right, we'll deal with it then. One-step at a time Rachel. By the way, don't tell me what to say or how to say it."

Rachel folded her arms over her chest with a pouty snort as the two continued on their path; now only about an hour from Tinley park.

When all seemed well and serene, a blue and red light accompanied by a loud siren went off directly behind them. The worst of their fears came true as the police were calling, undoubtedly for the stolen Ranger they were driving. The pit Steven felt in his stomach knotted tightly as a wash of warm blood flooded up to his head. He thought for a moment he'd pass out, but with a few deep breaths, quickly recovered. He pulled the Ranger to the side to face the music. Rachel held her breath as the trooper's cruiser pulled in behind them. When she looked over toward Steven, she saw that he had a pistol hidden beside his right leg. He looked at Rachel, lipped a "shhh" and rolled his window down.

"Good evening Officer. What can I do for you?"

"It's not your lucky night, is it boy? Hand over your license and registration."

The pit in Steven's stomach tightened anew as his grip on the pistol became firmer.

*

The more Matt stewed in his cell, the madder he became. Nurse Lisa had not only been sadistic but was cruel and cold in her tactics. It wasn't all her fault though, as she had undoubtedly been put up to the task by powers much larger than herself. For that matter, the entire system, in his opinion, was "fucked up." He told the men in his cell about what had happened to him in the courtyard. The true pedophiles told him to get over it and expect more harassment if he couldn't keep his mouth shut, while the others listened intently, telling the molesters to stand down in their verbal assault.

"We're not getting out, so why do we even bother trying to make waves?" One prisoner told him.

"Because I'm no quitter," Matt revolted, even though he knew that the men were probably right. "Besides, we have nothing to lose here. They're getting rid of us, so why shouldn't we fight? They're raping our women, humiliating us; what else do we need to succumb to?"

Nobody in the cell said another word; they simply crept back into their cots.

"That's fine. You guys do what you have to do and I'll do what I have to do. I won't stop fighting. So fuck you all if you just want to bow to the control machine."

Matt crawled into his bed and went to sleep. It was about one a.m. when he was awakened by guards and Nurse Lisa.

"Get up Lyons. You're coming with us."

Matt looked around the cell, but there was no movement. Either the other men were asleep or they were doing a great job of faking. Matt walked out with a guard on each arm. Nurse Lisa picked up a few of his things lying by the bunk: A toothbrush, a razor and his clothing. Matt wasn't sure, but he suspected he was being moved.

266

"What's going on?" Matt asked.

"Shut the fuck up!" Nurse Lisa answered. "If I ask you a question, you can answer. Until then, keep quiet."

After a long walk through the facility, the two guards, Matt and Nurse Lisa reached a room with a table and a chair. The room was gray and had a two-way mirror. Nurse Lisa nodded to the guards. They took Matt to the table and cuffed both hands directly onto the tabletop. Now his back was turned to the nurse with his torso bent at the waste. It was an uncomfortable position. Matt started getting nervous.

"We're going to start with a frisk." Nurse Lisa explained.

"Frisk me for what? I'm only wearing a thin jumper."

"You'll see. Now shut your sorry ass up before we gag you."

As she was frisking Matt, she placed her hand on his testicles, which hung freely between his legs under his scrubs.

"Hey!" Matt admonished. "You can't do that. That's assault."

The nurse squeezed hard and Matt gasped. The pain was enormous, filling his lower region and even his stomach.

"Talk again and I'll fucking squeeze them until they pop in my hands."

Matt shut his mouth and Nurse Lisa let up. The relief was phenomenal, but left him with a stomachache, as if he'd been drilled with a baseball in his private area. Nurse Lisa then pulled Matt's pants down and off, leaving his lower half-nude and rear-end up in the air. Matt felt humiliated and used.

Nurse Lisa asked some questions.

"Are you riling up the prisoners again Matt? They've complained and want you moved. You can't help but rock the boat, huh tough guy?"

"You guys are the real offenders. Feeling me up, humiliating me, and trying to break my spirit. I'll get even one day. You just watch."

The next thing Matt felt was beyond description. Nurse Lisa stuck something in his rectum that was far too large and unnatural for that part of the body. Matt wept with pain. The nurse then started taking pictures, her flash lighting the room for brief interludes.

"That's a great look Lyons; a baby doll sticking out of your ass. How appropriate, seeing you couldn't keep your hands off your little sister." Matt said nothing.

"Enjoy this room Lyons, because it's where you're staying until it's time for you to go north. No more talk, no more chances. I can't trust you and I won't have you encouraging other prisoners to riot. Oh, by the way, everyone who walks by can see you with that dolly sticking out of your ass. I think it's a good example for the other prisoners. It'll make 'em think before they speak."

Matt would've spit at her, but he couldn't turn around. The lights flickered off and the door slammed shut. He was stuck against the table, cuffed, with who knew what hanging from his rectum. Matt cried.

He stayed in that position for a total of twenty-four hours before a guard came in, *ripped* the appendage out of him and uncuffed him. He left his jumper pants on the floor. It took Matt a half hour to loosen his muscles up enough to bend down, pick them up and put them on. He slunk to the corner of the room and moaned. He knew there was nothing more he could do until he was sent to The Brick.

*

"Yes, Officer, what can I do for you?"

Steven was smiling and being very polite when the officer explained that it was his "unlucky" night and order him to come up with a license and registration. Steven knew he had neither and gripped the pistol tightly.

"I forgot it officer. I was in a hurry because my wife here isn't feeling well. I think she might have appendicitis."

The cop looked into the car and saw Rachel moaning, clutching at her stomach and oozing thick lines of saliva from her mouth to her lap. He bent up and scratched his head.

269

"Oh, wow, okay. The nearest hospital is down the road and to the right. You'd better get her there fast. She looks rough."

Rachel didn't care for the cops description of her, but kept up her act all the same as Steven negotiated.

"Sorry I slowed you down," The officer said. "Get on moving. Go as fast as you need to go. No worries."

Feeling like a ton of bricks fell off his shoulders; Steven nodded and put the Ranger in drive. Now he had permission to speed. The situation turned out much better than he or Rachel expected. He looked over to Rachel and giggled as she wiped her mouth and jeans.

"What's funny?" She asked.

"You played that perfect. The drool was a great effect. You looked like a mad woman."

Rachel only smiled slightly as she secretly marveled at her acting abilities.

The last stop before reaching the seclusion of Tinley Park was a trip to the gas station so Rachel could fill-up while Steven relieved his upset stomach in the station's toilet. His nerves had boiled over, but he felt like one lucky person. The only problem was with his digestive tract, which succumbed to the pressure. Steven sat on the toilet for thirty minutes until Rachel pounded on the door.

"I'll be right out for Christ sake. Can't a guy take a shit in private?"

Rachel wrinkled her nose. Knowing Steven was okay, she waited for him in the truck. When he finished and reached the vehicle, he put up a hand to his counterpart.

"Don't even ask Rachel."

She didn't.

Steven figured they were always one bad move away from big trouble, him obviously for being on the run and Rachel for hanging out with him. He knew the utmost care had to be used if they were to complete their self-imposed mission.

After freshening up, the two set out for the home stretch. The hideout was about fifty miles away. Steven did about eighty MPH, and they reached the destination in forty-five minutes.

As strange looking as it was, Steven still kept his cool and control. Rachel gaped at the sight. It was a tiny shack in the middle of Tinley Park, Illinois that couldn't fit a five-member family, let alone house on-the-run offenders. Steven kicked at the dirt and cursed.

"What the fuck is this shit? Now we've had it. Where in the hell are we supposed to go? This was our staging point, our set-up area."

"Let's go talk to the folks living here. You know their names. Maybe we're in the wrong place."

Steven looked left, and then right. He then looked at Rachel with a sarcastic grin.

"Let's see. There's no other house in sight anywhere. The address said 442, and this is 442. Unless this is all a huge joke, we're where we're supposed to be."

"Let's check, okay?" Rachel tenderly urged. "What can it hurt?"

The man in the green truck parked some five hundred feet away, carefully observing the situation through bloodshot eyes.

The two headed for the front door. Rachel knocked politely. A man wearing a blue polo and khakis answered. Steven knew when he saw him that this was definitely the place. His anger grew.

"You must be Rachel," the polite man said. "Hey Steven! Long time no see."

The man reached out and hugged Steven firmly.

"Welcome to your escape. I know it doesn't look like much, but…"

"But what, James?" Steven scolded. "You told me you were housing a ton of wayward offenders. In this little shack? No fucking way."

"Oh Steven. You never have any faith. Come on in you two. By the way, Rachel, my name is James Rogers. Nice to meet you."

Rachel shook his hand and followed him into the small but hospitable kitchen area. There she saw two men neither she nor Steven knew. They continued following James. He led them to the other side of the kitchen and opened a small pantry that measured about one and a half feet wide.

"Please step in Rachel. You next Steven. After they both cramped into the tiny space, chest-to chest, James slammed the pantry door and yelled out, "Is that enough space for you guys? That's your new home for the time being. Good hiding space, huh?"

Rachel was uncomfortable with her breasts pushing into Steven's chest, but he didn't seem to care, per his aggravation. Just when Steven was about to lose his cool for good, James added two words that slowed the momentum.

"Just kidding."

With no warning, the tiny room began to move. Steven and Rachel put their hands on each side of the space to stabilize themselves. The room seemed to gain downward thrust and the two weren't sure what was happening. It was dark, scary and moving very quickly. It was as if the bottom of the house fell apart and they were spiraling to hell. As suddenly as they'd picked up speed, they slowed, and finally stopped. The door creaked open and light flooded them. Steven gave the door another nudge and what he and Rachel saw was nothing short of spectacular.

Before them was a huge underground warehouse. Judging by the time it took to ride the pantry down, it must have been about one hundred and fifty feet under James little 'shack,' as Steven called it. There were cots everywhere, tables for eating and at least five hundred offenders, guilty and innocent alike, being shielded from the law. It was well lit and large. There were Ping-Pong tables, a computer area and even a basketball net with half a court. The place was awesome. Just when they thought it couldn't get more incredible, a large freight elevator opened and out drove Steven and Rachel's stolen Ranger. It was driven into another large room filled with vehicles. The two men Steven saw in the kitchen had brought it in. Behind them, the pantry opened and out popped James. He was smiling, surely appreciating their awe with the warehouse.

"Steven. You thought you were the only one who built underground dwellings?"

Steven could only smile as his face turned a shiny crimson. James led the pair to their cots and told them to take full advantage of the computer system in an effort to find Matt.

"I have a guy ready to help you. He'll find where Matt is staying. We think Detroit, but we'll make sure."

A giddy Rachel interjected, "Let's do it. I've waited long enough. It's been a torturous week."

The man James recommended quickly found, intercepted and displayed the prisoner lists from every F.E.M.A. camp across the country. They searched for Detroit and sure enough, Matt was listed. The list informed them that his group would be leaving for The Brick in approximately three days.

"Let's go!" Rachel jumped. "Let's find Matt and rescue him."

Steven motioned for Rachel to calm down. He knew they needed a plan.

"Give me a day to work something up Rachel. We have to see which train he's taking and its routes."

The man working with the computer punched a few more buttons and the train route was visible.

"He's starting in Detroit and headed toward Lansing. Then it's Lansing to Bay City and Bay City to the bridge. Your best chance to stop that train is between Bay City and Mackinaw. It's the least populated and woodsiest environment."

Rachel thanked the man for his help and went to work with Steven in determining where and how they'd stop the

275

train. It would take careful planning and a team effort to be successful in their venture. They studied the map of Michigan and decided that the area between Grayling and Gaylord served as the best possible hope of success. They checked the terrain, the weather forecasts and the approximate time the train would pass between the two points. After ten straight hours of work, they were exhausted. For the first time in many nights, they'd sleep peacefully knowing no one would get to them in this vast underground hideaway. They both knew they had to get plenty of rest, because the real action was yet to come. If they thought they were tired, they'd find out it was mere child's play in comparison to what they'd soon face. They both fell asleep quickly and slumbered through the night and half the next day.

*

The man in the green truck watched the men come out of the shack and take the Ford Ranger into a pole barn. He decided that he'd investigate at nightfall and report his findings to Sal, who was en route from Florida. Despite the fact that he was a bit more than tipsy, the man very quietly headed for the pole barn and slid in through the side door, which was to his surprise, unlocked. He pocketed his lock-picking tools and investigated the inside of the barn. He

276

couldn't turn any lights on in fear of detection, so he pulled up the infrared goggles he had hanging around his neck. Now that he could see as if it were daylight, it all came to him rather quickly. The floor was obviously cut out and replaced with a platform elevator system that was hydraulically controlled.

"Hmm, park the vehicle on the lift, press a button or two, and down you go to the floor below."

The man needed more. He was now suspecting an underground hideaway, but couldn't say with any confidence. Inspecting further, he found small cracks in the cuts between the old concrete floor and the hydraulic floor. Spying as deep as he could was to no avail, so he pulled out a scope from his small bag of tools. The scope was only two feet long, but extended to a surprising five-hundred feet upon stretching it out. It was a paper-thin device when open, but had a five-inch circumference when closed. It was the perfect snaking tool.

As he led the long apparatus down the crack, he was able to see light beyond the end of the scope. The room in which he was looking was where the cars and trucks ended up lowered from the garage for hiding. Luckily for the man, the door entering the large warehouse had been left open, giving him a view into the main hall of the facility. He could see people walking, talking and passing by. Upon further inspection, he saw the two men who had taken the truck into

277

the garage playing cards at a small table. Being within twenty feet of them, he needed to be very careful not to bump anything or make any sound that would get his device noticed. That's when he saw Rachel. She was standing next to the opening of the door, apparently thanking the men for their help, as she shook both of their hands. It was all the man needed. He slowly backed the scope back up and it disappeared into the darkness.

The man packed up his tools and headed back for his green truck. The air had a bit of a nip, increasing the briskness as he walked. The heater of the truck would be a very welcome feeling, along with his flask of whiskey. He warmed up and dialed up Sal's number.

"Hey Sal. Have I ever got news for you!"

TYRANNY OF A PEOPLE

Definition of *tyranny*

Tyranny is thought of as cruel and oppressive, and it often is, but the original definition of the term was "rule by persons who lack legitimacy, whether they are malign or benevolent." Historically, benign tyrannies have tended to be insecure, and try to maintain their power by becoming increasingly oppressive. Therefore, the rule that initially seems benign is inherently dangerous, and the only security is to maintain legitimacy. It's an unbroken accountability to the people through the framework of a written constitution. It provides for election of key officials and the division of powers among branches and officials in a way that avoids concentration of powers in the hands of a few persons who might then abuse those powers. Tyranny is an important phenomenon that operates by principles which can be recognized in its early emerging stages, and, if the people are

279

vigilant, prepared and committed to liberty, countered before it becomes entrenched.

Despite the fact that Henry and Rene agreed on the hit that was to take place on John Wisecroft, Jasper still felt the need to show Duchard on paper exactly how the president was manipulating the country and stealing their freedoms one subtle step at a time. The two had agreed, yet Jasper was very reluctant on a plan to whack the president. Henry was given the honors, although it would be much more discreet then he'd thought. When Henry thought of whacking someone, he heard the good angel in his mind telling him how wrong it was. Duchard showed him how much easier and quieter it could be to kill Wisecroft. Exercising care, mouths had to stay closed for the plan to work. The two believed in each other and figured there'd be no problems on that front.

Henry handed Rene the paperwork proof of Wisecroft's tyrannical ways and they went over it together.

"It's happening repeatedly across the country. A government that wants total cooperation from the people is threatening free speech. The freedom of expression is being phased out." Henry continued.

"Demonstrations are being diffused before they can get structured. If they could get organized and actually find a place to express their feelings, one of two things would happen: They'd be broken apart with tear gas and rubber bullets, or the groups would be allowed to picket way out in the middle of rural areas where no one showed up. It's the same for peaceful protests as well as not so peaceful. The only difference is that in a non-peaceful protest our government sometimes uses real bullets, not rubberized intimidators. The Bill of Rights, as it was known, is dead."

Henry marked each of the first ten bills of rights and explained to Duchard each instance where Wisecroft was lending a direct hand in the destruction of the document.

Amendment I

Congress shall make no law respecting an establishment of religion, or prohibiting the free exercise thereof; or abridging the freedom of speech, or of the press; or the right of the people peaceably to assemble, and to petition the Government for a redress of grievances.

"Congress, through Wisecroft, is running roughshod over the first amendment. In addition to breaking up gatherings, the president is making sure that the press is firmly stuffed with cotton; that is, quieted to a point of only allowing the anti-offender sentiment to ring in the newspapers and television. This does a few things; it squelches the freedom of speech, freedom of the press *and* helps Wisecroft give the people only what he wants them to hear and know. The press decided to remain muzzled after a few of its own was found dead, or murdered?."

Duchard stood with his mouth hung open. This was only the beginning of Jasper's explanations.

"Unless you're a part of the mass gathering and depositing of offenders to The Brick, you really have no idea that America's in a state of flux. Normal people go to the movies, do their grocery shopping and gather for parties. The average American still eats their fast food, has their heart attacks and fights over health insurance coverage. Wisecroft's a master at allowing everything to appear normal while in the background he crumbles the very walls on which freedom stands. Mexico and Canada have closed their borders so Americans can't come into their countries and spread what they consider poisonous habits. The two neighboring countries have also come to hate the leadership of the U.S.A., abhorring what Wisecroft's doing. The United States is slowly, but surely, becoming the second North Korea, or worse."

Amendment II

A well-regulated Militia, being necessary to the security of a free State, the right of the people to keep and bear Arms, shall not be infringed.

"The right to bear arms is going out the window. Wisecroft learned in *Mein Kampf* that an unarmed country is a safe, harmless country, so the military will go city-to-city, street-to-street, and house-to-house disarming the people. Of course it's virtually impossible to take every gun away, but Wisecroft will do his very best to make sure the people are as weak as they can possibly be while he's in power; power which I believe he also wants to extend past his term limits. Weakness hinders would-be demonstrations and the gatherings of any angry people. The free state of the people is already in peril, but taking away any possible militia or fighting faction outside of the armed forces goes a long way towards Wisecroft's goal of total power."

This seemed to hurt Duchard the most because he expressed his firm belief in citizens being able to stand up for themselves, whether against invading armies or sanity-challenged government.

Amendment III

No Soldier shall, in time of peace be quartered in any house, without the consent of the owner, nor in time of war, but in a manner to be prescribed by law.

"The military thinks they own the country now, especially with the way Wisecroft's been giving them free reign. He gives them total control over the people and that's plain wrong. They settle into whoever's house they want, drink their booze, eat their food and even, I've heard, rape their women. It's a wonder more innocent civilians haven't been killed, tortured or even jailed."

Henry stopped for a moment to compose himself. He felt terrible for the plight of the people and had guilt inside him because he didn't recognize Wisecroft's motives while running on the same ticket with him.

"The military follows orders to the tee. If they're told to invade, they invade. If they're told to pillage, they pillage. It's the nature of the beast. We have some of the best generals in the game and they absolutely will not tolerate sass or backtalk. The discipline is harsh and the penalty steep for turning their back on the armed forces. Wisecroft knows it. Let's move on."

Amendment IV

The right of the people to be secure in their persons,
houses, papers, and effects, against unreasonable searches
and seizures, shall not be violated, and no warrants shall
issue, but upon probable cause, supported by oath or
affirmation, and particularly describing the place to be
searched, and the persons or things to be seized.

"All sex offenders are dragged from their homes, usually in the middle of the night, by armed military. Houses that were on the list of suspected harboring of sex offenders are pillaged and taken over. As I said before, soldiers stay as long as they like and the people are powerless to stop it. Wisecroft has effectively plunged his poison needle into the collective minds of the public by using fear as his main ally. Fear allows the leadership to do as they wish without much of a chance at backlash. After all, who wanted to be the one that doubts Wisecroft's principles? Neighbors and friends would be the first to doubt *you*, followed by the government itself. No American wants to be looked at as weak concerning the majority's agenda. Looking good to others is a weakness Americans share. Whether by behaving, being the best family or having the best kids, Americans want to be important for being the charmed family."

Amendment V
285

No person shall be held to answer for a capital, or otherwise infamous crime, unless on a presentment or indictment of a Grand Jury, except in cases arising in the land or naval forces, or in the Militia, when in actual service in time of War or public danger; nor shall any person be subject for the same offence to be twice put in jeopardy of life or limb; nor shall be compelled in any criminal case to be a witness against himself, nor be deprived of life, liberty, or property, without due process of law; nor shall private property be taken for public use, without just compensation.

"Wisecroft is using the public danger card here. He says that ALL offenders are a public danger and must be stopped under any and all circumstances. This is how he's talked the public into such radical measures. You know; save the children, protect the kids, don't allow the pedophiles, sex offenders and rapists to get to our people. It's been a brilliant ploy, if I say so myself, because the public is so gullible. That's not to say that offenders don't prey on our children; I just don't think it's as prevalent as he makes it out to be. There are many offenders behind bars today that have done nothing more than become a victim of someone's twisted vengeance. It goes both ways."

Henry decided to level with Duchard on his family situation.

"I have two family members that are offenders, but they have a nice chalet in Vermont to stay in. They aren't getting the same treatment as the rest of the offenders and while I'm grateful, I feel a huge amount of guilt over it. It doesn't seem fair, especially when I see these men and women being hauled away."

Duchard concurred, but stayed quiet. Henry continued. "Fear is the number one biggest motivator in this country. Fear brings out the nastiest in people and it has to stop. I don't know if it will ever really end, but it can be controlled better than our president is doing it."

Amendment VI

In all criminal prosecutions, the accused shall enjoy the right to a speedy and public trial, by an impartial jury of the State and district wherein the crime shall have been committed, which district shall have been previously ascertained by law, and to be informed of the nature and cause of the accusation; to be confronted with the witnesses against him; to have compulsory process for obtaining witnesses in his favor, and to have the Assistance of Counsel for his defense.

287

"Offenders are being cast aside swiftly and with little justice. The juries, judges and prosecutors are excited to get convictions and defense attorneys do the least effective job possible to insure conviction. In the past, say 2010, it was all about the money, but now it's more about protecting the public and completely forgetting about justice. Defense attorneys fear being labeled as sex offender sympathizers, so they draw straws to get stuck with the cases. Wisecroft has taken over where John Walsh, Nancy Grace and other fear mongers left off. He's angry about the rape of his family. He's taken it personally, as Walsh did back in the early 2000's, and revenge seems to be the conquering emotion. Our court system has turned into a farce and it can't continue like this, lest we really do fall into totalitarianism. The lobbyists, who are paid off by the Congressmen and lawmakers, pay off the judges. It's a shame. Again, that's not to say that their aren't dirt-bag guilty child predators and scum-bucket pedophiles, because there are plenty. I just want you to know that there's also the falsely accused and wrongfully convicted. The point is that after you serve your sentence; shouldn't you be square with the house?"

Amendment VIII

Excessive bail shall not be required, nor excessive fines imposed, nor cruel and unusual punishments inflicted.

"Cruel and unusual punishment? You'd better believe it. The people in this country don't see it and don't care to see it. The fact that they're taking these people to Northern Michigan and sticking them in a bricked facility without family or friends is a shock to the system. There's no telling how many offenders are running around this country looking for places to hide. What else can you do if one doesn't care to go quietly? I know if it were me, I'd run. I'd hide and make them find me. The public seems to be okay with the fact that the offenders are being sent away and that's because they're not paying attention. Until it happens to them, there's no sympathy."

Amendment IX

The enumeration in the Constitution, of certain rights, shall not be construed to deny or disparage others retained by the people.

"I really don't know how to address this Rene, except that the bills are being shredded as we stand here."

289

Henry looked down at the notes he had in front of him. He was emotionally drained and felt like a ton of bricks were burying him alive.

Amendment X

The powers not delegated to the United States by the Constitution, nor prohibited by it to the States, are reserved to the States respectively, or to the people.

"Or to John Wisecroft; who must die." Henry was adamant.

"The plan is set then, Mr. Jasper. John Wisecroft will be assassinated and you'll take over the country. The first thing you'll do is what?"

Henry Jasper didn't have to think long before it came to him.

"Restore freedom."

*

Steven was still overly impressed with the facility that James had built under his "shack" of a house in Tinley Park. He wanted to know more about the actual building of it.

"It's simple my boy. We started this project some ten years ago assuming that this was going to happen. Bulldozers, earthmovers and other equipment were all we needed to get the hole dug. Once the concrete walls were poured, it was off to the races simply modeling the inside."

"So how long has it been in operation?" Steven inquired with more than a passing interest.

"Just a couple of months. When Wisecroft made his announcements, we commenced to getting the facility kicked in gear. It's not quite finished, but it'll suffice considering the other, less enthusing option."

While Rachel was impressed with the building, she was more impressed with the computer operator who finally found Matt's whereabouts.

"He's in Detroit, Rachel, and he's being hauled out in two days for the final trip to The Brick. You and your friend better get your running shoes ready, because you're going to need them."

Excited, Rachel shared the news with Steven. They would have to head for the northern part of Michigan the next day in an effort to head off the train. Steven knew it was going to be a very touchy place to linger, as Michigan was home to The Brick and they were to be within sixty or seventy miles of the entrance. To Steven, that was almost too close for comfort. Steven shrugged with an almost dis-interested look on his face.

"I don't know anybody up there Rachel, and I don't think you do either. We're going to have to be so careful to avoid detection. We'll be in the teeth of the machine."

"I get that Steven, but we'll be okay. I can't wait to rescue Matt."

Steven tried to calm Rachel but came off a bit untidy about it. "I understand how you feel about your man Rachel, but not even Matt's worth me getting caught. I can't repeat to you enough how very careful we must be to keep under the radar."

Miffed about Steven's comment that Matt wasn't worth his time, Rachel became defensive. "Don't go then. I'll rescue him myself. If it doesn't mean a hill of beans to you, then fine. Stay here and be a part of the underground."

"Screw you Rachel. I'm not putting my ass on the line for some schmuck who wasn't being careful and got pinched."

James sensed both tempers getting hot and separated the two with a polite invitation. "Rachel, there's a group of woman on the other side of the warehouse that would love to meet you. Steven, come see my workroom."

Rachel walked over to the women and immediately had a conversation going with them. Smiles permeated as they shared stories. James led Steven to his work area, where he began what would be the worst chewing out Steven had ever taken.

"So you're still acting like you're the only person in the advocacy Steven? I have news for you: This woman needs your help and you're being a complete asshole about it. The advocacy is for helping others, not turning your back at the last minute because of your tedious *'me me me'* bullshit."

"Fuck you James. I've been dealing with that woman since Montana and I'm the one who offered the help. I just don't like getting so close to The Brick."

"Why Steven? Are you afraid of capture? Listen to yourself son; it's all about you. 'I'm this, I'm that.' Stop it and man-up! Have some balls for a change."

Angry with James outburst, Steven cocked back to throw a punch. James was more than ready as he blocked Steven's right hand and flipped him over his legs. Steven was lying flat on the floor while James engaged a painful arm-lock.

"I'll tell you what Steven; if you don't go, I will. I'll take her and I won't be a pussy about it. However, if I do that, you're no longer welcomed here. I've had enough of the selfishness and fear. You make a choice son, because I need to know."

"Let me up James. Let go of my fucking arm."

"ANSWER ME GODDAMMIT! I NEED TO KNOW IF YOU'RE GOING TO BE THERE FOR RACHEL IN HER TIME OF NEED!"

Steven tried to picture himself at the advantage: James in the arm lock listening to how Steven said it was going to be.

Sticks and stones may break my bones...

It didn't help.

"Okay, okay." Steven begged. "Yes. I'm taking her. Okay? Now let me up."

James released Steven and then gave him a hand to help him off the floor. Steven refused the hand and rose.

"Now you go apologize to Rachel and tell her what you told me. You're an advocate Steven. Act like one. I expect leadership out of you."

Steven begrudgingly did as James requested, apologizing to Rachel and promising her he'd do whatever he could to help set Matt free. Rachel hugged Steven tightly, thankful that he'd apologized and thankful for his help. He felt her tight body against his.

...But Rachel's pert body holding me close will never hurt me!

294

"We're leaving at sunup tomorrow Rachel. Make sure you get some good sleep."

Rachel, as giddy as a ten-year-old in a candy store, nodded her head in agreement. The women took Rachel to their quarters while James approached Steven from behind and invited him to a room for sleep. The days to come were to be more intense than they ever knew.

SAL'S PURSUIT

"Tinley Park, huh? Yes...okay, thanks for the info. Call the local police and get that place busted."

Sal, on her way back up from Florida after dispatching Davis, had received all the information she needed about Steven and Rachel's whereabouts from the man in the green truck, and now knew he would lead her right to them *and* Matt. She clicked off her phone and paid close attention to the road in front of her. She was only in Georgia and knew it would be hours upon hours of driving to reach the north and throw a huge wrench into everyone's plans. The thoughts ran through her mind as she drove.

"Davis is dead. I loved him but he's dead now. He crossed me and paid the ultimate price. I'm unstoppable and nothing will get in the way of my goal; killing Steven, Rachel and her pervert husband Matt. If I were them, how would I go about finding Matt? What steps would I take to make sure I

297

didn't miss my opportunity? Personally, I'd go to a spot
ahead of the train and wait. Where would that be though?
The man in the green truck will tell me. These three are mine.
I might even mount their heads on my wall as a remembrance
of the greatest capture and kill of my life. They have no idea
who they have messed with and what the penalty will
encompass. I'll find and kill them all."

The thoughts thrilled Sal as she headed north with a
purpose. Steven, Rachel and Matt and even the man in the
green truck knew she hated them, but they didn't know it was
to the extent of actual murder. Sal had been planning her
vengeance for a very long time and it was getting closer to
becoming a reality. The need and want shot through her like
adrenaline injected through a needle. She was completely
obsessed with the idea. The fact that she could actually be
flirting with insanity never crossed her mind. To Sal, she was
now the leader of the N.V.A.C. and made it her project to see
through no matter the circumstances. In Florida, no one
suspected Sal of the cold-blooded murder of Davis, and she
knew it would remain that way. Her mind kept flying
sideways with thoughts and ideas that were becoming less
coherent. She did, however, keep the thought of the three
advocates straight as an arrow.

"I know I'm the leader now. I have the greatest job in the world. God has granted me the leadership I so deserve."

More distant thoughts about her family crept into her mind. It was a surprising turnaround from the views she was having about the advocates. It seemed that her mind was beginning to play tricks on her. Whether it was driving fatigue from countless hours on the road or something else entirely, Sal had no idea. She had been driving for days on end taking care of business. Sal thought it to be a touch of the "tired syndrome."

"My mom and dad are in Texas somewhere and I need to see them. (Her parents had been dead for fifteen years) I'm sure Mom needs a helping hand with a few things. Dads like a typical man: Lazy and good for shit.

Sal's thought's continued to shift at an alarming rate.

"I'll get those three and slice their throats from ear-to-ear. Those fuckers belong to me. I've done everything to help this country flush out the offenders. I'll get a purple heart. President Wisecroft loves me and what I stand for. Why hasn't he met with me? Am I so unimportant that he can't make time for me? After everything I've done for him, how

299

dare he ignore me. What's that on the radio? ELO? Turn to Stone? They suck; I need some hardcore shit. Who does Steven Smith think he is? Turn to fucking stone?"

As she grew more and more tired with each mile she put behind her, her sudden madness made itself known in more profound ways. Sal was hearing things in her mind that hadn't been there before. The voices, the images and the people were flooding her mental plain.

"The dogs need food. I need to feed them before they die. Why didn't I feed them when I was in Florida? Wait a minute; the dogs are dead. They were poisoned by the scumbag offenders. Hux and Gritty are dead."

Sal looked to her right and saw both of her bloodhounds sitting in the passenger seat of the truck. Their tongues hung low as their bloodshot eyes stared at Sal in a loving stare. They were every bit as beautiful as Sal remembered them.

"Well there are my good boys! I'm so glad you could join me for the trip. I missed you two. What happened? Did someone hurt my babies? Well it didn't work did it? Those numbnuts couldn't hurt my babies."

300

When Sal looked at the road and glanced back, the dogs were gone, replaced by two dead mutts, maggots and worms escaping form their mouths. Their stomachs moved up and down as the bugs and larva curled and multiplied in the dog's stomachs. Their eyes were no longer red, but a pale shade of jaundice yellow. The stink of death permeated Sal's nose.

"What happened? Who killed you? It was those three mother fuckers I'm after, wasn't it? I'll get their asses just for you. My dogs don't deserve this kind of ending. My poor babies. Mommy's so sorry about this."

Weeping, Sal had to pull off the interstate and rest. When she parked the SUV and hopped out, she didn't feel much better. The insanity was creeping in; one brain cell at a time, but she still didn't realize what it was. The all-consuming power had turned its back on her, making her vulnerable to the short circuits that affect a human's brain. The stress she ignored was expressing itself in the form of strange pictures and thoughts. When she returned to the vehicle, she went to the old reliable Canadian Club whiskey sitting in the glove compartment under the passenger dashboard. Two shots later, she felt the heat of bitterness land in the pit of her stomach. The feeling was more of a relief for her than simple sobriety. She wanted the buzz that chased the ghosts away. What she was getting was only a temporary reprieve. Sal was painting over dirt. The ghosts and demons of sixty years were attacking her and she could only ward them off for so long. Time was spinning out of control. Sal needed to move fast.

Back on the road north, and three shots of whiskey behind her, Sal was beginning to feel that sense of normalcy *(whatever normalcy is)* that most everyone strives for, but rarely finds. She had temporarily seduced the demons and put them in their rightful places. Instead of continuing to focus on the thoughts that wanted to haunt her, she sang, talked aloud with herself and tried to focus on the task at hand.

Sal was stubborn and driven. The mental overload, while annoying, was not the motivating factor. The three enemies, combined with the alcohol, were the focus of Sal's motivation.

She drove until the light of sunrise before stopping. Sweat soaked her hair and greased it back in a combination of black and gray mush. She had failed to shave her armpits or legs in days, causing a stench of body odor that permeated the cab of the truck. Showering would be needed if she were to cut the odor floating into her realm. Sal was rapidly moving into a madness that would take over her life.

*

It was a short stay, but Steven and Rachel were ready to leave the comforting seclusion of James underground warehouse. Although they'd only been able to stay for a short time, they were leaving impressed and excited. Rachel thanked James profusely and honored the warehouse unyieldingly. Rachel was more excited than Steven to find Matt, but Steven had a different attitude, thanks to James and his fisted pep talk. James shook both of their hands and wished them Godspeed. He told them both they were welcomed back anytime and if needed, they could come back after rescuing Matt. Rachel nodded that it was a distinct possibility while Steven remained neutral.

The Ford Ranger was returned to the front of the small house where they had originally left it, the license plate changed to Michigan with new numbers and stickers. This pleased Steven, as he felt much better about the prospect of getting to Mid-Michigan unscathed. The advocates knew they were actually breaking laws that they felt were broken *against* them. The shoe appeared to be inflexibly forced onto the other foot.

After studying the maps and the highways, they agreed to head off the train north of Grayling, Michigan and south of

Gaylord. It was a more open terrain with a seemingly minimum risk. They'd use the thickest of the wooded areas to try to intercept the locomotive. Steven had to figure out whether he was going to stage an accident on the tracks or risk a derailment using live ammo. He'd ponder a bit longer, and then decide when he saw the type of area he was dealing with in full. Rachel beamed. She was unable to stop talking or smiling as the endorphins rolled through her system. The high was unmatched.

The two had one major worry on their mind: Sal "The Gal" Parker, who was most assuredly lurking in the shadows. The two knew how dangerous she was and that she'd resort to murder to stop them. James had told them that Davis Lowell was murdered in his home, leaving the pair stunned, but not surprised. Lowell, Steven figured, had it coming to him. Had they known it was Sal that pulled the trigger, the concern in their hearts would've undoubtedly grown. The fact that they didn't know was better. Rachel tried not to believe that Sal had really murdered her family members in Idaho, but the fact that it could be true wasn't lost on her. The pair would have to take the utmost caution in their future travels. While giddy in their pursuit of Matt, the man in the green truck was following closely. He had already informed the authorities of the underground warehouse and felt his allegiance to Sal was justified. After all, in his mind, Steven and Matt were true offenders and Rachel an accomplice. They all needed to be stopped so justice and law could run its course. The man would do his best, short of killing, to make sure that would happen.

*

Sal had reached southern Ohio: Cincinnati to be exact. She smiled as she passed the city, knowing that she'd left Steven's roommate dead in the apartment just days earlier. As she drove, the alcohol began to wear off, causing more strange thoughts to fill her slowly dilapidating mind. She had a discussion with her dogs.

"There out to get us boys. The three wayward offenders are going to try and get me first, but I have news for them!"

At that point, the dogs were looking fit and alive on the passenger seat.

"They tried to kill you. Those goddamn offenders don't know what in Hell they're doing. Try to kill my fucking dogs will they? I'll torture them. I'll make it hurt so bad that Hell will be child's play."

305

A driven look permeated in Sal's eye. The dogs
howled approval for their master's plan. When Sal looked
back, the two were gone. No dogs; just an empty passenger
seat. One and one didn't make two to the slightly delusional
stalwart of the N.V.A.C. She was trying to figure out what the
answer to the disappearing dogs was when her cellphone rang.

"Sal, It's me. Did you hear?"

The man with the green truck had just heard the news
about Davis Lowell and wanted to tell her all about it. Acting
completely innocent, Sal replied. "Hear what? What are you
talking about?"

"Davis is dead. Someone shot him in the head. This is
bad; really bad."

Sal shrugged and questioned the man. "So what do
you want from me? I'm in Ohio on the tail of three crooked
asses. What's up with the N.V.A.C.?"

"The rumor is that they want you to take over Sal.
They want you to be the leader. By the way, I'm on Steven
and Rachel's asses. They've bypassed Chicago and are headed
into Michigan."

Sal smiled a toothy grin and felt the aura of excitement
wash over her. She was now a notch higher; cloud ten, if you
will. She didn't hesitate in her response. "You're Goddamn
right I'll take over the cause. I should have been leading this

thing anyway. You tell the people who need to know I accept."

"You got it Sal."

"By the way, is there any word on who killed Davis?"

"No Sal. It's assumed an advocate did it, but who knows. Anyway, don't worry. Do what you're doing and I'll help you capture those creeps."

Sal hung up the phone and giggled at her newfound power. No sooner than the euphoria reached a peak, Sal's mind played more games with her. The dogs were prevalent in her thoughts.

"I thought you guys were alive. I'm so sorry. I let them kill you. I'll get their sorry souls and send 'em to Hell in a hand basket. Those dirty Sons-of-Bitches! How dare anybody mess with my family, my pets, my life! We're going to end this nonsense once and for all. "

The dogs again lay dead on Sal's seat, but only for a moment. They disappeared again. Sal then saw her Mom sitting next to her, talking. The image of her mother was as real as the day was light. Sal truly believed her mother was sitting next to her. She felt a combination of fear and longing. She missed her mom and needed her support.

307

"Oh Sally. What's gotten into you child? I raised a better girl than this. I didn't raise a murderous woman. Oh Sal, oh my Sally."

Sal pleaded. "You don't understand Mom. They have it coming. The others had it coming too. There's no other life on earth as low and scummy as a rapist. I have to kill them. If I don't they'll surely rape and pillage again. You don't want that, do you Mom? Mom?"

Sal's mom was gone. For the duration of the trip, the psychosis would come and go like the road signs she passed. For Sal, she didn't know the difference. She was slipping into madness. Help was badly needed, but unavailable. The woman was functioning according to her emotion and gut feelings. It was a dangerous and potentially lethal combination.

*

Sitting in his lonely cell *not* reading, *not* writing and trying very hard *not* to think was Matt. Thinking complicated the matter and no books or papers were given to him in solitary anyway. There was nothing to do but sit in silence and wait. He had been beaten, humiliated and chastised. He was no longer on the favored lists of his former cellmates.

Matt was alone but knew it would eventually come to that. When he found himself drifting, it was about his love, Rachel. He missed her terribly and wanted a hug from the woman of his life. He still knew deep down inside that she was coming, but he wasn't sure where or when. He just knew. They had a special connection that couldn't be broken by bias, hate or contempt. The two were so in tune with one another that it surprised even them. The pair was in harmony when it came to life, politics and everything else important and always answered for each other correctly. It was an amazing feeling. Like peanut butter and jelly, the two were made for each other. Despite all of the synchronicity they shared, he felt a doubt deep within the recesses of his mind; a doubt that questioned if she could actually succeed in her goal of rescuing him. It was an unarming conflict of thoughts that punished Matt. She was coming, but probably wouldn't succeed.

On top of all his mental tests, Nurse Lisa had been trying to break Matt. Physically, she did to an extent. Mentally, Matt was as sharp as a tack and no one sadistic nurse would be able to take that away from him. He was in a class by himself when it came to keeping his cool and having a shrill edge about him. He had a feeling it wouldn't be long before it was time to move toward The Brick and was no longer scared. Matt figured that whatever he did, whatever decision he made and whatever role life would give him, he would be prepared. He finally reserved himself enough to fall asleep. It was his only sanctuary in the inglorious glow of broken constitutions and freedom.

The next morning, a guard woke Matt and told him to gather himself, as he was moving to the final staging area before his train trip north. Feeling the relief of finally getting out of the isolation and moving onto something with purpose helped Matt's social state. The guard led him down the hallway to a large meeting room where many other offenders were placed. Worrying terribly about Mary, he scoured the room from one end to the other. He finally found her with her head between her knees in the corner. There was no need to ask what was wrong. Matt knew why she was in pain and could little to help except offer some comfort.

"We'll be okay Mary. Soon we'll get to that bricked place and they'll be at least some freedom within the walls."

"I'll never be okay, Matt. They've done to me exactly what they preach against: Rape, sodomy, abuse and indignity. It's a hypocritical oath and it stinks like a bad nightmare."

Matt knew and could do little about it. The government was moving to the beat of its own drum, and the offenders were no different from common household cockroaches to the authorities. They were the reason for all of the country's problems. The writing was on the wall and like

310

it or not, it wasn't good for Matt, Mary or any of the others being shipped to upstate Michigan.

The guards entered the room rolling a cart of fresh jump suits. All of them were a bright red and had BRICK knitted on the upper right chest. The prisoners in the room were all ordered to strip naked and line up.

"Another strip-down," Matt sighed to Mary.

"Yes. I'm tired of being naked, but I'm getting used to it."

This time when the two stripped down, something spoke in each of their minds. Like Adam and Eve, this time they looked at each other's nakedness with a slight hint of embarrassment. Matt felt a twinge of excitement near his groin. Mary also sensed sexually driven moisture developing within her lower region. They both smiled and looked away from one another. Matt knew this was a problem because he felt guilt immediately. He had just thought to himself how terrific Rachel was and how they clicked so well together and now he felt like he was getting excited over another woman. How could he show any interest in Mary? How could he breech Rachel's trust like that? These questions crossed his mind as he waited for the guards with the red scrubs to reach them. Perhaps he was anticipating being separated from Rachel forever and wanted to keep Mary close as a possible companion. It felt to him like selfish thinking, but he couldn't help it. As bad as he felt, he still snuck one last glance at the naked Mary. He was thrilled deep inside as her small, pert breasts welcomed him. He noticed that she had glanced at him once more, slightly smiling at his chest and arms, which were well toned. He was more than relieved as they finally received their jumpers.

"Everybody with ticket number one form a line," the guards yelled. "We'll be loading the first group in five minutes."

Matt and Mary looked at the small ticket stubs they had been handed with the jumpers and both carried number eight. They would be traveling together, which made them both happy. It took about two hours when the number was finally called on the loud speaker. As they lined up, Matt put Mary in front of him to keep her safe and shielded. He didn't mean to, but when he wasn't paying attention and the line slowed, ran up against Mary's back, pressing his partially erect penis into her. This caused Mary to shudder with internal excitement. Again, Matt found himself becoming aroused and thought about anything besides Mary so he wouldn't become completely erect. He thought about bugs, birds, jail uniforms and anything else that he could to divert his mind. He was a man in serious emotional trouble and knew it.

312

*

In a strange twist of roles, it was now Steven deliriously asking questions and trying to plan his attack with Rachel trying to calm him.

"How do we know which train and at what time? How will we know what to do? There's more questions than there are answers."

"Relax Steven. They're group number eight on the 275 Western Rail. The engine's blue and orange and the train will be passing between Grayling and Gaylord tomorrow at about two p.m."

Steven blew a huge exhaust of relief as Rachel gave him the information. He was glad she was doing her homework because he certainly wasn't at that point.

The two passed into Michigan from Illinois on I-94 at six p.m., hightailing it for their interception spot. They were some six or so hours away, but Steven was fresh and Rachel offered to drive if needed. Steven decided to take I-94 to I-69 north until he reached 127, where he would head north until it met I-75. From that point, it'd be only an hour or so to their destination. They would drive all night.

Bored after a few hours, Steven had to ask the very question Rachel was trying to avoid. "What if we can't find him, or we fail?"

313

Rachel, bordering on a nap moments earlier, gave Steven a polite lecture. "There's no 'what if's' in this game Steven. 'What if' defeats every purpose we've tried to accomplish. I hate those two words more than any others in the English language. We *will* find him and we *will* succeed. We *will* free him from the Hell he's in right now."

"Not to be a total dick Rachel, but there is a chance this won't work. I can't lie to you. Honesty is still the best way to explain things, especially when we face a task as daunting as this one."

Rachel smiled as though she had a tickle in her ribs. Steven was a bit perplexed at first, but soon understood. He chuckled too. Rachel explained. "We're both tired and running on pure adrenaline. It's not funny and I'm very hopeful that we are successful in our attempt. I'm not trying to be negative, just realistic. No more 'what if's' though. I promise."

"All we can do is what we're doing now Steven. That's all anyone could ever ask. Matt will be coming home with us soon. I have to keep that attitude or I'll give up."

Steven nodded and told Rachel to get some shut-eye in case she needed to drive. She snuggled against the door with a pillow and slowly drifted away. It was to be her last peace for some time.

*

Back in Tinley Park, all that was left of James small shack was a bump in the yard. Parked to the left and right were government owned tractors and digging machines. Although some people lay dead in the yard, most were unharmed and being led out of the underground bunker and into the buses that were lined up in the street. The authorities were stripping the offenders and handing out jumpers, while other officers were surveying the bodies strewn about. Lying in the front of what used to be the shack was James, dead from standing out in front of the oncoming bulldozer. The machine never hesitated as it crushed him and moved forward. The hideout was gone and the surviving people headed to their F.E.M.A. facilities to be prepared for their trips to The Brick.

Sal "The Gal" Parker had succeeded in ruining more lives.

WISECROFT'S PLAN BROADENS

President Wisecroft organized another meeting with his unknowingly lame-duck cabinet, including VP Jasper to go over his future plans within his presidency. The room was filled with tense and worried men and women. Wisecroft had taken a normal presidency and turned it into his own personal tyrannical funhouse of ill-gotten gain. Congress and the House approved the Brick in Northern Michigan because Wisecroft had made it seem like a reasonable enough idea. Now he had manipulated the media and other social outlets to, in turn, brainwash the public into thinking that what he was doing was actually for the good of the country.

The cabinet members felt like they had dropped the ball and underestimated the president, along his way of thinking. There were still three of four cabinet members that went along with the program, but the sentiment was turning against him. Wisecroft now had total control of Congress, the House and more importantly, the armies in the United States.

Conservative Army Generals agreed wholeheartedly with the president's agenda and vowed no disobedience. The majority of the cabinet members, however, were desperately trying to figure out a way to slow the man down before more damage could be done.

Wisecroft entered the room to a series of glum faces, give for an occasional smile here and there. He quickly went into his future plans for him and the country.

"Ladies and gentleman of the cabinet, vice president Jasper, defense secretary, speaker; I've brought you all here in this room for a top secret meeting about the next two years in planning for our country. I'll start by going over a few of the wonderful things we've accomplished so far. The Brick has been a huge success, as we are eliminating the sex offenders from our population. Men and women who had harmed children and adults sexually are already taking up space in the facility standing in the U.P. of Michigan. We have a long way to go, but so far, my staff of advisers has informed me that sex crimes are at an all-time low. Soon it will be eliminated. Give yourselves a round of applause for being such a key helper in this cause."

Four people clapped enthusiastically, while a few lightly clapped. Some, Henry Jasper included, stood with their arms crossed. There was no applause from them.

"I'm surprised some of you don't clap. Is there a problem with cleaning the dirt out of the vents? That disappoints me greatly, as I thought you'd be happy to be rid of the offender. Oh well, it doesn't really matter because I don't care what you think."

Nobody spoke. Wisecroft glared unapologetically before continuing his plan for the United States.

"Next, we eliminated the pornography industry from our country. No longer will there be filth to spread around to the young people of our nation. Pornography is one of the monsters that had speared the offender. Without it, there will be no more offenders, give or take the few cases that may crop up in the years to come. The bottom line is that it's another problem eliminated. I won't ask for applause this time because your long faces speak volumes to me. I'll simply move on with the next steps in my plan."

The cabinet members who were against such radical change sat stupefied and in wonder of what the man was going

319

to say next. To them, there was no telling what kind of beast had been unleashed on the nation.

"The next phases are to include: An elimination of term limits for the president and vice president of the United States. All leaders of this great country should be allowed to serve until death, just like the Pope in Rome. When an effective job is being done, it makes no sense to mess with it. I've been assured by enough conservatives in Congress and the House that the measure will pass. This is a top secret, classified addition to the constitution that will be made public after the law is enacted."

There were no audible gasps in the room, only a lone hand raised high. It was one of the members wanting to comment on Wisecroft's idea. The president gave him a nod to speak.

"So what you're saying Mr. President, is that you've decided that this "idea" will be presented and passed by both houses, and that your power will become permanent?"

The president affirmed this question with a "yes."

"Okay, so you're going to personally take the constitution of the United States and wipe your ass with it?

This time, there was no mistaking the gasp in the room. The cabinet member stood and walked toward

320

Wisecroft at the other end of the table. Two men quickly walked over and flanked Wisecroft's left and right side. The Cabinet member stopped and continued his assault.

"You talked us into a bricked facility by telling us it would hold offenders and help the country. I agreed, but only because I thought it would be done peacefully. Now I find out that people were violently ripped away from families, that men and women alike are being stripped naked and displayed to everyone so they can be spat on and humiliated. The fucking guards in the prison are raping the offenders. How is that forward progress, Mr. President?

After that, you took an industry; porn; which I'm personally not fond of; and strip their freedoms, however disgusting they may have been. You threw men and women from that industry into The Brick because they practiced the freedom that goes along with being American. It doesn't matter that it was pornography, because it was a right for them to make and sell movies. You *personally* stripped that right away. You are dangerously close to fascism sir. I sense totalitarianism and tyranny. I don't like it one goddamn bit. I'm going to the press, the media, and whoever else will listen and I'm telling them what you're up to. This has gone far enough. It's time for you to stop...*sir*."

321

"I suggest you have a seat." Wisecroft advised. *"You're perilously close to trouble."*

"Excuse me Mr. Tyrant...uh...I mean President, but FUCK YOU!"

A nod of Wisecroft's head was all that was needed to get his guards moving. They grabbed the cabinet member and shooed him quickly out the door. The rest of the cabinet, including Jasper, sat quietly. President Wisecroft walked over to a TV set stationed at the corner of the room. He flipped a remote control switch and on it came, showing a live picture of the Rose Garden in the center of the White House grounds. Wisecroft turned and told all his cabinet members to watch closely. They did as he asked and they saw the two men, cabinet member in tow, enter the screen. They turned the member toward the camera and forced him to his knees. While one guard violently struck the member in his face, knocking him to the ground, the other guard pulled out a high-powered pistol and shot him through the ear. The blood spurted out as the cabinet members inside the meeting room watched in horror. There was a gasp and a muffled scream. The terror was unmistakable. Wisecroft shut off the TV and turned toward the rest of the cabinet, hands on his hips and an unyielding look on his face.

322

"Does anyone else have a fucking question?"

Nobody spoke. The cabinet members sat in stunned silence. Henry Jasper boiled inside.

*

Jasper called Rene Duchard on the special number they had between the two of them and demanded that the assassination attempt go forward as soon as possible. He explained to Duchard what he had seen and couldn't wait much longer to eliminate the man who was, in essence, taking over the country. Duchard agreed to meet with Jasper at the secret location and go over the final plans with him. Thrilled, Jasper quickly called for a limo. The cold-blooded murder of a fellow cabinet member was the straw that broke Jasper's back.

Duchard met Jasper and immediately handed him a pin of the American flag. It was an inch long by an inch wide and had a stickpin about a quarter inch long. It was just enough to put on a man's lapel. Jasper attempted to pin it to his own lapel but was stopped by Duchard.

"That, Mr. Jasper, is the assassination weapon."

Jasper looked at Duchard as if he'd lost his mind.

323

"This? This measly little broach? Do you truly expect me to believe that?"

"That pin, my friend, has enough poison in it to kill ten elephants. As you look at the pin itself, it has a protective cover on it. When you remove that cover, you expose a hollow point filled with venom from the black mamba; the deadliest snake in the world. One drop of this on your tongue and you'll be dead in two minutes. The nervous system, brain and internal organs shut down quickly, causing a tremendously hideous death. To the people standing around, it looks like a heart attack, but to the recipient? Oh, the pain will be legendary."

Jasper giggled at the lunacy, while at the same time savoring it. The plan was so complex, yet a tiny stickpin will kill Wisecroft in seconds.

"This is unbelievable. Now the question is how do I use it?"

Duchard grinned underneath three days of dark stubble. He was both astonished and amused by Jasper's child-like attitude toward murder.

"You stick him with it Henry. It's that easy. At the next big event, you act as if you're giving him a token of appreciation and you "accidently" put the pin in too far and stick him. You'll have time to apologize and put it in right before the convulsions hit."

"And what if it doesn't, you know, kill him?"

"Oh it'll kill him Henry. Fear not, it *WILL* kill him."

Henry placed the pin in its holder and snapped it shut. He placed the tiny death gadget in his pocket.

"Be careful that the cover does not come off that pin before you use it. It'll take only seconds for the poison to drain out and dry up. Then you're screwed."

"Got it." Jasper assured.

"I'm leaving now Henry. You'll never see me again. I'm not going back to the Bahamas or anywhere anyone will know. I'll read about the death in the papers."

"But Rene..."

"No buts. You'll never see me again; that is, unless you spill the beans. Let me rephrase that Henry; if you spill the beans, I'll come back for you, but *you'll* never see me again."

Henry nodded and Rene left out the door. He was gone. It was all in Henry's lap now. A simple stick and it'd be lights out for the crazy Wisecroft.

*

Another cabinet meeting was called, with Wisecroft only allowing his four closet advisors: Henry Marsh, the tether business mogul; A. Davis Goddard, the billionaire whom Wisecroft often conferred with for advice; Ivan Cross, another tether businessperson and Henry Jasper. These were the four men Wisecroft trusted and relied upon the most. He wanted to go over another step in his plan to be the undisputed and extended leader of the U.S.A. He had made a point to the rest of the cabinet by having one of the members murdered in cold blood before their eyes. He had no doubt this meeting would go smoother. Henry brought the broach pin with him. If the opportunity presented itself, he would strike. Wisecroft greeted each man enthusiastically and asked him to have a seat and hear him out.

"Thank you for attending this special meeting gentlemen. I'm thrilled to have the four men I trust the most present at this meeting.

Let me open by mentioning how "unfortunate" our last meeting turned out. Henry Jasper was here, but the rest of you don't know about the incident. A certain cabinet member that you've heard on the news as "disappearing" has been replaced. This man disappeared as a direct result of insubordination toward me. I make it a point to let you men know that you're here to listen and offer advice. I, however, own the bottom line and have the final say on any and all ideas. Oh, and I don't take too kindly to vulgarities;

especially those directed toward me. I do hope I make myself
perfectly clear."

Each man nodded an affirmative toward Wisecroft.
All except Jasper, who took some extra time giving his
reluctant agreement. Wisecroft stared straight into his eyes
until he received the nod he was seeking.

"I've decided to ask for your opinions today. I've
already explained to the cabinet that I intend to end term
limits and stay on as your president until death. I'm very
confident that the House and Senate will have no problem at
all passing this bill, as I have a certain amount of "influence"
when it comes to such matters. Does anyone here have any
objections about that plan?"

Goddard was in agreement with Wisecroft, as he
smiled widely and smacked his hand on the table in a happy
manner.

"I'm all for it John. I like you being our president and
I like the idea of keeping you on. Bully for you sir."

"Bully...bully!" Marsh and Cross exclaimed. Jasper
nodded with little care.

"Very good! Now onto the rest of my plan. As you know, I've been eradicating our country of all sex offenders and it's been a huge success, hasn't it Henry?"

Wisecroft looked at Jasper with a sneaky grin. Jasper sighed. Again, Jasper reluctantly nodded as Wisecroft waited for his response. Henry knew his reaction was unenthusiastic. He hoped Wisecroft didn't take it that way. He needed to keep the peace so he could strike with even more deviance and mastery.

"I feel that we need to take it further. As you know, offenders hurt our children, so we eliminated the problem. Let's eliminate two more problems: the middle and lower class family. For years we've had presidents that have tried without success to get rid of these "Obsolete" people. Right-to-work, tax cuts for the rich and many other programs have been implemented but failed terribly. The obsolete are a tough bunch, but they're also a stubborn bunch that destroys the rich "trickle down" tax bracket by constantly stopping and starting as far as work goes. They collect unemployment, welfare and use other "easy money" programs that are destroying the upper echelon of our society. We can send everything, and I mean everything offshore. We can get

everything we need as a country for pennies on the dollar, so
what are we waiting for?"

Goddard and Marsh, already multi-millionaires, loved
the idea. Cross was okay with it, while Jasper stewed.
Goddard spoke for the others.

"Another great idea sir. My question is how to
implement this idea. What measures are you going to
introduce to help the process?"

"Great question Mr. Goddard. This is how: We
eliminate all assistance programs in the country. We
eliminate unemployment, social security, Medicare and
Medicaid...all of it. No more welfare and no more "free
money" coming out of the rich man's pockets. My political
power owns the House and Senate, as I had previously
mentioned. It's time to get rid of the riff-raff in this country.
When they go broke, they'll get desperate and commit crime.
We now have an enormous amount of room in our prisons and
F.E.M.A. camps. All of these facilities are completely
privatized, so they're self-sufficient. That's the only funding
the government will have to worry about, and seeing how the
dollars will be saved by shipping all work offshore, it'll be a
cakewalk. We can even use the healthiest of the obsolete to do
our backbreaking work within the country.

329

Gentlemen, the rich, and only the rich will own this country. Chalets, vacation spots, everything. How does that grab you? Needless to say, this plan stays in this room. The only thing I need from you guys is a little cash to buy off the doubtful politicians."

Goddard, Marsh and Cross all stood and applauded. Jasper stood with his arms crossed, deciding in his mind that it was time to spring his plan into action. He approached Wisecroft with his hand extended.

"Mr. President, what a great idea. I'd like to thank you by presenting this broach to you in appreciation for all you've done to help our country."

Wisecroft, always a sucker for attention, happily shook Jasper's hand and accepted his token of appreciation. Jasper pulled out the broach and carefully took Wisecroft's lapel in his hand. He would "accidently" stick Wisecroft in the chest. Within ten minutes, the president would be dead. Change was about to happen.

Jasper struggled with a case of the shakes as he prepared Wisecroft's jacket. He took the token from his pocket, opened the case and removed the gleaming broach. He then pulled the pin cover off the toxic pin.

"Wow Henry, that's really nice. I'm honored and I feel really good about the fact that you're on board. I was starting to think you had cold feet about the whole presidency, but I see you've come around."

"No problem sir. Just stand still and I'll put it on for you."

Jasper put the pin up to the lapel. He was now in more control of his shakiness, making the job a bit easier. As he was a mere half an inch from doing the job, Wisecroft's phone rang.

"Excuse me Henry, I have to take this." Wisecroft answered. *"Yes. Yes. I'll be right there. Don't get excited, I'll be right there."* He hung up.

"Sorry Henry. Our little award ceremony will have to wait. Why don't you just give it to me and I'll make sure to get it put on later."

"Oh, umm, I'd rather do it sir. It means a lot to get a picture taken as I put the broach on you. You understand, yes?"

331

"Of course Henry. We'll pick this up in a few days when I see you again. I have to go. I have a family emergency."

Wisecroft quickly shook hands with the group and departed. Jasper frustratingly put the cover back on the pin. He knew he hadn't spilt a drop, so that was the only relief he felt. He couldn't believe the blasted luck as the phone rang just in time to save the president's life. He put the broach back in its case and pocketed it. The other three millionaires approached Henry to ask his opinion on Wisecroft's ideas. Henry thought about it for five seconds and responded.

"Swell." Was all he could muster. He departed the room.

*

As the days passed, Wisecroft communicated and pled with Congressional representatives over his ideas. Initial laughter turned into positive votes as money filtered into the hands of the reps, especially those on the fence. Support for Wisecroft's new changes quickly gained momentum with the infusion of cash, lobbying and a very shrewd presidential attitude. What at first sounded like a gimmick, or to some, a ridiculous idea, gained momentum as the reps had time to think over the country's economic savings there would be by shipping approximately ninety percent of the jobs offshore. The dominoes were rolling and Wisecroft knew it. Soon, the lawmakers would pass laws for the elimination of presidential term limits along with the elimination of the middle and lower classes incentives. Ultimately, the rich upper echelon would be in charge of the country. Armies would be formed using the poor prison outcasts and former middle and lower class citizens. There would be no rich folks ever smelling any front line in any war; that would be for the obsolete. Many jobs would be shipped offshore, insuring the low cost of products used by the "noveau riche." There would be taxes for the rich, yes, but they'd be minimal enough to keep everyone happy. The country, Wisecroft thought, would be self-sufficient; or not needing any help from anyone else in the world. No longer would the U.S.A. worry about the Middle East, China or Russia. They could take their own problems and deal with them however they liked. North Korea? Who cared? Let them bomb and destroy whoever ruffles their feathers. It simply wouldn't matter to the rich execs of the United States.

Henry Jasper sat awake all night worrying about his failed attempt to take Wisecroft's life. He started to think the man might have been blessed with a lucky halo floating over his head. Henry couldn't understand how Wisecroft had the ability to convince so many important people that his ideas were actually good ones. Yes, there were threats from the president for not complying with his radical plans, but never in the history of the country had anyone ever given into the threats. It was perilously close to a true tyranny in the U.S.A. and Henry knew he had to make it stop. Rene Duchard was long gone, so there'd be no pep talks coming from that end. It was all up to Henry and whether or not he had the stomach for the hit.

Henry, widowed, had no wife to confide in. He wouldn't have to worry that the plan would leak. If that happened, Duchard would make a return visit, but not to exchange pleasantries: That is, if Wisecroft didn't get to him first. It was a very tumultuous time for the vice president, who never would've taken the job if he'd known Wisecroft's true agenda. Now that he did know, it made him sick to his stomach and caused his head to ache. One thing was sure to Henry now, and that was that he was in a position to make it stop. If he could get his talons into the country, he'd call for the elimination and destruction of The Brick, a resounding veto of the new elimination of the middle and lower class law that would surely pass by his desk, and any other nonsensical laws or practices that Wisecroft may have adopted. Henry doubted The Brick's immediate elimination, at least not until Congress and the House was more liberal. It would probably take years for that to happen, but eventually it would. He

334

would also veto the term limit elimination policy Wisecroft wanted in place. It was an obvious grab at totalitarianism if he'd ever seen one. There was no telling what Wisecroft would come up with as the years rolled forward.

The best thing Henry could possibly do was to sleep on it and see how everything looked the next day. If it were meant that he would kill Wisecroft, then it would happen.

*

Wisecroft continued drumming up support for his big plans and convinced most lawmakers that it was a good idea to follow suit and stay on board with his wishes. Most reps knew what Wisecroft was capable of and wanted no part of his wrath. It looked like the presidential term limit elimination was a sure thing, while the destruction of the middle and lower class would obviously take a few years to come to fruition. It would be impossible to simply off billions of Americans without someone smelling a rat. The public, as lazy as it was, wouldn't fall for such a ploy if it were perpetrated on them too quickly. The best strategy the president could employ would be a slow and easy approach, passing laws here and there until it eventually squeezed the life out of the obsolete sector of the public's pocketbook. There would be some politically savvy Americans, however, that wouldn't fall for the ploy in any way whatsoever, so Wisecroft would have to resort to the tactic of breaking apart demonstrations much like he successfully did with the offender program.

President John Wisecroft was neither democratic nor liberal. He was smart, talented, and he knew how to manipulate people through propaganda and alienation. He was good at convincing the people of things by setting a problem on a platform before them and then fixing it. He used the same strategy Hitler used in Germany during the 1930's and 40's. He wanted to own the U.S.A. and if the chips fell correctly, he most certainly would, to the cries and agony of the "little people." The copy of *Mein Kampf* was always the "go to" for Wisecroft in his pursuit of total dictatorship.

INTO MICHIGAN

As Sal headed north, getting ever so close to the Ohio-Michigan border, she cracked open another pint of Blackberry flavored whiskey in hopes of alleviating the mental pain suddenly overtaking her. The weather was rainy and chilled, with a soft mist gathering on the windshield every five minutes or so. Running the wipers only made the dirt-mist mix worse, causing Sal to stop at every rest area along the route to clean it. She finally smartened up and pulled into a local gas station to purchase a gallon of solvent. After doing that, her trip turned into clear and smooth sailing, at least vision-wise.

She continued to stay in communication with the man in the green truck, who told her of every move made by the wayward Steven and Rachel. She smiled and tingled all over when thinking of killing them. However, the thought of the letdown that would follow their deaths bothered her. Sal wasn't sure if she was prepared to face the deep depression of life without the three pests. After all, they had been her focus for the last year, and the arguments, fights and debates had been legendary. As her thinking whirled, she convinced herself that there would always be more offenders to hunt, hate and destroy. She took great joy in making people's lives miserable by harassing them at their work, home or wherever else she could throw her weight around. The internet, to her, was a Godsend, as she could be everywhere all at once. She haunted the cyber-world. She'd been told on more than one occasion by authorities to be very careful about how wide her swath of misery stretched, as she risked being sued and having harassment charges pressed against her. Now that The Brick existed, she didn't need to worry about it. The government had so turned against the offender that she could do just about anything she wanted and get away with it.

The thoughts about her dead dogs haunted her while fueling her vengeance. She was angry not just with the person or persons who killed her beloved pets, but at everyone on the registry. She never cared much about murderers or arsonists, as she didn't feel the same hate as she did for people who harmed children. Sure, murderers and arsonists sometimes hurt kids, but it was different to her, as they didn't molest them.

Drinking the whiskey continued to help Sal forget about the strange feelings she'd been having earlier. The fear that knocked on her door was scary and unpredictable. She wasn't sure how else to approach the sudden change in her personality.

Just when she was getting herself worked into a nervous fit, the phone rang, interrupting Sal's train of thought. The man in the green truck was on the other end.

"Sal, I can now say they're definitely headed into Michigan. I don't quite know yet if they'll head toward Detroit or north. I'll let you know soon."

Sal responded. "I'd say its north. They know just as well as we do that Matt's leaving Detroit soon. They have no chance of breaking him out of the F.E.M.A. facility, but robbing a train? That goes way back to the days of the wild west."

"Wow Sal. You're really smart. I'm impressed."

Rolling her eyes, Sal answered the man. "Just keep an eye on them and don't let them out of your site. Oh; and don't go near them. They belong to me."

"10-4 Sal. I'll keep you updated."

Sal smiled. She put her right arm out along the seat of the truck and thought she felt something fleshy. When she looked over, her hand was lying on her mother's dead, rotted flesh.

"That's not my Sally." She shook a skinless finger at Sal. "I didn't raise my Sally to carry guns and hurt people. Your daddy would blister your behind."

339

Completely shocked, Sal had to stare for a moment before her crusty personality took over. She acted as if it were everyday that you saw a decomposed corpse sitting in the front seat of your vehicle.

"Too bad Ma. I'm killing these people and that's final. Nothing will stop me from my goal."

Looking back into the passenger seat, she saw no one. Confident and cocky, Sal felt that she'd gotten her deadly point across and chased the ghost away.

*

Steven and Rachel were heading east toward Detroit. Rachel pulled a fold-it map out and began studying the routes of the mitten-shaped state.

"It looks like we stay on I-94 until we reach Battle Creek, where we pick up I-69 east toward Lansing."

Steven nodded his approval, an eye always concentrated on the rear-view mirrors for signs of a police presence. The anxiety and paranoia coursing through his veins felt cold and slow.

As they drove a stretch of I-94 between Benton Harbor and Kalamazoo, they saw trains that had left out of Chicago headed toward The Brick. The site of the large "F.E.M.A. CHICAGO" letters blazing out from the side of the boxcars was chilling. The trains from Chicago were on a B-line through Grand Rapids, up toward Cadillac and on to The Brick. It was a straight shot for a train that didn't need to worry about anything other than the tracks that lay ahead of it. Rachel imagined the sad faces inside the boxcars, most having resolved themselves to the grim reality before them. She thought about Matt and what he must've been going through. She felt sadness intertwined with fury; a touch of hope also mixed with her emotion.

"Why did these awful things have to happen?" Rachel mused, "Human beings are being sacrificed for what? A president's agenda?"

Steven gave Rachel a slight peek as he drove along. He thought he knew what the answer was and gave his opinion. "It's definitely the president's agenda. His family was raped and now all "perceived" rapists are going to pay the price. Wisecroft is no different than John Walsh or Nancy Grace back in the early 2000's. The key now is that Wisecroft became president, so he holds all the power. He's made it his personal vendetta."

Rachel agreed and added some key points that made sense. "The N.V.A.C. has a lot to do with this too. They put pressure on the government way ahead of Wisecroft being elected. The pressure they applied was a starting point for The Brick idea. When the president came forward with his ideas,

the seeds had long been planted. The Brick, realistically, has
been in the works since the early 2000's. If Walsh, Grace or
Lunsford could've done it then, they would have. Our
brothers and sisters in the advocacy warned of something like
this and it came true."

The two stared straight ahead as the countryside of
Michigan breezed past them in blurred flourishes. The man in
the green truck was following behind, but not so close that
he'd be recognized as a threat. In Northern Ohio, Sal was
only a few miles from Michigan with her own version of why
The Brick now stood.

*

Sal Parker always had a flair for being opinionated and
blunt. She also had some mental difficulties that were
attempting to interfere with her thought patterns. When it
came to N.V.A.C. vs. The Advocacy, however, she was well
studied about the reasoning of both sides. When discussing
the ongoing conflict between the two groups, her insanity took
a back seat to purpose. In meetings she had with Davis and
other N.V.A.C. members, she was remarkably lucid and able
to express wide-ranging conversation with the issues.

"The problem we have is that the offenders ALL say
they're innocent. How are you supposed to differentiate

between the ones who really ARE guilty and the ones who aren't? I handle it this way: If the offender expresses deep concern for the accuser while professing their innocence, then they're probably innocent. However, if there's no sympathy for the accuser, then it shows that they don't care about anything EXCEPT their innocence. Now, having said that, how are we going to handle it? In my opinion, if a jury states you're guilty, then something *must have happened*. Whether it's as severe as the accuser says is up for discussion, but I'm convinced that ninety-nine percent of sex offenders tried and convicted are as guilty as sin. The one percent that are wrongly convicted? Again, something happened between the individuals involved that brought out such allegations. If one percent of our population has to pay for ninety-eight percent of the perverts, then so be it. I hope in my heart they find a way to escape and never have to go through the Hell. Personally, I just don't have time to sort 'em out, so let God do it."

In some ways, it appeared that Sal was absolutely right. The N.V.A.C. agreed that the high percentage of accused were guilty. Whether that number went as high as ninety-eight percent was certainly up for debate. The Advocates argued that once the sentence was served, then you should be free to live your life. Of course, that never happened, as potential jobs, being anywhere near children, and finding a sympathizing public was all but impossible.

*

Steven discussed his points with Rachel, who didn't know as much about Sal as she originally thought. Steven explained how close he had been to Sal when she was trying to talk him into going the N.V.A.C. way despite the fact that he was an offender.

"She was trying to infiltrate my cover. She was always tipsy or flat-out drunk when I spoke with her and it was impossible to change her mind about the state of the offender in the public eye. She tried to act as if she was a nice person with a golden heart, but I saw right through her. I never once considered joining her side of the cause, although I think she really felt deep down that she had me. Sal "the Gal" Parker is one batshit crazy woman and cannot be trusted. She's also a murderer and destroyer of families."

A surprised and enlightened Rachel countered.

"Families? Let me tell you about families. The lawmakers who passed these sex offender laws back in the 1980's never thought about the affect it would have on the children *of the* offenders; the children they swore to protect. Sure, they wanted to protect the kids from molestation, but the bullies came out and started beating up the kids of the offenders themselves. How does that protect children? I've wondered about that and still can't wrap my head around it."

Steven countered. "Because they didn't take into account all of the possible repercussions of having a registry. The lawmakers wanted votes, so they knee-jerked these laws into place. Now I'm not right about everything, but I know a flawed system when I see one. Now that it's become so flawed and we have a vengeful president in office, you have The Brick as a result."

Rachel could only shake her head. She knew there were some God-awful people out there who molested children, but she also knew there were people registered who didn't belong registered. She honestly believed her husband was one of the victims caught in the net of the law. She re-focused her thinking as Steven guided the truck onto 127 headed north. They had reached Lansing, Michigan and headed up the middle of the state where they would eventually run into I-75. That would bring them very near the destination where they intended to derail the train's route. The pressure of mounting a rescue operation, keeping their eyes peeled for Sal and getting a train to stop was beginning to squeeze within her guts. Steven felt it too.

*

345

Sal crossed into Michigan just north of Toledo. She was running I-75, which she'd been driving since leaving Cincinnati for Florida and then back up to Michigan. Criss-crossing the country had left the assumed N.V.A.C. leader exhausted and in serious need of rest. She mapped her route and decided to stay on I-75 until she reached the Livonia, Michigan area, where she would merge onto I-96 headed west to Lansing. From there, she'd take 127 north just as Steven and Rachel had done. She'd make up ground as fast as possible, considering the pair had about 150 miles on her. All of Sal's figuring and assumptions were hunches as to what she thought Steven and Rachel would do. Wanting an update, she called the man in the green truck.

"You tell me when they stop for rest. I need rest too, but I'm driving for another hour after they stop. I need to make up ground."

"Do you want me to sabotage their vehicle so you can make up more ground Sal? It'd be easy. I can let the air out of a tire or two. They'd take an extra thirty minutes or so getting it fixed up and it wouldn't look so obvious."

"Good idea. That'd help me catch up faster. I want to follow them until they decide where their thinking about heading off the train. It's very important because I want Matt's ass too."

346

"You got it Sal. I'll be calling soon. Say Sal, why are you worried about Matt? He's already caught."

"Do me a big favor and mind your business. Just do what I ask and help me out, okay? The reward will be plentiful."

"Okay Sal. Sorry. I'm just curious, that's all."

While ruffled by the man's nosiness, Sal was pleased with his idea of slowing them down with the flat-tire idea. She wanted to catch up, but at the same time, she didn't want them to be suspicious. A couple of flat tires that need air would do the trick.

Steven and Rachel stopped in the small town of St. Johns to get food and sleep. They were both tired, but Steven felt it more as he had done all the driving. Being the control freak *(sexist?)* that he was, he wouldn't allow Rachel to take the wheel at any point. She had asked him more than once if she could relieve him so he could sleep, but the stubborn offender/advocate refused. He felt he needed to be abreast of every situation put before him. He wanted to know every car that passed, every cop that was hiding and every inch of the road of which he was driving. That was Steven's way. Rachel let him do as he wished, but kept her eye on him to make sure he didn't snooze at the wheel. The two finally ate and arrived at their room when Steven's cell phone rang. It was a call he wouldn't soon forget.

The man in the green truck parked in a wooded lot, oblivious to any passing motorist. He popped open his bottle of whiskey and re-filled his flask, and then took a few shots of the hard stuff to give himself what he called a "snort of fresh air." He waited two hours to make sure the lights were low and walked over to the parking lot that held the Ranger. He quickly hissed two tires flat and ran back to his hiding spot. After returning to his truck, he slumped over for some much needed shut-eye. He set his personal alarm on his cell phone to buzz every hour so he could make sure the Ranger was still in the lot. Losing them now would be enough to set Sal off the deep end. Her deep end could end up with him being six-feet under. He wasn't interested.

*

Sal made it as far as Fowlerville before stopping for the night. She had been driving eighteen straight hours and had had enough of the arguing with her mother's memory. She was also sick of the images of her two dead mutts back in Florida and just needed to shut her eyes. She was no more than an hour and a half from the two "escapees" as she called them, and knew she'd make up much, if not all of the ground in the morning hours. That was, as long as the man in the green truck didn't screw it up. If that happened, he'd find

348

himself whacked and in a strange place. She wasn't interested in his excuses. Sal was on the edge.

Getting to sleep turned out to be a major challenge, as she tossed and turned with the thoughts of her mother rattling around in her mind. Her mother was the nice, gentle character that her father wasn't. No matter how much she tried to resist, a resounding voice kept echoing in her head.

"I didn't raise my little Sally to be such a nasty person. I raised a nice, well-kempt young woman. Why do you kill, Sally? Why do you live by the sword that'll surely get you killed?"

"SHUT-UP MOM! I've heard enough of you. I can't take another minute of your guilt trip. Why don't you go back to Heaven...or Hell or wherever you came from? Leave me alone to do my work."

"If you don't mind Sally, Heaven's where I live, but if you don't stop this infernal nonsense, Hell will be your home forever. You don't want Hell Sally. I've seen it. The Lord allows everyone a look at what you were in for if you didn't change your ways. It's not fire and brimstone like everyone here says...its total darkness and weeping. No light, no touch and you're trapped in a six-by-six foot box. It lasts forever

349

Sally. You'll want death, but the relief won't come. The pain and the torture will be more intense than the days you walked the earth. The anxiety and panic from claustrophobia is never-ending. You have a chance to change and come to the light, where it's total freedom. No worries and no stress Sally. Total freedom."

Sal glanced over and saw her mother, at the young and peak age of twenty-five, sitting in the guest chair near the nightstand. She sat with her hands on her knees and a smile upon her face. She gazed at Sal with the love only a mother could show. Sal took offense and pled her case. She said to herself that this was the last time she'd explain.

"Look ma, I'm killing people that have hurt children. They hurt and abused the very little ones God so adores. I'm not stepping back from my goal. No one, not even you ma, can make me stop. I think you're nothing more than a figment of my imagination anyway. You're the guilt that corrodes my insides. You're the vessel that the holy spirit uses to intimidate me. I refuse to take the responsibility of your life or death. That's on you ma."

"Oh Sally. You're fate will be a painful one. Allow God to deal with the people that hurt his children. That's not your job, dear. Let life run its own course. Don't try to be a

350

hero to God, who loves every creature. Don't end up in a six-by-six box for eternity."

"Go away ma. This is the last time I'll talk with you. Go mind your business and allow me to do what I'm determined to do. I believe my God will reward me for my heroism and protecting his children. I don't want to hear from you ever again."

"Very well Sally. I'll be out of your hair. You make me weep with sadness, but my Lord will erase your memory from my mind. I'll never have to think of you again. I won't have to worry about the suffering that's coming to you...soon."

With that final word, Sal's mom descended up and through the ceiling, apparently disappearing into the darkness. Sal watched her go and without another flinch, set her head on the pillow and went to sleep. Sal's mom had done and said everything she could, but it wasn't enough. Sal was determined and nothing, besides death, would stop her.

*

Steven took the call that he wasn't expecting.

"It's your Aunt, Steven. Where are you?"

"I can't tell you. What's up? What's made you call?"

"Casper's dead Steven and the law's looking for you with a vengeance. They found him shot in the head with all your hidden advocacy items on top of him. They think you're a murderer."

Steven took a long pause to reflect, as Casper was a childhood friend of whom he cared deeply.

"Well, I didn't kill him. It was probably that fucking Sal Parker. Oh my God, are you sure he's dead?"

"As sure as sure is Steven. Now give yourself up and you'll be able to defend yourself in court.

Not being fooled by his aunt's sudden kindness, after years of believing Steven was a pedophile, he shot back before ending the conversation.

"Court? What a joke. Do you have any idea what's going on in this country? Do you know how the offenders are being treated? Have you heard of a place called The Brick? I know you're having the call traced. Don't try to find me; I'm too smart for the law. Goodbye." *Click.*

Steven's aunt looked at the police officers surrounding her with the tracing equipment.

"Did you get his location?"

"Nope, it wasn't long enough. Nevertheless, we're sending out cell signals from all the towers across the region. We'll get him."

"Good," said Steven's aunt. "The pervert needs to rot for what he's done."

Back at the hotel, Steven went to the yard behind the building and threw his cell phone into a man-made pond. The minute the phone hit the water, it eliminated any tracking of his whereabouts. He took Rachel's phone and did the same. He knew it was getting hot, and the cops were on their tail. He was also very saddened by his friend's death. He would sit up for a couple of hours in sorrow, and then go back to bed. There was little time for mourning; too much work lay ahead for the pair.

*

Matt's train pulled out of its stall. He and Mary were together for the final ride to The Brick and he was seriously considering more than a friendship with the woman. Mary felt the same. She knew if Rachel happened to come to Matt's rescue, he'd be gone. She resigned herself to the possibility but clung very close to Matt on the train.

The train was to head due north, not far from the I-75 corridor. It would head toward Pontiac, Flint and through Bay

City. From there it would continue north past Grayling and Gaylord before finally pulling into Mackinaw City. The boxcar was stocked with water and food, and this time, it had fans running. The weather outside was chilly, but the heat that rose in the car was getting very stuffy. With some fifty other people in the boxcar, there was plenty of room to move around and stretch their legs. The government was again being very careful to bring their offenders to The Brick alive. For every live body that arrived, more money was made for the train lines and other related entities.

Matt and Mary found a secluded spot and sat down to talk about the fact that they had obvious feelings about one another.

"I think you're great Matt. I know that you have a wife who's trying her damndest to help you out of this mess. I can't help but tell you, though, that I really like you. If you don't get rescued, I'd like to be around you when we reach, well, you know."

Matt felt a twinge go through him. He was both tickled and excited at Mary's revelation.

"I feel the same about you. I like you, and the "like" could easily turn into "love." If I'm rescued, you'll be rescued too. I won't let them take you away."

"No Matt. If you're rescued, you let me go. I have nothing here anymore. I'll have more luck in The Brick.

354

Even though it's a huge prison, I'll feel somewhat free without fear of those guards. You promise to let me go if you get rescued?"

"But Mary…"

Before Matt could finish his sentence, Mary moved in close and put her lips against his. The kiss was long, sensual and deep. Both closed their eyes and danced a tango with wet lips, tongues and raging hormones. Matt placed his hand on Mary's breast as they continued their kiss. Mary clutched Matt's hand tight so the grip on her breast was firm and unmistakable. She caressed his neck and ear with her free hand. Finally, after what seemed like an eternity, they separated. They looked deeply into each other's eyes and leaned back against the wall behind them. There was no need for words. They simply laid their heads against one another and slowly dozed off. The two felt their first bit of true freedom since their captures.

*

A journey of hundreds of miles…

The fact that their tires were flat wasn't necessarily bad, just annoying. Steven knew they'd have to walk to a hardware store and get some Fix-a-Flat, or call a wrecker to get the vehicle to a gas station. Looking over the two flat tires, Steven figured they had just run out of air and nothing more. He did take a long look around at his surroundings, but found nothing contemptuous in the small town. After mulling over their choices, the pair opted to call a wrecker and get a lift to the gas station. To their surprise and good luck, the wrecker had an air compressor on board. For fifty bucks and an hour of their time, the problem was repaired and the two were on their way.

"No harm, no foul." Steven exclaimed.

...always includes at least one flat tire.

Steven and Rachel were on their way. The man in the green truck was following. Sal Parker was fifteen minutes behind the man. The train holding Matt headed north quickly. It was all coming together the way Steven, Rachel *and* Sal had hoped it would. Soon the conflict would take place: A conflict that would settle the score for good.

"EACH TIME A MAN STANDS FOR AN IDEAL, OR ACTS TO IMPROVE THE LOT OF OTHERS, OR STRIKES OUT AGAINST INJUSTICE, HE SENDS A TINY RIPPLE OF HOPE, AND CROSSING EACH OTHER FROM A MILLION DIFFERENT CENTERS OF ENERGY AND DARING, THOSE RIPPLES BUILD A CURRENT WHICH CAN SWEEP DOWN THE MIGHTIEST WALLS OF OPPRESSION AND RESISTANCE."

-Robert Francis Kennedy

SHAUN WEBB

THE BRICK I

The four frantically headed north. Steven and Rachel were followed closely by the man in the green truck, who was in turn followed closely by Sal. The race was on as Matt's train was headed north and had no intention of stopping along the way. There were no F.E.M.A. Camps between Detroit and the entrance to The Brick, so stopping the train was not a necessity. Of course, Steven and Rachel had other plans and that included violence if necessary. Whatever it took to rescue Matt was of no consequence, even if it meant other people *died*. It sickened the pair to think in such a way, but they had to. Rescuing Matt would be no minor feat.

The pair had gotten their tires aired up and were told by the mechanic that poor air sockets were the cause of the flats. No such a thing was true, but Steven opted to have new air sockets placed on the rims just in case.

"These guys will say anything for a buck." Steven deduced.

Despite the small inconvenience, they had reached Mt. Pleasant and were speeding north with purpose. Rachel found the F.E.M.A. train reports on the radio dial and found out that Matt's train was just south of Bay City. The pair knew they had to keep up a brisk pace, as the train had no stoplights to slow them down. On a geographical plain, the two were actually ahead of the train by some ten miles. They needed to widen the gap to at least forty or fifty to have any kind of chance of heading it off. Steven increased his speed to some eight-five MPH, hoping that the train was maintaining about a seventy M.P.H. clip. They were about two hours away from their planned hijack spot, so fifteen miles every hour would help immensely in the timing. They had no idea where or when, but they definitely knew what. They'd figure the rest of the scenario out very soon.

*

The man in the green truck kept constant phone contact with Sal and the two finally met up in Alma, just south of Steven and Rachel's location. They ditched Sal's tired SUV and rode together in the green truck, which the man had souped up for such extensive and rugged travel. After the initial greetings and small talk, the two were back on the road, the man doing as high as ninety MPH to close the gap between the two ahead of them. The man had kept a sighted distance between himself and the pair, but had to slow down and wait for Sal, which allowed the two about a half-hour gap. The distance would surely be made up soon as they sped along 127 without a care of potential police intervention.

It was when they passed Mt. Pleasant and could almost sniff between the gap that Sal began getting maniacally excited.

"Don't fucking lose them! I can't wait to kill them all. I've been waiting for this day for a long time and now it's almost that magical time. I think I'll slash their throats slowly. Then I'll let them linger as the life seeps out of them in pools. I want them to watch each other die."

The man was at first slightly, and then definitely creeped out by the look in Sal's eye. She was as evil and sinister as he had heard but never believed. The sadistic way in which Sal seemed to be taking pleasure was orgasmic to her and unsettling to him.

"Sal. Are you okay? I thought you just wanted to catch them. I didn't know you were serious about killing them. I'm not so sure I like this method and what you're talking about."

Sal, with a cold sneer on her face, reached over, grabbed the man by the back of his hair, and jerked his head backward as he drove. She placed a knife on his suddenly fast-beating carotid artery and threatened him.

"You shut the fuck up! This is my dream, my goal and my dying wish. I want to see them suffer the way Steven made that young girl suffer when he raped her. I want Rachel to suffer the way all the raped children suffer. These two have advocated for the offenders for years. They've advocated for the most gruesome child molesters in the land. They WILL die today. Would you like to join them?"

"No Sal, I wouldn't. Put the knife down so I can drive. I'm with you. I understand your concern and anger."

Sal stared for thirty indignant seconds into the side of the man's face before finally pulling the knife down. She was seconds from gashing his throat ear-to-ear, but he convinced her of his will to see the two, and maybe three, dead. The man blew out an audible sigh as Sal turned on the radio so she would know at what point the train had reached.

Up ahead, somewhere near Harrison, Michigan, they spotted Steven and Rachel in the Ranger.

"That's them," the man said. "There they are."

With a scowl and a raspy, cigarette burned voice, Sal replied.

"Soon they die."

*

The train chugged along quietly as Matt and Mary had fallen asleep in an embrace. Matt had cupped his hand on Mary's breast, keeping her warm and feeling wanted and loved. Mary had placed her hand on Matt's bulge, giving him much of the same comforting feeling. Upon waking, Matt immediately moved his hand and separated himself from the woman. The guilt gripped his emotional psyche. He loved Rachel more than life itself but seemed to be bound and determined to set himself up in a "just-in-case" scenario. As he watched Mary sleep, it came to him in a flourish. He didn't think there was any way in Hell that Rachel could save him and he *was* lining up Mary to take her place. To Matt, this couldn't have been a worse deduction. There was no way he could possible give Mary what she deserved and be honest about it. Matt pulled his knees up to his chest and clasped his hands around himself. The tears slowly streamed from his sad eyes.

Mary awoke some thirty minutes later to find Matt had moved away from her. She carefully approached him to ask if he was okay.

"I'm not okay Mary. I love Rachel. I can't just throw that all away even if she can't rescue me, which I don't think she can."

"If she doesn't rescue you Matt, you'll never see her again, unless of course she commits a sex crime and gets thrown into The Brick. Matt, do you think she'd do that?"

"NEVER!" Matt insisted. "That's not Rachel. She would never hurt a soul if it was her life on the line."

Mary put a finger on Matt's cheek, catching a tear as it ran down and then licking it off the tip. He turned his head away in an apologetic manner. It hurt him to be drawn to Mary while still loving Rachel. The torment made him sad, angry and frustrated. The fact that he was being thrown into The Brick was worst of all. In his mind, the government, not caring about shredding families apart, was to blame. The fight that was inside Matt during his F.E.M.A. stay was draining away from him. The man that swore he'd never give up was giving up. The facts standing before him were indisputable in his mind. Unless Rachel did the impossible and stopped the train, he'd be a beaten man.

"I respect whatever decision you make Matt." Mary softly told him. "I don't want to be "settled upon" either. I want to be with someone who loves me, not somebody who's with me because they lost their first choice. Is Rachel your first choice Matt?"

Matt laid his eyes on Mary. They were glimmering with tears. It took all of his being, but he finally nodded "yes."

"Then we'll be friends," Mary exclaimed. "You never know what could happen down the road. That is, if you're not rescued, we can hang together with no expectations. If it turns out to be meant for us, then it'll happen. Right?"

Matt was hearing the exact words he'd hoped to hear. It made him smile as he continued looking at Mary. He gave her a hug; an innocent hug. Mary had one more very important question for Matt.

"If we end up at The Brick together, can we at least stick with each other until we get settled down somewhere? I want to make sure I'm around someone I trust with my soul."

"Of course Mary. I would never desert you under any circumstances. I'm here for you."

It was a heartening moment for the pair. Matt felt the pressure of guilt alleviate while Mary felt safer knowing a strong man would help her when they reached the "not so" promised land.

*

"It won't be long Rachel. I'd say another hour or so until we reach the destination. You do know the odds of this working are very slim, right?"

"Look, you've said that a hundred times. You don't have to keep reminding me how difficult this is going to be. I already know."

Steven, perplexed, wanted to know exactly what she had in mind. "I want to hear your plan Rachel. What ideas do you have to stop that train?"

Rachel, sneering and touchy, came right out with it. "We're going to put this truck on the tracks. The train will stop and we'll find which car Matt's riding in. We'll spring him and off we go."

Steven began laughing in earnest. The laughter and snickers became a small roar as Rachel face soured into a deep frown.

"What's so fucking funny Steven? What is it that makes you laugh like a stupid-ass hyena?"

After calming himself, Steven hit Rachel hard with a dose of reality.

"So you'll stop the train with the truck and just "find" Matt's boxcar and spring him? What about the guards Rachel? What about the fact that they're not just going to sit back and say 'oh, no worries; go ahead and get what you need. We'll wait.'"

"It'll work. It has too. What else can we do?"

Steven patted Rachel on the thigh. She repeated the sour frown and slitted her eyes to a coin slot shape.

"We have guns Rachel. However, there are *two* of us. I'll have to cover while you check railcars. You'll need to scream his name constantly until you find him. From what I've seen, these trains have about ten boxcars behind the engine. You'll need to hustle. When you find his box, you'll have to shoot what surely will be a lock on the door. In the meantime, I'll do my best to hold the guards at bay. Like I said, the odds are long. I figure there to be at least six or seven guards. They may all have to die. They'll be shooting at you too. You'll need to stay low and be quick.

Rachel turned her frown into a slight smile.

"Yeah, well I was track champion in the one thousand meters. I can move pretty fast."

"But can you outrun bullets?" Steven inquired.

Rachel changed the subject by tuning the radio back into the F.E.M.A. station. She had to wait for a few minutes until they heard about Matt's train. It was running just south of Standish. The pair was pleased to know they'd made a half-hour gain on the locomotive. Steven figured by the time they reached their set spot between Grayling and Gaylord, the gap would be about forty-five minutes to an hour, which would give them plenty of time to find a nice wooded spot. The thicker the woods, the better shot they had at succeeding. There was only one slight problem; one mean woman was tailing them.

*

"Don't you fucking lose them. I'll kill you if you let them get away."

Sal was intense and getting worse as the minutes passed.

"Sal! I've been trailing them for how many hundreds of miles? I haven't lost them yet, and I even got a hideout leveled. I think I can keep up, okay?"

Sal leered at the man with the same tenacious snicker she had owned since getting in the truck. The leer was scary, threatening and intimidating. The man feared for his well-being.

"Just don't lose them, do you fucking understand me?" Sal was pointing her crooked finger in the man's face. "I haven't come this far for some fuck-nut like you to screw it up."

The man, now completely afraid of Sal, was staying back about two hundred feet. It was enough to look inconspicuous, while at the same time keeping a clear site on the pair. The traffic was much thinner in this northern part of Michigan, making driving and tracking much easier. The man broke out a flask of whiskey and asked Sal if she wanted a snort.

"Yeah okay. I'll have some of that. It takes the edge off the nerves."

Sal grabbed the flask and took a deep, gurgling snort. She coughed slightly as she pulled it away from her mouth. She wiped her whiskey lips with the sleeve of her shirt. When she handed the flask back, there wasn't even a shot left in it. The man tried to cheer Sal up further.

"That's better Sal. You need to relax and let this happen. I'm still not crazy about you killing them, but I understand your point. You have to do what's necessary in your book."

"You're Goddamn right I do. When I'm through with these assholes, there will be less children molested. For every child I save, an angel gets their halo."

The man cringed and rolled his eyes over the tastelessly borrowed remark, but tried to keep the peace between the two. He had begun to question his allegiance to the troubled woman, and was trying to remain steadfast in his loyalty. He didn't care for sex offenders either, but killing them was over-the-top as far as he was concerned. The Brick was enough punishment for the offenders and getting them there was supposed to be the goal. He had turned into a sex offender bounty hunter. If he would've known about the deaths at the warehouse in Tinley Park, he probably wouldn't have called the authorities. He didn't realize how killing was a part of the package, but Sal's knife to his throat technique convinced him for better or worse.

Sal leered through the windshield, not wanting the pair to get out of her site. The man had a full tank of gas, which meant it'd be non-stop from there on out. As Sal continued focusing her stare, she spoke to the man, exposing all of the clues needed to label her crazy.

"I've been talking to my mother about Steven, Rachel and Matt. I told her they had to die, but of course, she disagrees. I finally had to tell her not to bug me anymore so she finally disappeared."

"Disappeared?" The man asked. "Was she with you?"

"No. She's dead."

The man's face showed a slight whitish pale as he turned toward Sal.

"Did you say 'dead'? I could have sworn you said 'dead'?"

"I did say dead. She showed herself to me in my truck and at the hotel. She was trying to convince me that I was being evil; that she didn't raise such a nasty woman."

It wasn't so much as *what* Sal had said as it was *how* she said it. She really believed that she was speaking to her dead mother. The man decided to ask more questions, now knowing for sure that she was as nutty as a fruitcake.

"So what did she look like? What was she wearing?"

"What fucking difference does that make?" Sal spit. "What she was wearing doesn't mean shit to the situation. If you can't ask a decent question, then just stay quiet."

"Sorry Sal. I was just wondering. I wanted to know more about her, that's all."

"Well, you don't need to know more than what I'm telling you. Say, are you really in with me?"

Sal took her eyes off the truck in front of her as she asked the question, curious as to the man's facial expression.

"Of course Sal. I told you. I agree with you and understand why you feel the way you do. I'm in one hundred percent."

Sal, squinting, focused back on the road.

"Then you'll understand that these fucks killed my dogs. They poisoned them with antifreeze. The dogs visited me on the trip too. They support me in my endeavor. They want vengeance."

"Okay Sal. I'm not trying to piss you off here, but you're creeping me out. You say your dead mom and dead dogs have visited you. What the Hell? Are you losing yourself in your hatred? What you're saying doesn't make sense."

The man in the green truck was getting aggravated with Sal and now turned his mood into that of anger. Only moments earlier, he had agreed with Sal to appease her, but the addition of dead dogs visiting her was the straw that broke the camel's back. He gripped the pistol that he carried in his left pocket, while continuing to drive with his right hand. He too was a trained killer and was concerned that if he didn't do something soon, Sal would get him first. He planned to splatter her brains on the passenger window of the truck. Sal kept her attention straight ahead as she responded to the man. "If you're saying I'm batshit crazy, that's fine. You have a right to your opinion. Despite your belief, do me, and especially yourself a huge favor and let go of that pistol in your pocket. I have a gun aimed at your head as we speak and you won't so much as get that gun moved an inch before your blood's running down that dashboard."

The man peered over and sure enough, Sal had the jump on him. She was looking straight out of the windshield while lying in her lap was a gun with the barrel pointed straight at his face. If he moved an inch, it'd be over before it even began. The man took his grip off the pistol.

"No problem Sal. I was just sitting with my hand in my pocket. I had no intention of shooting you."

"Good, because I'll add you to the list just as easy as everybody else. You don't mean shit to me except to get to my goal. When this is over, I'll pay you and you can shove off. Just don't cross me. I'm warning you for the last fucking time."

372

"Okay Sal. No worries. Let's just get the job done. I think it might happen soon. We're getting too close to The Brick for them to wait much longer."

Fifteen seconds after speaking, Steven and Rachel pulled to a stop ahead of them. A moment later, they moved ahead some one hundred feet and turned down a dirt road. The man and Sal saw this and their eye's widened. They stayed far behind and turned down the same road. Something big was up and they knew it.

*

The destination was less than two miles away. Looking at the map, Rachel informed Steven that they had to turn down the gravel road ahead of them and head toward the train tracks. The nervousness was gripping them both with a choke of anticipation. Rachel was feeling a plethora of emotion including hope, fear, frustration, angst and depression. Steven's only emotion was fear; the fear of being captured and taken to that blasted Brick. He swore he'd never go alive and reaffirmed the thought in his mind.

"They'll have to shoot me dead. I'll take some with me though."

As they traveled through the wooded area east of 127, they noticed the trees becoming thicker while the road narrowed. Steven hoped the dirt road would remain wide enough until they reached the tracks so he could use the truck to block the train's path, forcing it to stop. They were off 127, helping Steven feel some relief as he had seen more than his share of army vehicles passing him. It was quite a desolate route, but the fact that they were so close to The Brick was the reason behind the camouflaged traffic. He was sure that I-75 would have been much worse. In the seat next to him, Rachel became intensely talkative. "Do you think the tracks are coming soon? Do you think the road will stay wide enough for us? Do you think...?"

"I think it'll be what it'll be Rachel. Only God knows what lay ahead. We have to take it one-step at a time and see for ourselves what happens. It's simple but at the same time but very complicated."

Steven rolled the window down to get some fresh air when he heard it. The roar of something, although he wasn't sure what, was behind them. He pulled to the side for a moment and listened closely. Rachel asked him what was wrong.

"Shh. I think there's something behind us."

"What do you mean? Like a car?" Rachel curiously inquired.

"Shut up Rachel." Steven sneered at her. "Damn." .

Rachel bent her chin down in an embarrassed frown.

374

After a few minutes, Steven dismissed the noise as an errant off-road vehicle: *Kids acting up and riding the berms.* He put the truck back on the path and continued the trek deeper into the wooded area.

*

"Stop." Sal ordered. "Shut the vehicle off."

The man did as he was told and waited. Sal explained to him that the dust trail ahead of them had calmed, indicating that Steven had stopped his vehicle. She wanted to wait until the dust picked back up before they proceeded.

"I want all three if possible, so we want them to reach the train. If they spring Matt, I get three heads instead of two."

After a few minutes, the dust cloud picked up and she ordered the man to continue. He continued on the narrow path. They passed a sign that read "Higgins Lake," which was a few miles south of the original point of attack, although it wasn't far off from the planned destination. Sal was getting even nastier and more degrading than before. She muttered to herself and became restless, moving her rear end around in the seat while the man watched with curiosity. After a few minutes of squirming, Sal pulled a gun out of her breast holder, one out of her leg strap and a knife from her hip

375

harness. Sal began checking the weapons, making sure they were ready for action. She made sure her Sig Sauer 1911 was locked and loaded, looked over her Browning HP Mark III and finally gave her Glock a quick look. She made sure the knife was sharp and balanced. The man glanced as he drove; ruing the fact that he simply had a small six-shot revolver, not to mention that he was stuck with a crazed woman.

"So Sal, where'd you get those awesome guns?"

Sal looked at the man with slight disdain and huffed as she turned back toward the windshield.

The man spoke again. "All I have is a little pea-shooter that's not worth a shit."

Sal responded with attitude. "Why don't you do both of us a favor and shut the fuck up? You can't stop running that mouth and it's annoying as Hell."

"I'm just trying to relax us, okay? Sorry Sal. Holy shit, you're so different than the woman I originally met."

"I don't need to relax, and I don't give three shits what you think of me since we met. Now are you going to shut-up, or should I just lose the loose baggage?"

Having heard more than enough, the man moved his head forward. He felt savage hatred worming through his soul. Within a few short hours, he'd grown a great dislike for the woman. He couldn't believe it was the same person he'd met only a year earlier; the one that was nice, polite and helpful. Oh, she had her anger issues, but they were funny and seemed harmless. Now she was acting out in a murderous way. He shook his head and soldiered forward.

*

Steven had seen the sign for Higgins Lake and knew they had pulled off the highway a bit early. At that point, it didn't matter. The only focus was stopping the train itself and trying to get to Matt. Even though he thought they needed more people with guns to be successful, he had to give it a go. He remembered what James Rogers had said in Illinois about being a true advocate and helping those in need. Rachel was more in need than anyone he knew. The woman worshipped Matt like no other. Having never had a true steady girlfriend or wife, Steven found their connection to be rather intriguing. He often wondered how two people could love each other so unconditionally, especially when the risk of an unwanted break-up was a possibility. With separation comes pain, with pain; acting out. Steven always found a friend with alcohol or drugs when he was younger and going through his teen-age angst-filled experiences. Now that he was older and wiser, he figured out that the chemicals only served to make the pain worse and last longer. He asked Rachel why she felt the way she did.

"Because I love the man so much. He's polite, kind, understanding and patient. He's always been supportive and has never wavered in his decisions. His touch is magical. Every time I smell his odor, I go crazy over him. When he's not home, I smell his clothes, cologne and even catch his intoxicating odor when I shower. We usually shower together, but when we don't, I miss him terribly; even if he's sitting in the other room; and he has a beautiful penis!"

Curious and now wide-eyed with Rachel's last remark, Steven asked what she would do if she lost Matt.

"I'd die. I wouldn't want to live anymore. Matt is my rock. I will never stop loving and adoring him."

"So you *do* really love the guy? I can't imagine what that feeling must be like. I've never experienced love so deep."

Rachel's eyes had grown soft and longingly distant. She was experiencing a moment of catharsis. Steven had to poke her to bring her back.

"He's like no other man. What else can I say? I thought I knew love, but I didn't. Without him, I'm nothing. I'd simply fizzle out."

Steven had hoped she'd be somewhat open to a relationship with him if she lost Matt, but now knew that she would simply cry herself to death. People had been known to die of a broken heart. Would she be the same? He resolved himself in the fact that there'd be no shot at Rachel under any circumstance. No other man would *ever* touch Rachel.

*

The train chugged along its path, approaching and passing West Branch, Michigan. Steven and Rachel had about thirty minutes to get in position. The pressure was immense. The two braced for a monumental showdown.

On the train, Matt and Mary talked and reminisced about their respective pasts. The adventures they'd been through caused giggles and tears. They spoke in a more personal way about the registry and why they were each taking up space on it. The stories were interesting and sad, but the two agreed that reality was slapping them in the face. It appeared as though the pair were accepting their fates of a life Behind the Brick.

Matt couldn't help but take long looks at Mary, her blond locks tenderly surrounding her youthful appearance. She was very beautiful and the ten or so year age difference between them meant nothing. She didn't look at all like a woman approaching her forties. Mary reciprocated Matt's gaze, noting his broad shoulders, manly five o'clock shadow and when shirtless, his firm upper body. When completely undressed. She was pleasantly surprised with his impressive

379

size. Women in general usually didn't pay attention to *that* part of a man, at least when asked about it, but Mary not only noticed, but also felt a touch of lust. She desperately wanted him inside her. She wanted to gaze into his brown eyes as he made love with her. She imagined a tender, loving man that cared about his woman, made her smile and opened up her deepest feelings. She knew he would be a great lover who attended to her needs. She imagined him whispering to her in a very loving way, saying just the right things to give her peace and make her feel protected. Mary had to calm down and focus, as she was drifting in and out of concentration, a shudder occasionally coming over her..

Matt was doing the same. He wanted her too, but couldn't commit to anything until after he knew whether Rachel could spring him. He felt that if she did rescue him, their relationship would be somewhat sullied by his lust over Mary. He couldn't stop thinking about snuggling with Mary, hand on her breast as she spooned herself as close to him as she could.

For the pair, daydreaming was their only means of relief. It would be very soon before they'd find out which way the chips would fall. Despite slightly pushing Mary away and giving her the "let's be friends" speech, he knew they would be destined to live their lives together if they reached The Brick.

They were falling in love.

DICTATORSHIP NATURALLY
ARISES OUT OF DEMOCRACY, AND THE
MOST AGGRAVATED FORM OF
TYRANNY AND SLAVERY OUT OF THE
MOST EXTREME LIBERTY.

-Plato

THE

FOURTH

REICH

JASPER ACTS

Studying the sharpened end of the needle was mesmerizing for Henry Jasper. He couldn't believe that the tiny little appendage could carry the poison that would fell the president. He was overwhelmed with the "gift" in which he'd been given. He wondered why it was himself who had to do the dirty work. Jasper sat down with a hot cup and mulled over his predicament.

Those who forget history…

"Out of all the people on the face of the earth, I've been given the opportunity and curse of a lifetime. There are some ten billion people in the United States: Some rich, most poor and many crazy. Not one person could step forward to put out this political fire? No one could recognize the absolute power that President Wisecroft is trying to establish? The people of the U.S.A. are okay with this ridiculousness? I told Rene Duchard the truth. I told him that the people were

lazy and sedentary. As long as they get theirs, life is grand. What will killing Wisecroft do for the country? Will the people listen to me as I try to convince them that The Brick is the biggest mistake ever? How hard will it be to show them that this regime has been no different from when Hitler ran Germany into a tyranny? Murder, pain and absolute power corrupted and ruined the German people. To this day in 2050, the German debacle of over one-hundred years ago is still remembered. Remembered but forgotten."

Henry continued to admire the broach. The red, white and blue of the American flag glimmering forth filled him with pride and nostalgia. The vice president remembered the days of the early 2000's.

"I remember the day the World Trade centers were so savagely attacked by terrorists. I was just a young lad, but I knew somehow that that would change everything about the future of this country. George W. Bush was the president then and wars broke out all over the Middle East and Afghanistan. Later, Barack Obama became the first black president in the history of our great country. After his eight-year term, the first female president, Hillary Clinton, served a four-year term before being replaced by the radical Donald Trump. That's where the tide really turned. Trump tried, but failed, to instill

a term limit elimination bill. The Congress and House shot it down, but the vote was much closer than it should have been. After Trump came two four-year presidents before Wisecroft came along.

The young, good-looking John Wisecroft has turned the gamut upside down. He's built that God-forsaken bricked facility, entered a term limit bill that just might pass and wants to eliminate the middle and lower classes altogether. Will we revert all the way back to slavery, as we did in the 1800's? Will the elimination of everybody except the rich effectively destroy this country? Worst of all, will Wisecroft act like Hitler and think he can take over the entire world?

...are condemned to repeat it.

Henry shut the broach into the casing that protected it and squeezed so tightly that his hand hurt. He felt a great deal of guilt for allowing himself to run with the tyrannical Wisecroft. Of course, had he known what the stakes really were, he'd never have lowered himself to that level. He didn't know, however, and stood with the future of the country tightly in his right hand. He was to use it soon. He was to stick the broach into the president's skin and bring death to this madness. Jasper rued feeling like God, as the Lord was the only decider of life and death, in his heart. He did feel,

389

however, that sometimes people were used as pawns to carry out the sentences that the Holy Spirit imposed. Could it be that Henry was a carrier of such orders? Was he a soldier of God? Henry knelt and prayed.

My Father,...

"My Lord, what have I done to deserve such a job? Am I to be the one who carries out the assassination of Mr. Wisecroft? Is this your will, my God in heaven? If so, I ask that you give me the dignity and strength to carry out the duty with honor and bravery. I pray that you give me the courage that's needed to inflict death upon a brother in Christ. Whatever happens, thy will be done Lord. Give me strength. Amen"

...why hast thou forsaken me?

The maid entered the room with another cup of tea and a few crumpets to offer the V.P. She sensed something with him but couldn't pinpoint it. She felt the urge to communicate with him.

"So I must ask, Henry. What's getting to you? I know you have a tough job with many difficult decisions, but you seem more, I don't know, stressed lately."

"Oh, I'm fine. There's a lot on my plate and I need to decide which routes I'm going to take."

"Meaning what?"

Henry picked up a crumpet and bit into it. The slight scowl on his face indicated that he was disappointed with the flavor, texture or both. He placed it back down on the plate and took a sip of his tea.

"Meaning I have so many decisions to make about the country's future. I'm worried about John, I'm worried about the people and that's only the start of it. I have lots of worries."

The expression on Henry's face turned from an "eyebrow's raised" worry to a scowl of contempt.

"You don't understand at all and I don't expect you to. I do, however, appreciate your concern."

Henry's maid responded. "I'm trying to give you an outlet. Sometimes you need the ear of a trusted confidant. That's what I should be to you; a trusted friend."

"I'm sorry." Henry said. "I'm a bit uptight and nervous. I didn't mean to snap at you. I really do apologize."

Henry's maid walked over and laid her hand on his shoulder and gave it a pat. She stared for a moment at his face; a face with deep lines that widened as they stretched downward toward the corners of his mouth.

"If you need to talk, don't hesitate to call on me. You know I'm here for you."

"Thank you. I appreciate your concern and understanding."

"Oh, by the way Mr. Jasper, sorry about the crumpets; I know they were dry."

The V.P.'s maid picked up the tray of tea and crumpets, exiting the room as quietly as she entered.

Henry rose to his feet, knowing that he would soon carry out the grisly plot against Wisecroft; a plot hatched and carried out by him alone. Jasper pocketed the broach and headed to the Oval Office where he was to meet Wisecroft for a very important meeting; a meeting that would be their last together.

*

The tone was surly as the president presented his new plans to a very nervous cabinet. Henry sat to the left, waiting for his opportunity. Since the last cabinet meeting, the members had learned a hard lesson; that death would come through disagreement. Instead of challenging Wisecroft in any way, they stood and applauded his ideas and decisions. It was a pathetic scene to the disgruntled Jasper, but he applauded all the same to give the impression of satisfaction. Wisecroft accepted the applause and continued with his rant.

"I'm happy to see that this cabinet has decided that the ideas I have are much better than anything else anyone can come up with. As you learned a few days ago, I can be quite...determined in my will. It's not that I act like a "spoil-sport," but rather it's what's best for our country. If we can get the term-limits eliminated, I can reign on and on, giving the country a solid regime with no worries of having to change ideas so completely with another president. Eliminating the middle AND lower class insures a great flow of cash into and out of our country. With almost all jobs and products offshore, we save billions and will thrive like never before. The middle class and poor can fight our wars, protect our freedoms and keep our jail system in place."

A few of the cabinet members were feeling nauseated as Wisecroft explained his theories. Others were listening without *listening*, not knowing what else they could possibly do to stop the madness. The president had Congress and the House in his back pocket with cash and promises. There was no way any cabinet members could keep the check on the president that was so sorely needed. Frustration permeated through the room as Wisecroft continued.

393

"Without a doubt, this will continue to be the greatest country on the face of the earth. We'll be as powerful and as rich as we've ever been. That includes you cabinet members, who will see substantial raises very soon. I hope that sounds good to all of you.

Okay ladies and gentleman of the cabinet, we're going to take an hour-long break and I'll see you back here promptly at 12:30. I have an even bigger surprise for all of you. Oh, and apparently, Vice President Jasper has a nice surprise for me. See you all soon. Henry, can you stay so we can chat? I have lunch ready for both of us."

Henry nodded and the disgruntled cabinet filed out to go wherever they go. Henry followed Wisecroft into his personal nook, where lunch sat on the table. Jasper thought to himself, "Last meal for the president. How dramatic."

"So what's the story John? You wanted to speak?"

"Yes Henry. I'm curious as to what your take is on the plans I'm making. Is there anything I'm missing or should add?"

In a flash, the coffee Henry was drinking seemed to stick in his throat as if it were molasses. He knew he had to answer and look as convincing as possible.

394

"I'm good. I told you I wasn't going to argue any further with you. You have the ability to pull my family from Vermont and dump them in The Brick. I'm kind of over-a-barrel on that, wouldn't you say?"

"If you don't mind Henry, I'd like to ask the questions here. You just answer, okay?"

"Sure. Shoot."

"So what you're saying Henry is that you don't have a problem with my techniques. You're one hundred percent on board with my plans for the country?"

"Sure John. There's nothing else that needs to be said. I'm with you all the way."

"That's good Henry. I was starting to think you'd had some major second thoughts about my agenda."

Henry looked closely at the president as he spoke. A general feeling of unease was washing over him like a warm rush of water through his veins. Something seemed peculiar to him, but he couldn't put the finger on it.

"Is everything okay John? Is there a problem?"

"Again Henry, I said I'd ask the questions here. I need to know, do you still have the broach that you intend to present me with today?"

"Of course, I have it right here." Henry patted his suit coat ever so carefully. "I was looking forward to doing it before the cabinet. Does that please you sir?"

"May I see it Henry. I'd like to have a look at it."

The balls of Henry's feet suddenly went flat and wet. He was starting to worry that Wisecroft knew something. He reluctantly handed Wisecroft the case with the broach in it. The president opened it and took a long look. He handed it back to Henry.

"Very nice. I just wanted to make sure it matched my suit. You do understand?"

Relieved and feeling the stones falling from his shoulders, Henry nodded.

"Of course John. I get that. You want to look your best at all times."

"Good. We'll go back out there at 12:30 and that will be the first order of business."

Henry was getting closer. The clock was about to strike zero.

*

The railroad car was motoring down the track as Matt and Mary continued sharing their life stories. The two had come to an agreement that they'd hold off on the lustful feelings until they learned more about their futures. It would either be The Brick or escape for Matt, while Mary would go to The Brick regardless of Matt's situation. Deep down she prayed that Matt's escape attempt would fail and the two would be forced to find a place together in the U.P. of Michigan. As they entered the train in Detroit, they were handed maps of the entire bricked facility so they could study where they might like to live when entrance was assured.

"It appears that The Brick starts, or ends in St. Ignace and runs around the whole U.P. There also seems to be an area around the perimeter that stretches a couple of miles from The Brick to the water. We have our choice of any city we want to live in, so the selections are abundant."

Mary looked at the map with Matt, interested in what all of the x's, circles and other symbols meant.

"I think they represent guard posts, borders and other stuff I don't understand. We'll have to see when, uh, *if* we get there."

"You know I'm going for sure Matt, so I guess I'm trying to learn as much as I can before we arrive."

"And it won't be long Mary. The way I figure it and timed it out, we're only some three hours from the entrance. That'll mean freedom, or prison; whichever way you'd like to look at it."

"What city will you live in Matt? Have you thought about it?"

"I've been looking at this place called Escanaba. I like how it runs well to the west and sits near the water. I don't know if the whole city's within The Brick, but it looks like there are few small towns just west of the city. Cornell, Hyde, Schaffer; they look to be out-of-the-way towns."

"Have you thought about the cold and snow? It seems I've heard that it gets pretty nasty in the winter."

"I lived in upstate New York Mary, so I'm used to snow by the bucket load. You're from the Seattle area, which isn't as cold. You'll get used to it either way."

The two continued studying the map when the train suddenly shook violently. The car they were in swayed hard left and right at least three times before settling. The people in the boxcar began to scream, as the assumption was that they'd derailed. Matt grabbed a hold of Mary, who'd almost slid all the way to the other side of the car. The shaking was forceful and nauseating. Matt wondered if an earthquake had hit. After a few seconds, he knew; Rachel was outside and this was an attempt to stop the train. He wasn't sure if he was right or wrong, but something told him it was the correct thought. Soon he'd find out.

*

Steven and Rachel reached the tracks just east of Higgins Lake. The two stopped, exited the vehicle and studied the terrain along with the tracks. Steven looked at his

398

watch. It appeared that they were a good thirty minutes ahead of the cursed locomotive.

"What do you think Rachel? Are you sure you're ready for action in about a half an hour?"

"I'm more than ready. My blood's pumping through my veins fast. The adrenaline's kicking in. So what plan do you think is best?"

"We're going to put the truck on the tracks and wait for the train to stop. We'll have to work very quickly and get Matt out of there. I'm going to get up on that branch and cover you with fire while you do your thing. Remember, you have to keep yelling his name loudly. He needs to hear you."

"I'm concerned Steven. There could be dozens of cars on the train. Then what? You only have so much ammo."

"The train we saw from the Chicago F.E.M.A. had six cars connected to it. It should be easy to get his attention. We have to get him and get out fast. They'll zone into my location and shoot me right out of the tree. When you get Matt, we have to run and I mean fast. The first good hiding spot we find, we hunker down and wait for the train to leave. I don't believe we'll have a truck left though, because I think they'll call a wrecker to take it. They may move it away themselves. There are a lot of questions but few answers."

Steven pulled the truck onto the tracks and took his perch about twenty-five feet up the tree, which was well covered. The season was late, but he crawled up a pine. It was painful but easy to climb and hide inside. Rachel stayed at the bottom of the tree, hidden from the trains view. The hiding spot, as good as it was, wasn't good enough. Watching from only fifty feet away was Sal and the man. They watched as Steven climbed the tree and took his spot. Sal also saw Rachel hide under the tree, almost completely out-of-sight.

"Well well," Sal told the man, "There they are, trying to outsmart everyone. They can't outwit me though. I'm way too slick for them."

The man tilted his head in unsure agreement. He stood just in front of and slightly left of Sal. When the knife plunged into the side of his neck, he felt the air shortening and the blood dripping from his wound. While holding the knife in both hands in an attempt to remove it, he turned to Sal and lipped the word "why?"

"Because I don't need your sorry ass anymore. Thanks for the work, but the rest is my responsibility. I don't need a witness to murder, so bye-bye birdie."

The man gurgled slightly before falling to his knees and then to the ground. Neither Steven nor Rachel heard a thing, as Sal was a master at killing quietly. She pulled the knife from his neck, wiped it on her pant leg and placed it back in her harness. She watched the man bleeding to death before finally passing out. She knew his death was near and focused her attention to the two advocates. She knelt, pulled a pistol from her breast holder and took aim at the top of the pine tree. She panned down slowly until she saw Steven in her sights. It was a tough sightline, as the pine's fir was thick and concealing. After a few short seconds of lining up her prey, a shoot rang out: A shot that changed everyone's perspective. Rachel turned quickly to see where the sound came from while Steven blurted out a gasping shriek. The branches broke as he fell from one level of the tree to the next, his legs caught on the branches and he finally came to a stop upside down five feet above Rachel. The blood from Steven's back wound dripped onto her face, as she looked up her the stricken friend. Steven was choking and gasping as he choked words out to Rachel.

"She's here. Sal's here. She shot me in the fucking back like a coward Rachel."

"Don't talk Steven. Stay quiet. Save your strength."

Rachel turned around 360 degrees and spied Sal making her way toward the tree with high-powered pistols in both hands.

"Come out, come out wherever you are!" Was Sal's giddy, singing order as she came closer to the tree. Rachel took aim at Sal and pulled the trigger. A deep gash formed in Sal's arm as one pistol flew out of her hand and stopped her in her tracks. The N.V.A.C. leader smiled. She looked at her wound and cringed toward Rachel. "That didn't hurt. That was just a scratch. Now it's my turn."

Sal rang off three or four shots in a row, but Rachel had the good sense to hide behind the trunk of the tree. She was thin enough to give herself full protection. She felt the impact of the shots when they hit the tree, shaking her up. Rachel took off low and quick to find different cover to try to confuse Sal. She prayed Steven would stay quiet, but it didn't matter. Sal approached an upside down Steven hanging from the tree and grabbed him by his hair.

"Well Steven, you thought you could get away huh? Now you're going to die."

Steven struggled, and then spoke.

"You fucking coward. You shot me in the back like the pussy you are. You can't even play fair. See you in Hell you piece of shit."

Steven spit in Sal's face. Sal smiled.

"I'm going to enjoy this more than I've ever enjoyed anything in my entire life."

Sal put the gun to Steven's head and pulled the trigger.

Rachel heard three successive shots, shuddering with each bang, and put her head down, assuming her advocate friend was now dead for sure. She was right. Sal had murdered Steven.

At that same moment, Rachel could hear the train coming. It was traveling fast and the horn was honking, presumably at the truck parked on the tracks. She was in the toughest of spots. She had no cover from Steven and Sal was walking toward her. The train was to arrive within thirty seconds. The situation was falling apart quickly. The anger seethed within Rachel's gut. Sal was ruining her best chance to save her beloved husband. She had to make a choice and it was obvious. If she went for Matt, then Sal would surely shoot her down. Rachel chose to go after Sal and figure out what to do after killing the woman. As she checked her weapon and thought about these things, a cold steel pressed against the back of her head.

"Finally Rachel. I finally get to meet you in person, and I get to blow your silly little brains out of your skull just like your friend Steven Smith. What a wonderful day it is to be alive. Wow, I never realized how pretty you were. This is going to be pure euphoria."

"Fuck you Sal. You cowardly cunt. You go on ahead and shoot. I'll haunt you until your dying day."

"I've already been haunted Rachel. You've got nothing on my ghosts. Now say goodbye, because I'm blowing this pretty little head right off your shoulders."

Rachel closed her eyes as Sal cocked the gun. A shot rang out just as the train arrived; a train that *didn't* slow down, running into the truck and driving it thirty feet in the air and off to the side.

"The train wasn't going to stop anyway." Rachel thought with the surprise that she was even thinking at all. She was sure she'd been shot. She looked at Sal, whose grip on Rachel's shirt was loosening. Sal's smile turned into a frown as a tiny trickle of blood dripped from the corner of her mouth. Rachel watched as Sal's eyes dilated and then went blank. Sal slumped over her in a heavy lean. A surprised Rachel pushed Sal off and looked to the rear flank. The man in the green truck, his throat slashed but covered with a handkerchief, had managed to crawl down the path and shoot Sal from behind. The bullet entered under Sal's neck directly into the spine, rendering her completely paralyzed. She soon died from choking on her own blood. It was an awful site for the meek Rachel.

"I told you Sally. No girl of mine is a murderer."

Rachel ran to the man on the ground. He was sliced across his throat and struggled to breath. Rachel asked who he was.

"I-I'm the m-man in the green tr-truck."

His voice was gravelly and bubbled with the phlegmy rattle of death. She looked down the path and saw the truck.

404

She asked him for the keys, but he was dead. He'd shot Sal mere minutes before his death. She searched him and found the keys. Out of her mind and frantic, she peeled out in the green truck to pursue the train that continued toward The Brick despite the efforts of the advocate team. There were three dead with Rachel left uninjured.

*

Henry and John re-entered the meeting room, but they were the only two present. Jasper, a bit confused, asked John about the rest of the cabinet.

"Oh, it's just the three of us Henry. May I please have the broach?"

"What do you mean 'three'? There are only two of us here."

"The broach Henry…Let's do this."

Henry agreed, removed the cap from the needle, and began to pin the broach on Wisecroft's lapel. The president suddenly grabbed Jasper and balled his hand into a fist, stabbing the broach deeply into Henry's palm, needlepoint first. He squeezed tight to drive the pin deep. Jasper's eyes widened immensely as Wisecroft let go and he saw the bloody, poison filled wound. The president was onto his plan

405

and had turned the table. After five seconds, Henry began to feel the initial effects of the poison.

"But how?" Jasper nervously asked.

Wisecroft smiled as Henry desperately attempted to suck the poison out of his hand and spit in a futile attempt to ward off the effects. He knew his method wouldn't work. He also knew he had only moments before the venom brought death.

"What's the matter Henry? You look spooked. Is there a problem?"

Wisecroft allowed a slinked snicker to pass by his lips. Henry coughed and then coughed again. He grabbed at his chest as he felt the squeezing within the walls of his chest cavity. The door behind them opened and in walked Rene Duchard, who also snickered at the stricken Henry.

Wisecroft introduced the pair. "Oh, Henry, have you met Rene? This is Rene Duchard. Do you know him?"

"Hello Henry." Rene offered a handshake, and then pulled back. "You look peaked. Are you okay?"

"YOU!" Henry seethed. "You fucked me you son-of-a-bitch!"

The effect of the poison worsened, sending Henry to his knees. His vision was now tripling and he felt his nervous system beginning to seize in a paralyzing grip. His arms went numb and limp, followed by his legs and torso. Foam began oozing from the corners of his mouth. The pain shooting through his body was incredibly vivid. Death was approaching. Wisecroft lifted Henry's chin with his hand so he could look in his eyes.

"Do you really think you could've pulled this off Jasper? You stupid bastard. Rene's one of my most trusted men. Now he'll be my new vice president. Goodbye Henry."

Wisecroft released Henry's chin as the V.P. slumped forward. The poison took full effect and Henry entered darkness. The pain was fading as death descended upon him. Henry Jasper died thirty seconds later. It would be dismissed as a heart attack.

Wisecroft picked up the phone and called medical personnel within the White House. He then called his number one advisor's desk and gave him an order.

"Gather up the Jasper sex offenders in Vermont and send them to The Brick. Kick the rest of the family out of the house. Do it today."

"Yessir. Consider it done."

Henry Jasper had played with fire and lost.

V.P. Dies in White House

AP- Vice President Henry Jasper has died. Jasper was stricken with an apparent heart attack while in a cabinet meeting with President Wisecroft and the cabinet members themselves.

Jasper was about to present the president with an award for outstanding service when he collapsed. 9-1-1 officials inside the White House responded, but Jasper was pronounced dead at the scene after the paramedics worked on him for an hour.

Jasper 67, was Wisecroft's V.P. since his election victory in 2044.

President Wisecroft mourned the loss of Jasper and promised to speak at his funeral in a few days.

More details will be shared pending the release the autopsy and lab reports.

Henry Jasper, a widower, leaves behind two kids and many other family members. Funeral arrangements are pending.

A DESPERATE PURSUIT

The green truck moved as fast as lightening, or so it seemed to Rachel. She had pulled onto 127 and raced north at a smooth ninety miles per hour trying to catch up with the train. The radio station that covered the train routes to The Brick said nothing about the incident involving the truck that Rachel and Steven had parked on the track. Of course, it was only thirty minutes earlier, so it was still quite fresh and deep in a wooded area. Regardless, Rachel had to try to catch the train that carried Matt to the large prison in Northern Michigan. It was only a matter of minutes before 127 merged into I-75, still headed north. The train had a thirty-minute jump on Rachel, making catching it before it reached the Mackinaw Bridge virtually impossible. She felt she needed to try anyway.

The skies opened up and the rain came down, complicating matters dramatically. She held at a solid eighty MPH, but knew it was too slow. If she had increased her

409

speed any further, it would undoubtedly result in a huge crash. Her being injured or killed wouldn't help Matt.

The thoughts began to flow through her nearly defeated mind as she thought about the time the two had spent together through the years along with all the good times she'd miss if she didn't rescue him.

"Lord I miss him. The best thing that ever came along in my life is getting away from me. I can't bear life without Matt. I want to have babies with him and raise a family and be in love. I want to walk the beaches and feel the warm sand between our toes as we laugh with each other. He's my whole life. He's my being, my soul mate and my confidant. There's no other man in this world that could come close to my Matt. What would I do without him? I can't imagine my life alone."

The tears ran down Rachel's face and spilled in her lap as she drove. She couldn't believe the laws that were passed which ruined families and marriages. The government appeared to no longer care about the welfare of the spouses or children of the offenders.

"The point," Rachel thought, "was to protect the children."

The point had been missed, at least according to her. For many around the country, The Brick was doing exactly

410

what it should do: Shield and protect the public from the vermin walking the streets. Rachel's mind wandered back to Matt. She picked up the pistol on the seat next to her and brought it to her temple.

Ready...Aim...

"*I'm trying to save you my love. I don't know if I can do it. The train might be too fast and determined for me to catch it. The laws, rules and fear may also be too fast for me to catch. I've worked hard at this, seen people die and still it's still not enough. I've given, but the system continues to take. I've sacrificed, but this government wants more. I've bent, but the country wants a broken back.*

If I can get you out, I will Matt. If I can rescue you, I will. I've given my all, but I have no more in the tank. Somehow, the thought of you keeps me going. I'm tired, I'm hungry and I'm scared. Sal's dead, but so is Steven. He didn't even have a chance to fight. She shot him in the back like a coward. She snuck up behind him and gave him no opportunity to face her down. She died shot in the back too. It was an eye-for-an-eye, she lived by the sword and also died by it.

What will we do apart Matt? How can I live my life without your touch, your caress and your skin next to mine?

411

How can I live my life without making love to you again? I need your warmth, hugs, kisses, and love. I need you to wash my naked body with a soapy cloth when I bathe. I want to kiss you on the forehead when you're sick. I want to feel your presence. I can't live without you."

...misfire.

Rachel put the gun back down on the seat. She had one last run in her and pushed the pedal down. Against time and all odds, Rachel raced toward the Mackinaw Bridge as fast as she could safely travel in the torrential downpour. She knew it was almost hopeless, but hopeless didn't mean over. She weaved in and out of traffic, fishtailing and praying that the police wouldn't spot her. If they did, they'd attempt to pull her over for sure. She decided ahead of time she wouldn't stop driving. It would have to be a race to the finish line. She prayed she'd be in time.

She had reached Indian River and knew she was very close. She grabbed an old decrepit map off the floor of the truck and looked it over while driving. It was only about forty-five minutes before she'd reach the bridge. She upped the speed another five MPH, hoping she was at least even with the train, which was running parallel but still a good two miles

412

to her right. She couldn't see it but hoped against all hope that she was fast enough.

*

Horns blew and metal screeched as the train pulled into Mackinaw City. Matt, Mary and the rest of the travelers felt the momentum of the train slow to an eventual stop. Matt hadn't known that it was Rachel and Steven who had caused the train to rock so violently earlier, but he suspected Rachel, at least. Why else would there be such a violent shaking in the car? When the train came to a complete stop, he intended to ask the first guard he saw. He wasn't sure he'd get an answer, but he'd try the best he could.

As the guards made their way along the side of the train unlocking boxcars, Matt and Mary moved to the front of the door so they could exit quickly and ask questions. It did no good, however, as the guard that opened their car said nothing when asked. Matt and Mary looked up after exiting the train and saw the huge span of the Mackinaw Bridge before them. The train had reached the end of the line and so had the two brick-bound offenders. The buses that took the offenders over the bridge waited in a line-up just outside the toll entrance of the bridge. There appeared to be regular traffic in two of the three lanes that crossed the awesome

413

structure, so there must have been either visitation, people who worked outside of The Brick, or people using the U.P. as a cut across to Wisconsin. As Matt had never been to the U.P., he had no idea what the traffic signified. He and Mary looked at each other, shrugged and headed for the bus assigned to them by the guard. They both saw through the rain that The Brick extended to their left as far as their eyes could see. It was an incredible scene. To the right, they couldn't see much, as the city and traffic blocked the view. Then they looked straight ahead and walked onto the bus.

The entrance into The Brick was nigh.

*

Rachel raced against time trying to catch up to the train. She finally spotted it pulling into Mackinaw City as she raced toward the depot. She was down to only minutes before Matt would cross the bridge and enter the facility. She had to act fast. Rachel pulled off the road next to the depot and ran toward the train. She was stopped some fifty yards short as the guards allowed nobody from the public entrance into the depot. As she stood at the yellow gate watching closely, she spotted Matt walking in a line toward buses that were apparently waiting to haul the people over the bridge. She screamed at the top of her lungs.

"MATT! MATTHEW LYONS! MATT!"

"He can't hear you lady," the guard blurted. "It's too noisy and they're too far away. If you want to say goodbye, you better beat the bus across the bridge and wait near the entrance of The Brick. Once they cross, its right in and that's it."

Rachel took the advice and ran back to her vehicle. She noticed that Matt had stepped onto bus # 8 and knew she'd better hurry if she wanted to help him. Her plan was to run the bus into the rail on the bridge and use whatever means were necessary to spring her man. She peeled out with a noisy screech, prompting the guard to get on his radio and warn of an approaching green truck that might be dangerous. Rachel, not caring about anything other than her focus, screeched forward in a desperate and determined final attempt. Her facial expression changed from one of sadness to that of a nasty leer. Her hair was now pulled back in a curly snarl behind her head, a rubber band barely keeping it in place. Sweat poured from her forehead, and she felt heat in her chest and armpits. Her heart raced at one hundred and fifty beats per minute. *Thump, thump, thump, thump.* She refused to be stopped. Her breathing was heavy and tight while her hands shook on the steering wheel. Her eyes were sore and red. She was a scary sight indeed.

*

Matt and Mary stepped onto the bus and within moments, they were on their way. It was some fifty yards or so to the entrance of the bridge, followed by another six miles to The Brick's entrance. On the other side of the bridge, their futures awaited. They sat together on the bus and held hands. Matt looked out his window, hoping against final hope that he'd see Rachel, but he was disappointed. She wasn't in sight. There were three buses total taking offenders across. Matt's bus was in the rear. As the vehicle reached the peak of the bridge, he saw more of The Brick out his left window. It stretched along the Upper Peninsula as far as the eye could see. The wall was only fifteen or so feet high, but it was enough so that you couldn't miss it. He looked down at the traffic to his left and saw a green truck racing up next to them fast. It had been raining and the road was slick. He hoped the vehicle could keep itself straight, as it was fishtailing left and right. As he studied the reckless truck, it came close enough for him to see the driver. His mouth dropped open as Rachel herself was driving. He grabbed Mary by the shoulder and pointed out the window.

"It's Rachel! She's trying to rescue me."

Mary smiled slightly and watched the green truck along with Matt. As Matt looked down, the truck was close

416

enough to see clearly. Their eyes met. Rachel smiled at her man and he smiled back in return. It was only a three-second period, but was enough to feel that magical electricity between them. Mary watched cautiously, trying to smile through a frozen mouth. Suddenly the eye contact was broken as a sheer of wind caught Rachel's truck.

*

Summer Breeze…

Rachel was struggling with the high winds and slick highway as she obsessively chased the bus Matt was riding in. She looked up at the #8 bus and saw Matt, who was watching in return. Their eyes met and Rachel started tearing. She stepped on the gas in an effort to get ahead of the bus and cut it off. It had to be a careful maneuver, as to get too reckless could result in one or both vehicles going over the rail and plummeting to their sure deaths.

It wasn't only the wind that caught her truck.

Just as Rachel was about to make her move, the buses turned the tables on her, with the middle bus pulling into her lane and slowing. Rachel almost had to lock the brakes as the buses were now taking up both lanes in front of her. She couldn't pass on the left because traffic was too thick. In her rearview mirror, she saw the faint lights of a police cruiser. It

417

was catching up quickly. Matt and Mary had shifted to the rear of the bus, watching from the back window. Rachel looked up and met her man's eyes again. She desperately wanted to rescue him, but the buses were prepared for it. They had taken precautions to stymie her attempt. The guard at the depot had put a wrench in Rachel's plan.

As the bridge angled downward, Rachel knew her attempt to rescue Matt was in serious peril. She began crying very hard and smacking her fist on the steering wheel with frustration and anger. She continued on the tail of the bus as the police cruiser caught up with her. She could hear the siren and the loudspeaker as the officer ordered her off the road.

"PULL OVER IMMEDIATELY. YOU ARE IN VIOLATION OF THE LAW. PULL YOUR VEHICLE OVER NOW."

Ignoring the cruiser, the bridge ended. The buses went left. Rachel was going to continue following, but was met by a roadblock as soon as the buses passed. Six cruisers closed the opening, forcing Rachel's truck to the right. She drove just beyond the block, jumped into the grassy median, stopped the truck and jumped out. She ran for the entrance to The Brick as fast as she could.

...makes me feel fine...

Bus #8 pulled up to the entrance of The Brick. Matt and Mary were watching as Rachel was forced right, away from the buses. They watched as she drove into the grass, jumped out of the green truck and ran. The police were right behind her. She was fifty yards from the entrance when she completely ran out of gas and the cops finally tackled her. She fought, kicked, and scratched, but there were too many officers. She ran out of air, struggled for breath and was violently cuffed. She felt the knee of one of the officers pressing into her temple, pushing her face into the thick muck that was under her. She tried to yell, but nothing but a scant murmur came out. Matt watched Rachel being dragged away by the police. He turned his head down and wept. Mary gripped his hand tightly as the bus stopped at the entrance. Rachel turned to look, but Matt had turned back toward the entrance, succumbing to the reality set before him.

"LET'S GO! EVERYONE OUT! YOU'RE HOME." The guard's monotone echoed through the bus, along with each and every passenger's soul.

"Well Matt, here we are. We have to get off the bus." Mary pulled at Matt's hand with a gentle tug. Matt's reluctance was quickly replaced with acquiescence.

419

Matt reluctantly turned from the back of the bus and walked with Mary toward the new life that lay directly ahead. She held his hand tightly as they exited the bus and saw the entrance to The Brick. When they looked to the left, they saw the brick that was dedicated by President Wisecroft. Above the dedication were hundreds off dolls, teddy bears, plaques and other things hanging from The Brick. Each item had a name on it, most assuredly the name of a child who was the victim of a sexual assault or some other offense relevant to a sex offender. It was an awesome sight as the appendages stretched as far and out of sight. It was obvious that a "sick as hell of it" society had made their presence felt.

The walkway was closed off on each side with a large tarp. Matt and Mary walked up the small platform together. No guards spoke to them, telling them not to hold hands. It was at this point that Matt knew they no longer cared, as their fates inside The Brick were all but sealed.

They reached the front of the line, had their tattoos scanned for identification, waited for the guard to log them into a computer by running a scanner over their tattoos, identifying them, and in they went. They went through a small, normal sized door. When the whole group was inside, the door slammed shut behind them. Two guards on the inside pointed them down a ramp that was built over a synthetic moat that was fifty feet wide by five hundred feet long. When they reached the end of the ramp and everyone was inside, the gate was closed behind them. Matt and Mary were officially inside The Brick: Forever.

*

As hard as she tried and as much as she gave of herself, Rachel felt like a complete failure in her effort to rescue her only true love. The truth was that she did everything she could, but it was way too much to expect from anybody. The police had caught her, questioned her, and let her go. She wasn't considered a threat and they believed her story of trying to rescue her husband. Funny enough, she was never questioned about Steven, Sal or the man's deaths. It was apparent that they were considered obsolete and dismissed as no great loss. They found the bodies of Sal, Steven and the man in the green truck. The scene matched up exactly with Rachel's story. They believed that Sal had instigated the entire situation. As far as stopping the train, they could do nothing because the train was never actually hijacked. It was a failed effort and was brushed off by the police. Rachel was set free. Free to the world, but not to her mind.

Rachel wanted to die. She felt like a failure, got away with an attempted hijacking and missed her husband terribly.

She knew that the only way she could find him was to commit a sex crime and be thrown into The Brick herself but she wasn't that type of woman. She would never hurt another to get what she wanted. It was to be a long hard road for the normally happy woman. She had many pieces to put back together and she had a long haul back to upstate New York and her home, which waited for her return. The trauma of everything that she'd seen and heard was taking their toll on her mentally. Those scenes weren't for the squeamish or faint-hearted. While Rachel was neither of those things, it still hurt in her mind. She heard about the destruction of the underground warehouse in Tinley Park and it broke her heart. Those people, especially James Rogers, were simply trying to give refuge to a people that were persecuted by the Wisecroft Administration. It was just another in a long line of depressing events.

Rachel went home to New York to try to sort all of the events out in her mind. It was to be a long hard road back to "normalcy" as she would find out. The familiarity of home may have been of some help to the now less-than-fit woman. She'd lost thirty pounds, which contributed to a gaunt look. She'd started her journey at one hundred and forty-five pounds and returned home at one fifteen. Her hair, which used to shine with the gleam of youth, was now dull and flat. Her face, usually a bright red-cheeked natural beauty, had gone pale. Her stomach hurt and her heart raced for no reason whatsoever. The depression, anxiety and post-traumatic stress were taking over. If the woman were to regain her health, she'd need help.

The police confiscated the pistol that she pointed at her head, so Rachel didn't have the means to shoot herself. She did, however, have knives, which could do the job all the same. On more than one occasion, she'd stand in front of the mirror contemplating whether to slice her wrists or her throat. She never gained the gumption to do either, so she simply cut herself. The bleeding and pain seemed to help relieve the stress that was trapped inside her, if only for a short time.

It was in her darkest moment that help finally arrived.

...Rolling through the conflict in my mind.

ABSENCE DIMINISHES
MEDIOCRE PASSIONS AND
INCREASES GREAT ONES, AS THE
WIND EXTINGUISHES CANDLES
AND FANS FIRES.

-Francois De La Rochefoucauld

WISECROFT REIGNS

Now that Henry Jasper was dead, it appeared that nothing could stop the unquestionably tyrannical President Wisecroft. Following Henry's funeral, Wisecroft quickly named Rene Duchard the new Vice President, again breaking the tradition of the United States Government. There was no arguing, as the representatives in the House and Senate knew of the president's exploits. None of them wanted to end up six-feet under. So far, a cabinet member and a vice president had died under the president's watch. Many believed (secretly) that Jasper was yet another victim of Wisecroft's power trip.

Following his naming of Duchard as V.P., Wisecroft continued his stumping for an elimination of presidential term limits. A few more days and a few more greased palms finally did the job. Before the year was over, the lawmakers would enact the new amendment. Wisecroft would be free to rule like a Pope until death. Duchard was also pleased, knowing he had security for life. He was very loyal to Wisecroft and would never try to stop what he thought were great ideas coming from his administration. He also agreed that an elimination (albeit slow) of the middle and lower classes was paramount to the success of the country. Again, not many Americans paid attention, as the only things that mattered to them were food, a house and a general sense of security.

While it would take a few years to destroy the obsolete, the middle and lower class citizens would be powerless to stop it. They had already been in the process of disarmament, as Wisecroft had taken a page from the Adolph Hitler book. A society that was unarmed was harmless to raise Hell in the way of resistance, thus opening the door for the leadership to run roughshod over the people. Wisecroft was also taking control of the internet, severely limiting what people could watch and read. Pornography was eliminated, the offenders bricked, and most of the main U.S. jobs shipped offshore.

China, Russia, North Korea and other important countries were ecstatic; as they would see their economies flourish with the U.S. shipment of jobs to these overseas suppliers. Wisecroft took a slightly different approach than, say North Korea, in that he didn't completely shut the country off from the world. He also did the U.S.A. a slight favor by keeping them mostly uninvolved in other countries conflicts.

428

It was a new and exciting (for the rich) time in the still quite powerful country.

Soon the poor people found themselves drafted into the armed services in huge numbers. The middle-class weren't far behind. The president would eventually adopt a policy where all Americans at eighteen-years-old with parents earning less than $100,000 per household had to serve at least eight years of military service. He would also raise taxes to a ridiculous level for the middle and lower class, making it virtually impossible to keep up with the rising price of being obsolete. The IRS would then swoop in and take their piece of the pie and jail the non-compliant filers. In a short time, the middle class would be re-classified as lower class. Beyond lower class would be prison, deportation if foreign, and whatever Wisecroft could do to get rid of them, not short of having them "eliminated" from society. Although the process was slow, it was moving along. The American people remained oblivious. Within the next five years, it would raise many eyebrows. Within ten years, it would be obvious. The people were being duped, and would be eliminated from "existence" as it became necessary.

Some people, as they figured out what was going on, tried to march on D.C., but were always met with an impenetrable amount of resistance. The armies didn't use rubber bullets either, so the dead would lie in the street until the caretakers could sort them out. Soon, American obsoletes stopped trying to protest, as they knew death would be the sure result of their rabble-rousing. Wisecroft had a firm chokehold on the country and the people.

It was a new America, and the lawmakers, Senators and other V.I.P.'s also knew it. Resistance was futile and deadly. The writing was on the wall and Wisecroft had garnered enough power to do anything he pleased. He had the Army, Navy, Air Force and Marines all behind him, as they wouldn't ever disobey the president. Trying to overthrow Wisecroft wouldn't work. The rich were in charge of these armed factions and they were behind the president one hundred percent.

The lawmakers voted in just about any law Wisecroft saw fit to have passed. People were still committing sex crimes, but were shipped off to The Brick based on an allegation, bypassing the court system altogether. Laws *against* free press, free speech, freedom of expression and other formerly constitutional rights were passed. It didn't affect the rich as much as it did the obsolete, as the rich were much like Wisecroft in that they did as they pleased, never worrying about their place within society. The rich enjoyed living in the lap of luxury. The obsolete people who so much as uttered a word condemning Wisecroft were quickly and violently dealt with, resulting in imprisonment or at worst, death. The president kept that copy of *Mein Kampf* on his desk, reading it repeatedly and accepting 1930's and 40's Germany as the correct political and ideological techniques. He concluded that while Hitler was extremely smart, he failed to do the job appropriately. Wisecroft considered himself much more intelligent than Hitler and *definitely not insane*. Therefore, he'd use the same techniques with success. With great power comes great responsibility, and the president thought that he was above all the great leaders in history. He began wearing a military uniform to show off his might. He owned the country, in his mind.

Wisecroft organized military parades right down the streets in the middle of Washington D.C. He stood on a perch just as other dictators had done in other countries and watched the processions pass. Bombs, missiles and guns were shown off and the people of D.C. were forced to watch the proceedings, whether on the sidewalks or on their TV's. All this as the president saluted his troops and generals. It reeked of third-world hypocrisy.

The power of the people was torn from their grips. The powers of the Executive Branch of government to keep checks and balances on the president were dead. Congress and the House were in Wisecroft's back pocket. The members were also all millionaires, as the handouts, greased palms and favors were more prevalent and important than a wise decision. Wisecroft knew that a fat pocketbook was the key to his success, and he kept the money rolling in. Having the richest people in the United States on his side was the true secret of his continued success. Money equaled power and Wisecroft knew it. He had effectively created problems, had speeches about them and then solved them, thus fooling the masses. Now that it was too late for American people to do anything about his methods, they could only sit and take it. The American people had waited too long to express their dissent for such atrocities.

*

Rene Duchard led the band of strong-arms who took umbrage with any disagreement against Wisecroft. The large gang became known as the "Equalizers" as their reputation for bloody violence, public displays of strength and warnings were heard loud and clear throughout the country. The gang, which would've made Sal Parker proud, consisted of the very toughest people that Duchard knew. Some of the members had been relegated to a life in prison, but were given new life because of their deliberate ability to spread mayhem and stand down to absolutely no one. When the group reached 100,000 strong throughout the country, Duchard, through Wisecroft, went forward with another round of disarming the country.

Anyone caught with firearms was immediately arrested and thrown in prison. Arsonists, murderers, home breakers and other criminals were relegated to prisons. Since the building of The Brick, the prisons had plenty of room. The only option for prisoners who reached the end of their sentences was the armed forces, more prison or "elimination."

Elimination of the obsolete was another new law that wasn't passed through Congress, but through the Wisecroft agenda. It involved the mass murdering of anyone considered obsolete who wouldn't go into the armed forces or left prison and didn't report to the armed services. Once you were caught, you were out of options, as Wisecroft wanted to eventually rid the country of the obsolete. By running away or hiding, you were no longer trusted that you would do as inculcated. The executions took place on Saturdays around the country. It was yet another step in the systematic elimination of the middle and lower class.

As per the original plan, the disarming of all Americans kept any serious demonstrations at a minimum. Wisecroft was giggling all the while, figuring everything was going well. In the meantime, more offenders were offending, keeping the trains, F.E.M.A. facilities and The Brick strongly stocked. His new V.P., Rene Duchard was doing his part to keep the citizens wrestled to the ground. The rich citizens of the U.S. were having a grand old time, living in the lap of

luxury while everyone else (Chinese, Japanese, Korean, etc.)
did the grunt work. The countries were very happy though, as
they saw major boasts in their economical statuses.

*

The obsolete citizens would soon be feeling the
pressure from Wisecroft's regime, as they would no longer be
free in the traditional sense. For instance, the police, along
with Duchard's groups, walked into anyone's house at any
time and for any reason. It was much like the time when the
offenders were collected, but now there was a different reason
for the infiltration of freedom. The police took guns, arrested
the homeowners who had guns, and arrested anyone else who
hadn't met their extremely overbearing tax burdens. It was
shocking to the middle and lower classers who had no idea
that the extent of Wisecroft's plan was to have them
"exterminated" in different types of ways. The upper echelon
of society not only had little idea of what was going on in
these people's lives, but they didn't care either, as long as their
comfort levels weren't compromised. Oh, they saw things on
TV or heard them on the radio, but quickly dismissed the
atrocities as a necessary evil in light of the changing landscape
of the country.

The rich continued to spend, spend, spend; keeping the economy moving briskly throughout the U.S. They soon considered themselves the "cogs" that turned the machine and couldn't understand why it hadn't been done much sooner.

Wisecroft regularly had upper class guests at White House dinners and other functions. He made sure to hob-nob with the richest among the rich, insuring his future as the president of the United States; a president who would rule without term limits. The people that were invited as guests of the president never questioned his techniques. It, for them, was better to stay ignorant of the behind the scenes work. Besides, they didn't want to lose the president's favor. Being friends with the most powerful man in the country was a status symbol along with being advantageous in the lining up of offshore work. The rich business owners were able to keep a small but well-paid staff who oversaw the offshore work. Sending a man or two to China to make sure everything was going well was worth the $150,000-per-year salary the employees earned. The underlings were always precise and careful to please their bosses, in fear of being fired, losing the big salary, and falling to middle or lower class status. That would mean jail, armed services and an overall huge drop in their quality of life. Nobody wanted that: It was for the obsolete only. A few met that fate through overbearing bosses, but it was rare.

As long as life continued the way it was, the rich were happy and unassuming.

*

Duchard began spending more and more time with the president. Whether it was luncheons, meetings, diplomatic visits or hosting V.I.P.'s., Duchard was always at Wisecroft's side. The two were virtually inseparable. Duchard had come to Wisecroft weeks earlier with Henry's plan to kill him. Wisecroft instructed Duchard to carry out the plan with Henry until the fatal day at the cabinet meeting. The president felt that he owed Duchard for having his back and rewarded him handsomely with the Vice Presidency, the job as head of the goon squad running around the country enacting Wisecroft's laws, and anything else he wanted. Duchard had a different woman to sleep with each night. He also enjoyed marijuana, and was given his own personal supply of the plant. Duchard had it made and knew it. One man's plot was another man's riches. By turning the tables on Jasper, Duchard became a very rich man.

THE BRICK II

It wasn't the Garden of Eden. It wasn't Utopia. It wasn't even Detroit. It was simply a very large plot of land reserved for the worst of the worst, in society's eyes. That wasn't to say it was ugly; on the contrary, it was one of the most beautiful spots in the entire United States. To Matt, it was unfortunate that they'd deprive the public of such beauty, but that was the Wisecroft Law: A complete separation of the offenders and the public: A public that was undergoing their own struggles.

As Matt and Mary entered their new domain, Matt was still reeling from watching Rachel caught, pinned and cuffed by the police while trying to rescue him. It was a sad sight and made him understand how much the woman loved him. Mary felt bad for Rachel, but deep down inside wanted Matt to be with her in the new world they called home. She figured he would calm and eventually get over his longing feeling. Mary was very careful to be sympathetic and understanding,

437

as cheering Rachel's failure would surely separate the two permanently and that she didn't want.

The pair, along with many other offenders, decided to walk along I-75 for a while, hoping to get a feel for the terrain and possibly find people or some semblance of living spaces. Other offenders walked to the west in hopes of finding the same. What surprised Matt and Mary the most was that there was actually traffic heading both north and south beside them. It didn't take five minutes of walking before a vehicle pulled up to the pair.

"Going somewhere in particular?" The driver of the car, a blue sedan, asked.

"Um, yeah I guess." Matt exclaimed. "I'm not quite sure where yet."

"Well hop in you two and we'll talk about it."

"Why should we trust you? How do we know you're not some kind of crazed murdering bastard?"

"Har. Me? A crazed murdering bastard? I'm an old tired man, and I'm here to help you. You can ride along with me and find a great place to live, or you can go on walking. It doesn't matter either way to me."

Mary, and then Matt, confident of his honesty, jumped into the backseat of the sedan and the driver took off. He drove up I-75 for a short spell before pulling into a rest stop. He jumped out of the car and asked the two to do the same.

Nervously, Matt got out, signaling Mary to stay in the car. He wanted to see if any funny business was going on before taking any further steps forward. The driver asked Matt why Mary was staying in the vehicle.

"Because I'm not sure I completely trust you yet. You haven't even told me your name."

"The names Thompson, Ed Thompson. I'm a former third tier sex offender on the outside, but here I'm just Ed. I'm sixty-two years old and now I'm free. Here, I'm no longer an offender. And you?"

Ed Thompson carried a substantial waistline and a cherry reddened nose. Matt thought him to be an alcoholic, while Mary saw him as a cute old-timer

"I'm Matt and that's Mary. We're offenders too. We just arrived a few minutes ago."

"I know you just got here. Moreover, as for the offender label? Not anymore Matt and Mary. Here, you're regular citizens of the United Peninsula."

Confused, Matt attempted to correct Ed. "You mean the Upper Peninsula."

"No. I mean the United Peninsula. That's the new name for it. It's our own personal country."

Matt nodded, cracked a small smile and asked Ed why they stopped at the rest area. They'd only been in the car for a few short minutes.

"Because we need to get our bearings straight." Ed nodded. "I need to know where you want to go and I'll get you there. I'm your cabbie! A few of us do this to help out the newbies."

Ed smiled wide as his red nose beamed with the chilled breeze that bit at his skin. He pulled two jackets out of his trunk, handed them to the pair and then went into the car, pulling two roadmaps from his glove box. He smiled at Mary and told her it was okay to get out of the car. Matt leaned in and nodded, giving Mary the trust she needed. They put on the jackets, significantly cutting the chill. Mary stood close to Matt.

"Okay kids. Here's two halves of the United Peninsula. We have the Eastern half and the Western half. What's your pleasure?"

"Ed. We have nothing to give you to pay for the ride. How do you get gas?"

"Oh, don't worry about that. I'm your tour guide, real estate consultant and cabbie. When we reach your final destination, I get to pick one item from the dwelling you'll be living in. It's no biggie. I promise not to put the hurt on you. There's money up here, but it's hard to find. We trade items for gas. If we have money, it makes it a lot easier. I happen to have money and the new gas prices are a dime a gallon. Once a month, the United States of Wisecroft sends in gas trucks to replenish us. It's all privatized on the outside; bought and paid for, if you will. The same goes for food and water. It's all supplied to us. We just run the show on the inside."

"Alright. That sounds good. Are there any places you can suggest we live? By the way, how long have you been here?"

"I was one of the first groups. I've been here for a while and have learned the laws of the land. I'll help you with all that as we travel. Now, where do you want to live? The only places I won't suggest are the big cities. That's where the meanest of the former offenders have congregated. Some eggs are too bad to reform. Most people are nice and mellow though. Name a city or town and we'll talk."

"Escanaba?" Matt asked.

"Good choice. It's a nice quaint town out of the way and has good people living there. There's lots of available housing too. Okay, hop in you two. We're headed for Escanaba."

The three hopped into the shiny blue sedan and hit the road. Ed followed 123 east until he reached Highway 57. From there, he spilled onto Route 2, which would take them to the Escanaba area. As they headed west along 2, Matt and Mary could see the wall and barbed wire of The Brick. This time, they were looking at it from the inside. As they drove on and approached Naubinway, Matt asked about the large building that appeared to be just on the outside of The Brick.

"Power grid and a guard shack." Ed explained. "That's where we get our power supplied and the guards watch the walls. There are twelve that surround the entire U.P., and the main grids are on Drummond Island, just east of where you entered. It's a huge system put together a lot better than I ever thought it'd be."

The pair nodded and on they traveled. The terrain was beautiful, as the cliffs and lakes surrounding the areas they drove by were breathtaking. It was a striking land, one of which Matt and Mary were now a permanent part of forever. Mary was feeling as contented as she could under very tough circumstances while Matt still thought about Rachel every fifteen seconds or so. It would take a very long time for him to let Rachel go, if ever. Mary knew this and continued to play it smart, giving Matt all the room he needed. They were both patient people, so a year or two of Matt in mourning was fine with her.

"Okay folks, time to stop."

"Why?" Matt asked quizzically.

"It's sunset. We have a curfew of sunset through dawn until we get better organized. We're only one quarter of what it'll eventually be here, population-wise. We don't have many police patrols yet. We have a few cops, but not enough. It'll take time to fill in the cities, hospitals and houses up here. We're taking it slow; at least the ones of us who actually behave."

Ed handed Matt a pamphlet that underlined most of the basic rules of the day. He would go over it and read it extensively over the next day or two. The cabbie opened the trunk and pulled out a mattress. He had a compressor and filled it with air. The three lay out under the chilly U.P. air and covered with a thick comforter. The trek would continue the next morning.

*

Sitting at home with a blank face and frequent tears rolling down her face, Rachel stared out the picture window. She had three dogs, which the neighbors kindly watched over while she was gone to Idaho, Montana, Tinley Park, and finally The Brick. The canines did the best they could to cheer up their listless mother, but she wouldn't budge. Everything was a test of will: Feeding them, taking a shower, even sleeping. The depression, along with anxiety and plenty of anger was enveloping her. She hoped and prayed it would let up, but it was persistent in its indignation. With the deep emotional scars she now wore, it would have to eventually result in her seeing a doctor for help, if she could get off the couch long enough to do such a monumental task.

She had just arrived home, as three days earlier she was trying as hard as she possibly could to rescue Matt in Northern Michigan. It was a whirlwind of stress and trauma as she was apprehended in Mackinaw City, questioned, and then taken immediately on bus to Detroit, where she was extensively questioned again. Satisfied with her love story, the F.B.I. placed her on a plane bound for her hometown. She was extremely tired and mentally drained. The thoughts of what had happened began to fill her mind.

Steven was dead, Sal was killed right in front of her and a man with a green truck had his throat slashed. It was a Holy Hell of bad memories for the typically mild-mannered woman. The worst of it, however, was the loss of her beloved Matt. He was gone and she wasn't sure if he'd ever make it back. It appeared doubtful, as she watched the news, read the internet and saw exactly what President Wisecroft had done and would do to the country in which she lived. The depression was squeezing at her, and she wasn't sure what the result of such a horrible feeling would encompass. Would it be suicide, which she had been seriously contemplating, or just lying on her couch wasting away into a shell of her former self?

After a trip to her local doctor, Rachel was prescribed Prozac for the depression and Tranzine for the persistent anxiety that complimented the dreadful memories of those fateful and telling days in her life. She promised herself she'd take the meds as directed and try to get better. It wasn't three days before the entire shipment went down the toilet in one fell flush. Rachel was sinking and didn't care. She had no strength, felt anxious *all the time* and had to make extreme efforts to move from her living room couch to her bed at night. Feeding and watering the dogs, along with opening the door for them were the only real chores she completed. Her house was getting dusty, her carpet hairy from the dogs and her dishes piled up. It wasn't until her mother came for a visit that she realized how bad it was getting.

*

Rachel's mother arrived on a Sunday. She finally had made up her mind to check on her depressed daughter, despite her husband constantly telling her to relax, and made the long ride from Eastern New York. Rachel had called her only twice: Once to tell her she was home, and once to cry in the phone over her loss. Rachel's mom tried to convince her that being alive was a major accomplishment and that she should be proud of surviving the fiasco.

445

Opening the door and seeing her daughter in such a way broke her heart. She had matted hair, a dirty face and a very sad look permeating from her expression. Rachel was just as surprised to see her mom and rose to a sitting position on the couch.

"Rachel?"

"Mom?"

"What's going on in here Rachel? The house stinks, it's a mess, and you look like complete shit. How long since you've showered dear?"

Embarrassed, Rachel lied and said "yesterday", but her mom didn't buy it.

"Rachel. You smell bad and you have hair on your armpits. That's not you. You're usually very well groomed. What's the matter honey? Does it still hurt?"

The burst of tears shot out of Rachel's eyes as her mouth curled. Her mom walked over and embraced her tightly, stroking her hair as she held her. The smell that rose off Rachel's body was stiff and offensive. Her dogs tried to greet Rachel's mom, but she ordered them back as she held her little girl.

"It's going to be okay dear. I'm moving in for a while. I need to help you get back on your feet."

Rachel's mother did just that. Even though it was a monumental effort, she managed to get her daughter off the

446

couch and into the bath. She bathed and groomed her daughter, laundered her clothes, cleaned the house and did her dishes. She vacuumed, dusted and washed, bringing the house back to a "normal" state. She also took care of the dogs and most importantly, set up therapy sessions. She would take Rachel to rehabilitation as often as was needed until her girl perked back up. She coached and assured Rachel about losing Matt and guaranteed her that life would get better, despite all the losses. Rachel, earlier a woman on her deathbed, finally began to perk up after a few weeks. Although she was a long way from healed, it was a great start. Rachel's mom spent almost as much time as her daughter shedding tears, but knew she was the savior in her life. It was more of a happy weeping than anything else. Rachel's mom felt she did what she had to do to give her girl's life hope and confidence.

*

Matt, Mary and Ed arrived in the Escanaba area at midday and went about the task of finding an abandoned house to live in. The bonus was that since no banks or "government" had been set up, everything was free for the time being. They found a nice three bedroom, two and a half bath home sitting on the Days River in Brampton, Michigan.

It was cute, homey and satisfied both Matt and Mary, who at that point had decided to live in the same house.

As Rachel was struggling back in New York with the aftermath of everything that had happened in front of her very own eyes, Matt had had someone (Mary) with whom he could acclimate. Matt had gone through the worst experiences and was settling down. For Rachel, it was all uphill battle.

The house was a nice brick bi-level with a large upstairs along with a finished basement walkout. The lawn was a moderate size and woods surrounded them. The kitchen was quaint, while the living areas and bedrooms were roomy. There was also a spa type bathtub with the jets and all. Matt and Mary were very pleased.

"Great choice kids." Ed nodded. "I love it! This is a good part of the state. Nobody will bother you here."

Despite the roomy living space, the home was filthy. The family that had moved out of it left everything behind. The Government under Wisecroft paid all the homeowners handsomely and requested that they leave the essentials behind. Some elbow grease and a few adjustments would leave the home more than livable.

"Okay Ed. What do we owe you?"

Ed put a hand to his chin and began scrounging around the backyard and garage, looking for something suitable as payment. He settled on a walk-behind lawnmower sitting in

448

the corner of the garage. They shook on the deal and Ed left them.

"Okay kids. Be good and have a good life. Remember, you now live in the United Peninsula."

Matt and Mary waved and off Ed went. They turned and entered the house hand-in-hand. They were happy with their find but lots of work lay ahead. Matt figured that wasting any more time would be silly, so he rolled up his sleeves and got busy. Mary joined him in the happy effort. They both found that the United Peninsula, two days under their belts, was a wonderful place to live.

A few days later, the couple was pleased with their progress. They felt like they were free, even though The Brick loomed only some twenty miles to the Southeast. They promised each other never to visit the wall. They wanted to feel the artificial freedom they had with no-strings-attached.

They both wondered what uncertainties awaited the two *now* non-offenders. They figured themselves to be able to survive nicely while a society was established around them. These were only two of the thoughts that went through both of their minds as they continued the course of make their new home livable.

The flirting between the two became intense until the day came that they couldn't stand it any longer and made love. Mary stepped into the shower with Matt and hugged him from behind, reaching around to his front as she did so. There was no resistance as Matt turned around and the two engaged in a deep kiss. Mary still had her blouse, now soaked to the skin, on her body. Matt removed it slowly and sensually, exposing Mary's beautiful femininity to him. Matt picked Mary up and took her to the bed, still soaking wet. As he entered her, he felt the fireworks go off in his mind. Mary felt the same as her shrieks of delight echoed through the house.

It was a glorious coupling for both of them, although Matt thought about Rachel for a few minutes during and afterward. He didn't tell Mary of his distant longing, but she knew. She didn't ask and soon the feeling passed. Mary wasn't at all angry about Matt's thoughts, as she knew it was a normal reaction to losing a true love.

The pair made love day and night for weeks after their initial coupling. They settled down together for good, and a love connection was established.

*

With her mother's help, Rachel was slowly getting back into the swing of life. She had stopped laying on the couch with no hope, cutting herself and ignoring her duties as a human being. She was showing more enthusiasm, a better attitude and most importantly, taking baby steps in getting

450

over Matt. She could never completely forget him or let him go, but she tried to get a grip on moving forward with her life.

She was a young woman who could still marry and have children of her own if she so chose. It was too early to think about such things, but it was a definite possibility. Her mom was very careful not to pressure her or make her feel any more uncomfortable than she already did, especially about men. Rachel was taking her medication and going outside with her dogs. She kept herself cleaned up and began to eat a bit more. The stress had taken a great amount of weight off her and she needed the food. Even the coffee, which she always loved, but had lately ignored, tasted better. She was headed in the right direction. It was still early in her healing, so little frustrations could set her off. Her patient Mother listened intently, offered her advice and allowed Rachel to get her burdens out the best way she knew how without hurting herself or others. It was going to be a long road, but Rachel's mother hunkered down for the trip.

Under the circumstances, Rachel was doing as well as anyone could expect after losing her husband: A man who was her whole life.

TEN

YEARS

LATER

THE TYRANT STATE OF
NO-MERICA

As he woke up on a bright Saturday morning in the
White House, John Wisecroft reached for the remote control
and flipped on E-TV. He watched and he giggled. He saw it
and he laughed maniacally. The program was entertaining to
him in a most robust way. The maid came in and served him
and his still sleeping wife breakfast. She set the tray down on
the table. Breakfast consisted of oatmeal, eggs, toast and both
juice and coffee. There was a copy of the Washington Post,
New York Times and Los Angeles Times also taking up space
on the tray. Most of the news that the papers held were of the
local variety, or news about the country that was directly
governed by the White House. The lid had been firmly shut
on a free press in the U.S.A. Wisecroft always made sure the
"big three" newspapers, as he called them, were acting up to
snuff and following the rules set before them. There were
government officials working at every newspaper in the
country, reviewing and editing the content constantly.

Nothing questionable or anti-government would be released, or Wisecroft would see that heads rolled. Duchard also assisted in the filtering process.

*

What goes around...

The pair put their heads together and came up with even more laws. Besides the offenders being shipped to The Brick and disarming the country, the two decided that there would be no longer be alcohol allowed in the country. It was a new form of prohibition, that was, unless you were in the White House or very wealthy. It was another strategy to rid the country of the obsolete as it were. More laws followed, all tailored to hurt the "not-so-well-off" in the country. Food prices were raised dramatically, the cost of luxuries such as houses and cars went sky-high and a night out meant a month of savings for the average couple. Farmers were the only middle class citizens retained, as they needed to grow the food. The people that were used for such tasks as building skyscrapers, digging ditches and doing other manual labor were the ones that were plucked out of prisons, paid peanuts and sent back when the jobs were done. It reeked of slavery. The country had seemingly slipped back into the 1800's

456

fundamentally. It was exactly what Wisecroft wanted. The way he figured it, if Hitler, Stalin or other dictators had done their jobs correctly, they would have been unstoppable. He loved having his thumb on the people. It gave him a dose of power that he thirsted for since his days as governor in Texas. One of the ways in which he differed from other tyrannical leaders is that he actually took the advice of the important people around him. He felt it was very important to listen, but as always, he owned the bottom line. The final decision always rested on his desk at the end of the day.

The president traveled the world excessively; visiting every place he ever wanted to see. He gave his wife and children everything they wanted. He also visited The Brick at least once every three months, monitoring the upkeep and functioning ability of the facility. He left pleased each time. The people running the facility had made sure of that in fear of being severely punished for lacking in quality and operation standards. Wisecroft demanded, and was given, respect. Most everybody knew of his strong-arm tactics and wanted no part of it. If you treated the president well, he returned the favor ten-fold. If you messed with him, he punished you with purpose and intensity.

Wisecroft also enjoyed watching people being tortured and even killed. He demanded reports every week of people being humbled and murdered, as it gave him a higher sense of invincibility. The disturbing smiles he displayed while looking over the carnage was nerve-wracking even for Duchard, his right-hand man. Occasionally, Wisecroft even attended the punishment of the people, reveling in their pain and agony. Although it may have seemed sick to the people closest to him, Wisecroft knew that it garnered a level of respect not usually attained by a president. For Duchard, it was somewhat disturbing, but the fact that he was now comfortable beyond his wildest dreams kept him quiet. He could take some painful visuals in exchange for a comfortable lifestyle. He tried to talk with Wisecroft about his violent lifestyle. He was met with what he perceived to be logical explanations from the leader.

"I watch people being punished to gain respect. I don't necessarily enjoy watching people being beaten, tortured or even killed. As the leader of this country though, I have to show the people how serious I am about my regime. If anyone thought about doing anything to try to derail our plan, it's widely known that they could meet an awful end. Look at Henry Jasper. He thought he had the jump on us, but we proved to be too strong. He paid the ultimate price for trying to harm the plan. I'm tired of this country being a lazy, good-for-nothing land and I'm devoted to eliminating the riff-raff that makes it that way. If it's by violent means, then so be it.

Before too long, the citizens will realize how the ship is run and conform."

Duchard agreed with the president. He was proud of the fact that he'd been the one to put a wrench in Henry's plan, but allowed Wisecroft to take the credit for being smart enough to thwart the attack. It really didn't bother him, as the riches quickly straightened out his thinking. He listened to Wisecroft, learning a few pointers about tyranny as he did so.

"I keep my family comfortable. I keep my kids happy and my wife knows she has it made. I don't cheat on her and I'm still quite attentive. They know nothing of my business as president, nor should they. They simply live life to the fullest. Don't they deserve such luxuries and happiness? After all, they were terrorized years ago. It's my job to see that they don't ever have to face such humiliation again. I want to keep them happy and without fear. I will not waver in my efforts to keep them comfortable. It goes for you too Rene. You've been a loyal partner and I'll never forget that. You carry out my orders and never argue. I know sometimes it's hard to understand some of my motives, but that's what keeps it fresh."

The president's rationality was sound and helped Duchard move forward, trying to keep a positive attitude even in the throes of such violence. Duchard didn't have to deal with the viciousness of a flawed society. He simply sent out his goons to do it. It was a fair trade in his mind. It could've been made much worse having to go back to the so-so life he was leading in the Bahamas. It was a great place to vacation, but a lousy place to live. There was no money, no real artificial luxuries such as the digital exploits of the United States. It wasn't as special as people may have thought. He was in for the duration and dedicated himself one hundred percent to Wisecroft's cause.

*

The country continued on the "Wisecroft" course, which featured prejudice, slavery, wrongful imprisonment and brutality. People who had originally beaten and captured the offenders were now finding themselves the victims of an irrational idea.

As if to repeat the offender craze, people were yanked out of their houses and thrown in prisons. They were forced into military service that they wanted no part of, and they were humiliated into compliance. Some of the people realized they'd been duped and had to eat it like the offender did years earlier. The NRA was forcefully broken up, the media again had a rag put in its mouth and the country was turned on its ear. The people that had earlier helped Wisecroft reach his goals now had his back turned on them. No demonstrations, no letters to the president, nothing. It was no use trying to express your opinion because it no longer counted. All that counted was the Wisecroft agenda.

Innocent people were stripped of their property. Houses, cars and other goods went straight to the government. The people that resisted with too much vigor were placed on the "extinction" list to be shot at a time to be determined by the officials. While this was happening, Duchard sat with Wisecroft in the White House enjoying the scene. Citizens, even if armed, couldn't get within five miles of the building without being shot or arrested. The security was thick and relentless. The White House gates and fences were now outfitted with thickets of barbed wire. It was a severe change in scenery.

The countries personality was difficult to picture or fathom. Crying, wretching and sorrow again filled the streets of the U.S.A. The only people left to pick up the slack were the rich. They didn't pay any attention to anyone other than themselves. It was a cocky bunch who lived in mansions and had the money to afford the best in security and comfort. As these rich folks had dinner parties and get-togethers, the opinion was always the same; "It's a necessary evil." That seemed to be the riches catch phrase when it came to the antics permeating the country.

461

The United States was no longer the free, prosperous country it once was. Former presidents had to be rolling in their graves, ruing the day Wisecroft came on board. If there was a Hell on earth, the offenders and the obsolete had entered the heated gates without even knowing they were headed in that direction. The people, now awakened, could do nothing to stop it.

...Comes around.

*

As the morning continued, his wife finally awoke, bleary-eyed and hung over, as was the norm for her over the past five years. She looked up at the TV and moaned "again?" while slamming her face back into the pillow.

"I have to watch dear. It helps me to know that the people I hired are doing a good job."

"But every Saturday John? Don't you get tired of watching Execution-TV? It's disgusting."

John waved her off and paid attention to the TV. They lined up thirty men, women and children and shot them dead. They fell into a mass grave behind them. After that, they lined up thirty more. It went on like that every Saturday morning for three hours. The executions involved the middle and lower class obsolete citizens who weren't cutting their weight and

462

refused to conform. Wisecroft simply removed them from the picture. They were black people, white people, Hispanic, Japanese and so on. There were strong men who refused a life in the military who, along with their wife and kids, paid the ultimate price for their disobedience. The scenes were televised throughout America every single Saturday from 7-10 a.m. There were no other channels to choose from during that time span. Wisecroft wanted the people to see exactly what the penalty was for being "obsolete" and refusing to step in line with his laws.

*

The cities were getting rid of crime. The rich, long living in the suburban areas, poured back in and cleaned the towns up. Rarely did you see or hear of muggings, murder or rape. The gangs of the cities had been cleared out (executed, imprisoned or given military status) and there was a sense of safety among the elite. Of course, there was the occasional whacko who managed to get his or her hands on a gun and go nuts, killing a few people before being shot down in flames. It was a rare instance indeed.

*

The farmers ran the rural end of the country, planting and harvesting when the weather cooperated. They supplied the food that fed the rich Americans. They were, however, poorly paid and badly treated. The government officials would come in, take the goods that were needed and leave. The farmers themselves were off limits to the execution program and were protected by the government: Unless certain situations dictated action. If the crops weren't being taken care of, or if laziness was detected, the farmer was chastised and sometimes considered obsolete. They were usually given a warning or two. If they still did poorly or refused to conform, they, with their entire family, would be removed and executed. A replacement, assigned by the government, was placed in the farm and expected to do well.

As unhappy as the farmers were, they could do nothing to stem the tyrannical tide. The most they could do, as radical as it was, would be to pack up and live on the run. That was never the best idea, as the drones and nets were always at the ready to catch the runners; whoever they may be.

*

Canada and Mexico completely closed their borders to the USA, not allowing a mass exodus of *Americans* to infiltrate their countries. If the people seeking refuge were born in Canada or Mexico, they were allowed government immunity and entrance back into their respective countries. They felt bad but had to protect themselves from the American people who would slip in if allowed. The United States was considered a Fascist State and was therefore considered dangerous.

A lesson was learned when the United States when President Jimmy Carter allowed all Cubans who seeked refuge to come to America. Castro sent his criminals. Neither Canada nor Mexico wanted any part of a repeat.

Wisecroft never pleaded with them to open the gates, and many other European and Asian countries condemned him for such "acts" of atrocity in his own country. Wisecroft didn't care; he just went about his business of whistling Dixie. The same countries that condemned the USA stopped short of kicking the offshore jobs out, as it was too much of a boon to their local economies. Money spoke, as it always did.

*

The Brick was still welcoming offenders from around the country. The ones that were in hiding were rustled up and sent north. Other middle and lower class citizens, who were still committing rapes and assaults, earned a trip too. The classes were being eliminated, but there were still plenty to keep the railroads, F.E.M.A camps. Prisons and execution Saturdays busy. There would never be a complete lack of lower and middle-class people because Wisecroft hadn't yet figured out how to sterilize an entire population. He was working on it and had the determination to find out how he could do it.

There were no other countries willing to come in and attack the tyrannical country, as the military in the U.S.A was still quite formidable. Unlike the Russians and Americans in 1945 Germany, coming in and freeing the American people was a virtual impossibility. The country was surrounded by oceans and sat in the perfect spot to avoid such invasions. Canada and Mexico were simply too weak militarily to do anything.

*

Rene Duchard was policing the nation with an iron fist. After expressing doubt when he first took the job as V.P., he was now comfortable in his skin. He bought the president's plan hook, line and sinker, helping him to reason out the carnage and oppressive attitude. His goons pillaged and killed the innocent while leaving the upper-crust people alone. He was taking direct orders from Wisecroft and didn't flinch in carrying them out. If someone needed killing, then it would happen. The obsolete would try to reason with Duchard's men, but it didn't matter. The killing included children, women and even family pets.

*

It was a different nation from the one that had declared its independence from Britain almost three-hundred years earlier. Now Britain hated the U.S.A., as did most nations around the globe. People in the Middle East took great joy in watching the American people oppressed, as they had predicted it for many years.

The hate wasn't as intense as it had been nearly a century earlier when the U.S.A. seemed to have a habit of policing the globe. Now the United States kept its nose out of all other countries problems. The only country the U.S. dealt with were those who took the offshore work from the big executives of the day. The armies in the United States remained strong with the adoption of middle and lower class citizens knowing it was their only way to remain alive, and a part of the country they still loved.

Only some knew of the murders that were taking place around the country until Wisecroft decided to televise the executions. Now everyone knew and wanted no part of it. As frustrated and angry as the people would get, they could do nothing about the president's exploits. They were disarmed, dehumanized and taken for granted. Wisecroft had originally blamed the offenders for the country's economic ruin. After that, it was the lower 2/3 of the people squeezing the money. In both instances, he convinced *(through strong-arming)* Congress that the elimination of the obsoletes would save the country. As fanatical and over-the-top as Wisecroft was, his plan was working *economically*. That was all that mattered to the government. They had almost complete separation from the rest of the world and didn't have to listen to Canada, Mexico or any of the other angry nations if they didn't want to.

The UN in New York City was closed down and moved to Europe. Wisecroft had the Statue of Liberty taken down and thrown in the Hudson River. In Washington D.C., the Washington Monument, Lincoln Memorial, Jefferson Monument and other historical landmarks were removed and destroyed. History books began to be re-written with the changes reflecting what Wisecroft thought to be a "re-birth" of American ideals. History museums, such as the Smithsonian Institute and others around the country were re-developed to recognize only what Wisecroft wanted known. The brainwashing of the nation was in full swing and Wisecroft couldn't have been happier about it. His plan was going exactly as he'd hoped. He paid no attention to the downfall of other tyrannical or fascist societies, except for the fundamental points that worked. *Mein Kampf* was his instruction manual. He didn't once think his regime could be destroyed and anyone questioning his tactics paid the ultimate price with their lives.

Who was at fault for this radical change? The *people* of the United States of America. They sat on their hands until it began to affect *them*, but then it was too late. By the time they finally stood up off their couches and put a finger up, they found their voices were silent. They had no more guns, no more free speech and no more power. When elections were held, no one dared challenge Wisecroft, so he stood alone on the ballots. The rest of the Cabinet, Congress and Senate were all handpicked by the president. The days of general elections had long disappeared.

The people originally allowed Wisecroft to do his work, and now they paid the ultimate price. Had the people stood up at the beginning and recognized the president's ulterior motives, it could have been stopped. Now the middle and lower class was so weakened, it would be beyond impossible to change it back. The rich liked the way the country was being run and had no qualms. They were making their money and living comfortably in the cash that flowed to them by the bucket load. There was no such thing as "Trickle-down" economics, as the rich shared nothing except to pay the pennies for the work they sold offshore at dirt-cheap rates. It didn't matter if they had four-year-olds working in the sweatshops, as long as the work was done and they sold it to the other rich Americans, or to any other number of countries across the globe. Unions were also long gone. The law now read that if you tried to form a union, you'd risk jail or even death.

Where the American used to worry about being detained in foreign countries for trespassing or whatever ludicrous reason they came up with, the worm had turned. Foreigners now feared being detained in the onetime *land-of-the-free.* Many Americans who simply couldn't live in the oppressed society attempted escape to Europe or Asia. Some made it while many more did not. The drones and military that spotted escapists dealt with them by dropping bombs on the boat, or arresting them and having them executed for treason. It was an ugly America.

*

The United States now existed under a fascist ruler with tyrannical rules and laws. Wisecroft was cocky, arrogant and felt entitled. He had always been that way, only now he could flaunt in the face of a public that he believed wanted him. He felt that what he was doing was a Christian service to *his* people. Baptist was the only religion allowed in the U.S. Catholicism and other so-called "man-made" spiritual guidance's were outlawed. The only practice was that of the King James Bible and nothing more. It was a crime to shame, burn or otherwise destroy the King James Version of the Bible. Other books, especially those by literary heroes of yesteryear were destroyed. King, Salinger, Grisham and Stevenson to name only a few were all banished from America. Although the authors were long dead, it surely caused them to do somersaults in their graves.

*

Yes, the United States had changed and no one knew where it would go from here. From the years 2044 through to the present of 2061, Wisecroft had rule. It would continue until he either died or was murdered. Oh, there were plenty of poor people conspiring, planning and waiting for the day they could shoot him right between the eyes, but he was a tough President to locate. All people could do was keep their illegal guns cleaned, loaded and ready if ever the chance to change history reared its head.

It was only a matter of time. Napoléon, Hitler, Stalin, Mussolini and other had tried and failed. President John

Wisecroft never wavered in his dedication to his cause. The power that inebriated him was total and complete.

THE UNITED PENINSULA

Had the citizens of Wisecroft's tyranny known how good the people in the U.P. of Michigan had it, they may have done anything they could have to join them. Alas, the powers that were in charge never allowed contact from within The Brick, although notes did make it *into* The Brick from family and friends of people inside.

People tried sending notes over the wall to loved ones, even though they had no contact with them, no idea whatsoever where they resided in the U.P. or even if they were alive or dead. It was all a wild guess. The notes that did make it were either washed out in the rain or snow, or picked up by random strangers who walked along the inside edge of the wall. They usually read them, chuckled and threw them to the side, not having any idea who it was for or where they lived. If the notes read of the awfulness happening in America, the reader really got a kick out of it, as they had it much better *inside* The Brick. For the people on the outside, it offered them a slight ray of hope that they could communicate with

473

the ones they missed and let them know how oppressive the United States had become. It became a tradition to visit The Brick once a year and throw your notes over the wall. The guards didn't care. It wasn't hurting anybody and neither side could see each other. It turned out to be of no consequence. Very few, if any, reached a reader.

*

The facility stood strong through the seasons, even though it had collected a ton of graffiti.

Perverts

Pedophiles live here

Kill them all

Baby killers

Burn in Hell

Die

It was all there. The dolls also hung on the side of the brick by the thousands. Many had the name of the terrorized child on it, while others were play toys of the children that had been killed by offenders. People did, however, begin to realize that the laws were flawed and that not all the people in The Brick were actually guilty of *any* crime. It didn't matter to the government, because once you were locked in, that was it. There would be no getting out. The people inside had no idea of the tyranny going on in the U.S.A., while the people outside had no idea how peaceful it was on the inside.

A bricked wall separated two entirely different worlds from one another. It was a cruel plot twist in a rather cruel world. Life in The Brick had grown dramatically. The cities were filling up; the countryside was beginning to see farming development and growth, while the professionals such as police, courts, judges and doctors were found and employed. It was a slow, painful process, but everyone was trying to work together to get a democracy in place. Marquette served as the capital in the United Peninsula. The people were even forming sports leagues in the cities across the U.P. Football,

475

baseball, hockey and basketball were the main sports, although many others were growing.

Even though the people had been sprayed with sterilization concoctions in the F.E.M.A. camps, they were beginning to procreate. There were fifty men for every woman, but the birth of new children, while seeming cruel, would help even out the population quotient. As long as the birth rate between genders stayed at least 50/50, it would take about twenty years to begin seeing the adult population even out. At 50-1, more men were dying, so the averages improved each day.

The weather in The Brick was punishing, as the winters were brutal. Summers were spectacular while spring and fall tempered the seasons nicely. As far north as they were located, they still had a solid six-month growing season, so grocery stores were regularly stocked with vegetables. They were also raising livestock, so meat was plentiful. A print shop began manufacturing money for the people and the economy, while still a few years away, was doing as well as could be expected.

*

The United States Government still dropped goods over the wall once per month, so the other vital foods, such as canned goods, were kept well stocked. The Government also kept the gas in the pumps so the people could drive. It wouldn't be long, however, before the United Peninsula would become self-sufficient. Among the offenders were oil drillers, people who could run the factories, and folks to work in them. The talent was vast and all encompassing.

The cities were quickly filling up, as were the factories, facilities' for making prescription drugs and many other vital eco-structures.

The jails had to be opened, as some offenders re-offended against others in the U.P. Some people were obviously ill and couldn't control their impulses, but it was a very small number. About two percent of the entire population ended up being jailed.

Overall, the United Peninsula was running smoothly. There was no interference from the U.S. Government as far as laws and rules were concerned. The people inside The Brick had no idea, nor did they care, about the outside. Most didn't know what they were missing.

*

Matt and Mary didn't join the procreation party, as Mary was moving toward forty-seven years of age and didn't want to risk any complications. Matt was in his late thirties, but the age difference between himself and Mary meant nothing either of them. He fell in love with her and the two were determined to stay together through thick and thin. Matt still missed Rachel and thought about her from time-to-time. He hoped she was doing well and would be okay without him. Matt asked Mary to marry him and they wed in a small chapel within the town of Escanaba. The two were officially married in the United Peninsula. Matt had a job. He was a farmer. He harvested corn every summer. It was satisfying for him and he loved that he could stay busy. He also knew he was helping to feed all the people in the U.P., which was very much worth his effort.

Matt had moved on enough to live a happy life in The Brick.

*

Rachel was doing much better ten years later. She chose not to meet any men, as Matt was too strong of a husband to be matched by any other man. A few men tried to talk Rachel out of her self-imposed chastity belt, but Rachel decided that no man would ever be allowed to touch her again.

She took care of her dogs and managed a vet service out of her home. She went to school, learned about animal medicine, and was on her way. She easily surpassed the

$100,000 minimum income to avoid being considered obsolete, and loved what she did. She wasn't worried about sex, procreation or any of the other human impulses. It didn't bother her in the least to keep Matt as the memory of her last lovemaking episode.

There were no more advocacies or vigilantes as far as offenders were concerned, so she no longer had to worry about how, what, where or when, and that was fine with her. The last adventure had left very negative memories in her mind that took a good five years to get over. She was in no mood to repeat the process. She did, however, pay a visit to Steven's gravesite in Cincinnati once a year. She honored him as a true hero.

*

As Rachel looked out her window, a couple strode up with their horse. It was time for her to concentrate on her job as a Vet. Making animals feel better completed her. They neither lived in the past nor worried about the future. They were here for the present. Whatever the future brought, it brought. That was good for Rachel and she tried to think that way every day of her life.

She still thought about Matt for a few minutes each morning. She prayed for him and the rest of his days.

479

Matt did the same for Rachel.

A LETTER FROM THE
AUTHOR

A sex offender is defined as:

A generic term for all persons convicted of crimes involving sex, including rape, molestation, sexual harassment and pornography production or distribution. In most states, convicted sex offenders are supposed to report to local police authorities, but many do not.

This definition encompasses an entire gambit of sexual behaviors from violent rape and molestation to verbal harassment and consensual sex between minors. The act of saying but not touching can still label you as a sex offender for a minimum of twenty-five years.

The number of people currently registered in the United States is nearly 750,000. This number is growing at an alarming rate. People taking up residence in our prison system is app. 1.6 million and growing. Our economy is in a major funk, yet the taxpayers are continuing to be burdened by the ever-inflating costs of incarceration in the U.S.A. As an added fact, the United States imprisons, per capita, more than any other country in the entire world. You and I pay for these jail cells, the privatized companies that come in with food and clothes along with the medical and dental attention that these prisoners require. I know, many people have said that we should minimize the prison population by putting them to death: Especially the offenders. By doing that, you risk executing many innocent men and women. I can't accept the argument that if 1 in 10 are innocent but still are executed; it's a small price to pay for cleaning up the vermin. I know that if I were an innocent sitting in jail, being terminated would add the ultimate insult to injury.

Any of us could be jailed at any time. *You* could be jailed anytime! All that it takes is one false allegation, being in the wrong place at the wrong time, or even being caught up in a court system that promises to be "tough on crime." It happens every day here in our "free" country. Are we obsolete? Are all of us subject to a changing landscape and attitude within this, the self-proclaimed greatest country on the face of the earth? I certainly hope not, but it makes one think.

I love being an American citizen in 2013, because I'm free and have open movement to wherever and whenever I want to go. What if it changed? What if, all of the sudden, a madman entered the White House and completely fooled the public?

*

I wrote this book as my look into the future. If the current trends continue into the year 2050, without change today, the numbers and hysteria could hit new heights.

I started with "what ifs". What if...They built a huge brick wall around the entire Upper Peninsula of Michigan (My home state) to hold all the sex offenders? What if...The mentality of the public, with help from leaders, leaned more toward a Hitler-like attitude present in the 1930's and 40's in Germany? What if...I decided to tell it in a fictional sense but at the same time kept it real and relevant? Would it have an effect on people? Would it help people understand the registry in a new light? Is money at the root of the sex offender registry? All of these questions beg for answers.

The focus, however, was not entirely on any particular group such as the sex offenders. I used them because they seem to be the most reviled people in the country. Nobody likes offenders, with or without warrant. When people hear those two words, they assume (ass-u-me) that the person is a rapist or worse yet, a child abuser. It's not always true. We should be careful to get the facts before we strike out at these people. The same can be said for many other crimes and criminals. Without the facts, we swing blindly and wildly, hurting many more than we help.

I also focused on *Mein Kampf* by Adolph Hitler, as reading it myself gave me a whole new look into the intricacies and atrocities of his regime in Germany. I thought it'd be interesting to write something apocalyptic, tyrannical and quite believable as it came to politics and favoritism.

Speaking of, I explored politics, world history and the human spirit. After all, the human spirit has the real answers to all the questions presented before us.

Could the scenario I wrote about in this novel ever *really* happen? I happen to think it could. As I studied F.E.M.A. Camps, jails, state governments and other highly charged topics, I concluded that if our government ever wanted to, they could run roughshod over the constitution (some say they do already) and there'd be nothing we could do about it. Oh, we could get our guns out and fight, but against a military as powerful as that of the U.S.A? We'd be soundly routed.

Let's hope it never comes to that and our children, grandchildren and the future citizens of this great country can live in peace forever more.

Shaun Webb

Those who cannot learn from history are doomed to repeat it. Those who do not remember their past are condemned to repeat it ... "It would be insufferable if they did not."-George Santayana

ABOUT SHAUN WEBB

Picking up where the emotionally charged A Motion for Innocence...And Justice for All? leaves off, Shaun Webb spins an effective futuristic tale describing the state of America in the year 2050.

Weaving together politics, revenge, love, hate and plenty of action, Webb gives you a story that will leave you wanting more. Heavily influenced by Stephen King and John Grisham, Shaun's able to combine a haunting story with the political action that's needed to bring Behind the Brick to life.

A sharp wit, descriptive writing style and fast-paced plotting give Shaun the edge in creating tales that are both dark and thrilling.

Shaun lives in Michigan with his Border Collie, Cody.

Made in the USA
Charleston, SC
02 July 2013